PROPAGANDA
AND
THE FREE PRESS

KARL ROGERS

For Sasha Stone

1.

PROPAGANDA...

"Not ignorance, but ignorance of ignorance, is the death of knowledge."—Alfred North Whitehead

People often think of Nazi Germany, the Soviet Union, or Communist China when they think of propaganda. Old film footage of Nuremburg rallies, parades in Red Square, or gigantic pictures of Chairman Mao overlooking fields of people waving red flags spring to mind. There have been many studies of the use of propaganda in these authoritarian regimes, including all the various techniques used in the party-controlled production and distribution of cartoons, posters, and slogans, and political speeches on radio and television, and in newspapers, pamphlets, leaflets, and literature; and how the effectiveness of propaganda weakened in the face of the unfolding terrorism and destructiveness of these brutal dictatorships.[1] Propaganda was not only used to vilify "the enemy" and to praise the virtues of the regime and its ideology, but it was used to create a sense of national unity and patriotism among the people who gained nothing or very little from the regime. As Herman Goering commented during his trial at Nuremberg:

---

[1] David Welch, *The Third Reich: Politics and Propaganda* (Routledge, 2002); Jeffrey Hurf, *The Jewish Enemy: Nazi Propaganda during World War II and the Holocaust* (Belknap Press, 2008); Saul Friedlander, *Reflections on Nazism: An Essay on Kitsch and Death* (Indiana University Press, 1993); Milton Mayer, *They Thought They Were Free: Germans, 1933-45* (University of Chicago Press, 1963); Richard Taylor, *Film Propaganda: Soviet Russia and Nazi Germany* (Tauris, 1998); Maria Lafont, *Soviet Posters: The Sergio Gregorian Collection* (Prestel Publishers: 2007); David King, *Red Star Over Russia: A Visual History of the Soviet Union from the Revolution to the Death of Stalin* (Abrams, 2009); Anchee Min, Duo Duo, and Stefan Lansberger *Chinese Propaganda Posters* (Tanshen Press, 2011); Jennifer May, *Sources of Authority: Quotational Practice in Chinese Communist Propaganda* (Verlag, 2011)

1

"Why, of course, the *people* do not want war... Why would some poor slob on a farm want to risk his life in a war when the best that he can get out of it is to come back to his farm in one piece? Naturally, the common people do not want war; neither in Russia nor in England nor in America, nor for that matter in Germany. That is understood. But, after all, it is the *leaders* of the country who determine the policy and it is always a simple matter to drag the people along, whether it is in a democracy or a fascist dictatorship or a parliament or a communist dictatorship... voice or no voice, the people can always be brought to the bidding of their leaders. That is easy. All you have to do is tell them that they are being attacked and denounce the pacifists for lack of patriotism and exposing the country to danger. It works the same way in any country."[2]

These regimes borrowed many of the propaganda techniques developed by Western governments in Britain, France, and the United States of America during the First World War, which were further developed by the marketing and public relations industries.[3] Nazi and Soviet propaganda largely imported techniques learned from America and Britain during the 1920s and 1930s and further developed these techniques during the Second World War.

However, the word "propaganda" is much older. It was first coined in 1622 when Pope Gregory XV established the Office for the Propagation of the Faith (*Congregatio de propaganda fide*). In 1627, his successor Pope Urban VIII decreed that the mission of this office was to counter the spread of Protestantism and to aid the spread of the Catholic faith throughout the New World. The word "propaganda" did not have the negative or pejorative connotation of being based on lies, bias, deceit, or half-truths used for political purposes. In Thomas Brande's 1842 *Dictionary of Science, Literature, and Art* "propaganda" was defined in neutral terms as "any association, systematic scheme, or concerted movement for the propagation of a particular doctrine or practice." Similarly neutral definitions can be found in

---

[2] G. Gilbert, ed., *Nuremberg Diary* (New York: Farrar, Strauss & Co., 1947), pp. 278-9

[3] H.D. Lasswell, *Propaganda Technique in the World War* (Cambridge, MA: MIT Press, 1971, first published in 1927); L.W. Doob, *Propaganda: Its Psychology and Technique* (New York: Henry Holt, 1935); Jacque Ellul, *Propaganda: The Formation of Men's Attitudes* (Vintage, 1973); Samuel Huntington, *American Politics: The Promise of Disharmony* (Cambridge, MA: Harvard University Press, 1981); and, J. Michael Sproule, *Propaganda and Democracy: The American Experience of Media and Mass Persuasion* (New York: Cambridge University Press, 1997)

the dictionaries of the nineteenth century, such as the *Oxford English Dictionary*. The term "propaganda" was used to refer to such things as the teaching of religious doctrine or methods to improve public health, rather than the more contemporary usage of today as referring to media methods to promote a political ideology, personality, or policy.

Today, the following definitions of propaganda are commonplace:

(1) The deliberate and selective use of facts, rhetoric, symbols, or art to achieve social influence directed towards predetermined ends, without any reasoned or critical reflection on the desirability of those predetermined ends;

(2) The appeal to emotions rather than reason to connect discourse or symbols with associated meanings and implications;

(3) The expression of opinion or action by individuals or groups deliberately attempting to change the opinions or actions of other individuals or groups with reference to predetermined ends, without any reasoned or critical reflection on the desirability of those predetermined ends;

(4) Means of political manipulation and control.

While these definitions are correct, the problem with such broad definitions is that they make it rather difficult to distinguish between propaganda and genuine efforts to persuade/inform, and they do not tell us how propaganda gains its power over us. Even if we acknowledge that propaganda can be used for the public good, for example when it is necessary to provide simplified healthcare information or road safety information, we need to develop a definition and model of propaganda that allows us identify and analyze how propaganda causes a "pathological resistance to rational persuasion,"[4] and how propaganda, as Harold Lasswell noted,[5] can use vague and general concepts that make it immune to contradiction with experience.

Here, I shall describe how propaganda undermines the critical faculties and rationality of people by fostering a passive relationship with information

---

[4] Mumford, L., *Values for Survival* (New York: Harcourt & Brace, 1946), p. 39n
[5] Lasswell, H., "Propaganda and Mass Insecurity", *Psychiatry*, 13, 1950

and media. This leads to an irrational (unreflective, unreasoning, uncritical) relation with information and media, and conformity and subservience to the status quo. On such an account, the truth-status of any statement is irrelevant for consideration of its propaganda function. This allows for the distinction between propaganda and public information to be sustained in terms of *the relation* between the public and any statements of fact or opinion disseminated through media. It is this relation that determines whether any information is propaganda or a genuine attempt to persuade or inform. In this respect, propaganda can be used *educationally* to instruct the public, say on matters of public health or hygiene, disseminating true statements, rather than simply being a means to deceive or the public or arouse passions in order achieve support for political policy. The researcher or analyst of propaganda only needs to examine the public relation to any statement—whether it is passively received or actively questioned—and she does not need to know whether any statement is true or what the intentions of the source are. It may well be possible for a statement to be true and propaganda. It may also be possible for an attempt to persuade to be genuine and false. It is also possible that the disseminators of propaganda campaigns are as much victims of propaganda as is anyone else—wherein they are unaware of the propaganda function of their statements, as they uncritically and unreflective repeat statements that they irrationally hold to be true. This allows the researcher to move beyond a conspiracy theory towards a critical and social theory of propaganda.

The negative or pejorative connotation of the word "propaganda," with its connotations of deceit and trickery to manipulate the morale and opinions of people, and its connection with political ideology, began during the First World War. The word was first used in this way in the British press to describe German newspapers and pamphlets, and thereby discredit them, as part of the British and American war efforts to recruit from among the masses and fight "the Huns." The British and American press used "propaganda" as something the enemy did to demoralize American and British soldiers, and to impede recruitment and the public support for the war, as well as propagate misinformation and falsehoods. The Germans did exactly the same thing and accused the British and American press of disseminating propaganda, while, of course, described their own newspapers as sources the information and the truth. Propaganda was something the enemy did. The First World War witnesses the birth of propaganda as a psychological method and weapon used to undermine the enemy, increase public support for the war and levels of enlistment, and generate patriotism by appealing to social groups using visual, textural, and auditory techniques. By generating opinions among the leaders of social groups and associations, taking the social group as the basic unit rather than the individual, and appealing to fears and prejudices either directly or through the press, American public opinion was changed from isolationism (and pacifism) towards interventionism (and militarism) in a remarkably short period of time.

The modern conception of propaganda arose largely through the work of the U.S. Committee of Public Information (CPI) and the Office of Public Information (OPI) to create an all-pervasive propaganda machine to sell American interventionism during the First World War as being necessary "to make the world safe for democracy" and "to defend Western civilization."[6] The CPI discovered that social groups not only respond to particular kinds of propaganda techniques in predictable and reproducible ways, but is also the carrier of propaganda throughout society and therefore operational in the rapid and ongoing self-organization of society through groups. One of the leading figures in the OPI was Edward Bernays, a nephew of Sigmund Freud, who after the war went on the found the public relations and advertising industries. He remarked "There was one basic lesson I learned in the CPI— that efforts comparable to those applied by the CPI to affect the attitudes of the enemy, of neutrals, and people of this country could be applied with equal facility to peacetime pursuits. In other words, what could be done for a nation at war could be done for organizations and people in a nation at peace." Two of Eddie Bernays' early books on the use of propaganda are *Crystalizing Public Opinion* (1923) and his seminal textbook *Propaganda* (1928). After the war, these propaganda techniques were used and developed by Ivy Lee and Edward Bernays to establish the American public relations and advertising industries.[7] After all, if these techniques can be used to persuade people to fight a war, they can be used to sell soap or politics. This brought journalism,

---

[6] George Creel, *How We Advertised America* (New York: Harper, 1920), p. 3; Edward Bernays, *Propaganda* (New York: Liveright, 1928). p. 1

[7] Ivy L. Lee, *Publicity* (New York: Industries Publishing, 1925) and Edward Bernays, *Propaganda* (New York: Liveright, 1928); *Public Relations* (University of Oklahoma Press, 1952); and *The Engineering of Consent* (University of Oklahoma Press, 1955)

public relations, advertising, marketing, and broadcasting together to sell public policy and political candidates to the public.

Edward Bernays, Public Relations, and Propaganda:

Bernays insight was that to understand propaganda, we need to look at it as a sociological phenomenon, as well as looking at its psychological functions. The OPI propaganda model has formed the template for the marketing strategies used to sell each and every subsequent war to the American people. This was not only used for the Second World War, the Korean War, the Vietnam War, the invasions of Panama and Grenada, and the wars in Iraq and Afghanistan, but was also used for "the Cold War," "the War on Drugs," and "the War on Terror." As a result of these wartime efforts, the manipulation of "public opinion" became professionalized and placed at the service of industries and corporations. The advertising and public relations industries were born, alongside the continued usage of the term "propaganda" by the British and American governments and press against "the Red Menace" of communism to discredit the newspapers and pamphlets of the Russian Bolsheviks.

After his formative experiences in the OPI, Bernays embraced the idea of "the invisible government" and saw propaganda to be the means by which the majority of people could be educated and have their minds molded for their own good and the good of society.

"The conscious and intelligent manipulation of the organized habits and opinions of the masses is an important element in democratic society. Those who manipulate this unseen mechanism of society constitute an invisible government which is the true ruling power of our country." (Bernays, Propaganda, p. 1)

When developed scientifically, propaganda provided the foundation for successful public relations and advertising for both political and commercial purposes. Bringing together nineteenth century scientific positivism and the insights of his uncle Sigmund Freud, Bernays developed the methods by which the public could be manipulated and lead. Rather than place the emphasis on the zealous oratory of demagogues, Bernays placed the emphasis on teams of researchers, writers, artists, photographers, and film directors working scientifically to create gradual and irresistible cultural shifts and mass reactions. For Bernays, propaganda was an invaluable tool for education and social services, as well as for business and politicians. Instead of selling products, Bernays sold the need for the product. He sought to change culture in such a way as to make the products desirable. For example, if Bernays wanted to develop an advertising campaign to sell pianos, he would not sell the piano itself, but rather sell the idea of the cultural necessity of having a music room with a piano in the home. He sold the idea of music as a cultural necessity related to family life and personal identity. Hence, according to Bernays, propaganda was more than the means by which businessmen and politicians could sell their wares or policies, but the means by which the masses could become cultured and civilized through the efforts of exports. Hence, instead of selling bacon or toothpaste directly, Bernays would bring insights from sociology and psychology together to influence the public to change their habits. He would employ doctors and dentists to promote bacon and "the hearty breakfast" as part of a healthy diet, or the importance of regular use of toothpaste for dental hygiene. In this way, Bernays changed the culture in order to create a need for the products he was selling. The power of this approach can be seen in General Electric's Campaign in the 1920s, using the press and its own National Electric Light Association, to convince the public that public ownership of utilities was not in the public's best interest.[8]

For Bernays, a stable society requires that the masses must be organized and manipulated by this ruling elite, who govern by their "natural leadership" and their ability to mold minds and suggest ideas. Bernays understood that, given the complexity of the market, it is impractical for individuals to price and test every available alternative before purchasing it. Instead, our choices are shaped and led by propaganda. This is true of both our commercial and political choices. The *real* competition with the market or political arena is a competition between propaganda campaigns "to capture our minds in the interest of some policy or commodity or idea." They can do this because they occupy key positions within the social structure and they understand the psychology and sociology of the masses. Party machines control and limit the choice of candidates and the owners of newspapers control and limit public debate. Within these limits, citizens may vote for whomever they please from among the political elite. These leaders are used to shape events and opinions

---

[8] Ernest Henry Gruening, *The Public Pays: A Study of Power Propaganda* (New York: The Vanguard Press, 1931)

by selling ideas and policies. This is done with the consent of the masses via propaganda.

"From our leaders and the media they use to reach the public, we accept the evidence and demarcation of issues bearing upon public questions; from some ethical teacher, be it a minister, a favorite essayist, or merely prevailing opinion, we accept a standardized code of social conduct to which we conform most of the time." (Bernays, p. 3)

With the advancement of communication and media technologies, along with the overall complexity of society, the invisible government has developed the technical means by which it can shape and control public opinion and activities. Newspapers soon gave way to radio, which in turn gave way to television, and now the Internet dominates communication and mass media. The ability to transmit ideas around the world and to any number of people has led to greater national and social integration between people who have never met and live thousands of miles apart. The power of radio has been confirmed since the 1938 broadcast of Orson Welles's adaptation of H.G. Wells book *War of the Worlds* sent thousands of listeners into a mass panic across New England, thinking that they had heard the announcement of a real Martian invasion. The Second World War saw considerable development of the use of radio and movies to disseminate propaganda. Since 1952, when the Dwight D. Eisenhower campaign ran the first television campaign ad, television has become an essential technology for the dissemination of propaganda. Ironically, the same industrial-military complex that Eisenhower warned the American people about provided the means for his election in the first place, and also provided the means for that warning to be televised across the nation. His warning had very little effect. The lesson of this was that "the public" can be manipulated and organized through both their association via shared ideas and interests, and also by manipulating the many and diverse divisions with a heterogeneous society, between social, political, economic, racial, ethnic, gender, religious, and ethical associations, and the many subdivisions of each. Human identity and hostility can be created and manipulated through these associations and divisions.

"This invisible, intertwining structure of groupings and associations is the mechanism by which democracy has organized its group mind and simplify its mass thinking. To deplore the existence of such a mechanism is to ask for a society such as never was and never will be. To admit that it exists, but expect that it shall not be used, is unreasonable." (Bernays, p. 7)

For Bernays, what was needed was both a deeper understanding of this mechanism and a gradually evolving code of ethics regarding its use and practice.

"Whatever of social importance is done today, whether in politics, finance, manufacture, agriculture, charity, education, or other fields, must be done with the help of propaganda. Propaganda is the executive arm of the invisible government." (Bernays, pp. 9-10)

He argued that one of the myths of the Enlightenment was that the people would become fit to govern themselves through education, science, reason, and moral conscience. He argued that the people remain confused and chaotic, unless led by the ruling elite. Literacy was supposed to provide the means by which "the common man" would be able to inform himself and make rational judgements. Instead, Bernays observed, literacy has provided "the common man" with "rubber-stamps" that are

"...inked with advertising slogans, with editorials, with published scientific data, with the trivialities of the tabloids and the platitudes of history, but quite innocent of original thought. Each man's rubber-stamps are duplicates of millions of others, so that when those millions are exposed to the same stimuli, all received identical imprints." (Bernays, p.10)

His insight was that the American public receives most of its ideas and opinions through the wholesale dissemination of ready-made ideas and opinions, "rubber-stamps," that are transmitted and shared through the organized dissemination of propaganda to spread a particular belief or doctrine, and give people the feeling that these rubber-stamps are their own opinions and views.

Bernays maintained a value-neutral stance about propaganda. Whether its use was good or bad depended the merits of the cause and the correctness of the information, and whether some discourse was labelled as "propaganda" or "a statement of truth" depended on its propaganda-function, since the common usage of the word has sinister connotations. Hence, despite having placed his propaganda methods at the service of the tobacco industry for many years, Bernays changed track, once it became known that tobacco was carcinogenic, and placed his services at the disposal of public health and anti-smoking campaigns. Charities, businesses, educators, churches, and politicians all have to use propaganda. If a group of citizens uses propaganda to promote an opinion or cause of action they will label their own efforts as "free speech" and denounce any other group of citizens expressing an opposing view as disseminating propaganda. It was for this reason that Bernays attempted to reclaim the word "propaganda" and define it in value-neutral terms:

"Modern propaganda is a consistent, enduring effort to create or shape events to influence the relations of the public to an enterprise, idea, or group." (Bernays, p. 14)

It is all-pervasive throughout society and used to enroll public support for every important undertaking whether it is some public works program, a new building, and marketing movies, promoting university courses, selling bonds, or electing a president. Once public opinion has been established through propaganda, not only will the public continue to disseminate that propaganda through rubber-stamps, repetitions and reinforcements, but the public will also bring pressure on politicians and public officials to act on those opinions. If the public clings to stereotypes and prejudices, the task of the propagandists is to use them and manipulate the public to move in the desired direction. Without mass support and public approval, any campaign or movement will dwindle and fail, no matter how laudable it may be. Efforts to lower the infant mortality rate will be unsuccessful, unless they work on public opinion and regimenting rubber-stamps to galvanize public pressure and money through propaganda, using the same methods as are used to sell toothpaste, bacon, or pianos.

Propaganda changes the world view of people and regiments the public mind; it becomes the currency of exchange within the marketplace of ideas. Bernays pointed to how propaganda was used to generate patriotism and support for the war effort during the First World War to show how propaganda appealed to individuals by using visual, graphic, and auditory techniques, but it was most effective when it was disseminated by social groups, associations, and churches. By generating opinions among the leaders of groups and associations, and through the press, public opinion was changed away from isolationism and pacifism, and towards intervention and militarism. This was achieved in a remarkably short period of time. It did this by not only focusing on the fears and prejudices of the individual, but also on the social structure of interacting groups and associations, thereby generating and directing "patriotism" and outrange at German atrocities. The individual not only responds to specific kinds of propaganda technique in predictable ways, but is also a carrier of propaganda throughout society and operational in the self-organization of society through groups and associations.

The efforts of propagandists during the Second World War and the subsequent Cold War brought skepticism about the ability of the average citizen to resist propaganda, while progressive critics were labeled as 'muck raking' subversives or even as traitors, and the public settled into a passive consumer relation with media. This placed power in the hands of the owners of mass media. Bernays was aware that the use of modern propaganda tended society towards plutocracy.

"The invisible government tends to be concentrated in the hands of the few because the expense of manipulating the social machinery which controls the opinions and habits of the masses. To advertise on a scale which will reach fifty million persons is expensive. To reach and persuade the group leaders who dictate the public's thoughts and actions is likewise expensive." (Bernays, p. 26)

This tendency has created the new profession of propaganda specialists. Bernays termed this type of professional as a "public relations counsel." The public relations industry was grown up to communicate the ideas and enterprises of the invisible government and to interpret the public's response. This specialist mediates between the public and the ruling elite. This mediation is achieved by working with mass media and the groups and associations of which society is comprised. He sells policies, doctrines, causes of action, systems, and opinions, as well as products and services. Not only does this specialist advise the client on how to communicate ideas, but he also liaises between all the public contacts involved or interested in the client's products and services. The public relations counsel shapes both the client and public's actions so as the latter can better respond to the former. Advertising is part of his work, but it is not limited to it. The public relations counsel analyses psychological and sociological factors to better understand the client's problem and how to solve it.

By communicating with various groups and leader, shaping both the client's and public's understanding of their needs and how to satisfy them, the relations between the client and public can be formulated in terms of strategies, tactics, and policies that coincide the client's and public's interests. This often involves the client learning how better to listen to and interpret the public and the public shifting its attitude towards the client and its understanding of how the client benefits the public. For Bernays, public good will, and understanding are best achieved through confidence and frank information; false or misleading information may will backfire and result in public suspicions or hostility towards the client, Hence, although public relations is a pragmatic profession, it works best when it develops in accordance with ideals and ethics.

"It is to make the producer, whether that producer be a legislature making laws or a manufacturer making a commercial product, understand what the public wants and to make the public understand the objectives of the producer... It aims to bring about an understanding between educators and educated, between government and people, between charitable institutions and contributors, between nation and nation." (Bernays, p.32)

The conditions of the work forces an ethical code upon public relations, claimed Bernays, because while the counsel must present the client's case in the best light to the public, it is in the counsel's best interest, from the professional point of view, to refuse to help dishonest and fraudulent clients, or an antisocial cause. Should the counsel obtain a reputation for fooling or hoodwinking the public, his profession would come to an end.

"This invisible, intertwining structure of groupings and associations is the mechanism by which democracy has organized its group mind and simplified its mass thinking. To deplore the existence of such a mechanism is to ask for a society such as never was and never will be. To admit that it exists, but expect that it shall not be used, is unreasonable." (Bernays, p.7)

For Bernays, the study of mass psychology was essential for the public relations counsel to discover the propaganda methods through which the invisible government could manipulate the behavior of individuals in groups. Even though he admitted that mass psychology was not an exact science and there are many mysteries of human motivation, Bernays accepted the basic insight that the group has mental characteristics distinct from those of the individual. This idea of "group mind" expresses the way that individual behavior in groups is motivated by impulses and emotions that cannot be explained in terms of individual psychology. Bernays asked the following question:

"If we understand the mechanism and motives of the group mind, is it not possible to control and regiment the masses according to our will without their knowing about it?" (Bernays, p. 35)

He answered that it was, up to a certain point and within certain limits. Theory and practice had been sufficiently developed to reveal and operate some mechanisms to change public opinion with a fair degree of accuracy. It is possible to have some knowledge of cause and effect within the group mind and to predict and change group behavior in a consistent manner. However, human behavior is inherently unpredictable and there are always unexpected events. Mass psychology has the same kind of limits as sociology or economics and should not be considered to be a laboratory science like physics or chemistry, but, providing that these limits are taken into account, the modern propagandist can influence the ideas of groups, with or without their cooperation, through a systematic and objective study of the groups and the circumstances in which they exist.

"...men are not actually gathered together in a public meeting or in a street riot, without becoming subject to the influences of mass psychology. Because man is by nature gregarious he feels himself to be a member of a herd, even when he is alone in his room with the curtains drawn." (Bernays, p. 36)

Individual minds are shaped by group influences and the mental characteristics of the group are stamped on the individual mind through patterns of activity within the group. The individual may well imagine that they make their own judgements and control their own decisions, but they are shaped unconsciously by outside influences impressions that can be systematically and objectively manipulated. The group mind does not think, but through the impulse to follow the example of a trusted leader, the mental characteristics of the group, through manipulating leaders, the propagandist is able to effect the popularity of a summer resort, cause a run on a bank or panic on the stock exchange, create a best-seller or box office success, or get politicians elected to public office. When leaders are not available, the group mind is structured by means of clichés, stereotypes, and slogans that connect the beliefs of the group and the identity of the individual within it to words and images which stand for a whole ensemble of ideas and experiences. Hence it is possible to turn a group against a particular politician by exposing "the interests" that fund his or her campaign, simply because the idea of "the interests" invokes images and memories of corruption and deceit, regardless of who "the interests" might be, or what their goals and agenda are. Similarly, both "liberal" and "conservative" voters in America can be turned against any public policy, regardless of its actual content and purpose, simply by stamping it with the term "socialism." In fact, what terms like "liberal" and "conservative" mean, and the policies associated with them, is more a product of propaganda than of a principled political philosophy. People come to self-identify with a label and the task of the propagandist is to associate specific policy ideas and talking-points with that label.

It is well-known by psychologists that human desires are often suppressed or repressed and human beings seek "compensatory substitutes" for their desires. Suppressed or repressed sexuality, for example, can provide the mechanism by which the propagandist can establish a "compensatory substitute," say cars or chocolate treats, sports events, cigarettes or alcohol, or other consumer items, like clothing or firearms. The herd instinct for social position can be manipulated to sell the individual the trappings of success as a "compensatory substitute." Scapegoating immigrants, minorities, or ethnic groups can provide a "compensatory substitute" for the desired feelings of superiority held by downtrodden and alienated members of society. Nationalism, racism, or patriotism can be a "compensatory substitute" for a lack of personal achievement and happiness. The successful propagandist needs merely to aid the concealment of individual motives from the individual through the selection and use of "compensatory substitutes," and take full advantage of the psychological model of human nature that reveals human beings to be shaped and motivated by "compensatory substitutes" for repressed and suppress desires and attitudes, which the individual often remains unaware of or even conceal from themselves. Arguably, it is for this reason that often the most homophobic and aggressively anti-homosexual attitudes are expressed by repressed homosexuals who use their "moral" and "political" power as a "compensatory substitute" for their repressed sexuality. Hence it is frequently the case that the most zealous public crusaders conduct secretly the very same behavior that they publicly condemn. This is not merely a case of hypocrisy, which only treats the contradiction between public speech and private behavior in terms of individual choices, as it also reveals the social power of "compensatory substitutes" within the social dynamic of group identity and leadership, thereby placing the sexual identity of the individual in contradiction with their social identity.

"This general principle that men are very largely actuated by motives which they conceal from themselves, is as true of mass as of individual psychology. It is evident that the successful propagandist must understand the true motives and not be content to accept the reasons which men give for what they do." (Bernays, p. 39)

A successful propagandist needs to understand the structures of society, its groups and their relations with each other, its divisions and classes, and human design within these groups. Who is it that influences how humans pursue their desires? Answer that question and it becomes possible to manipulate large sections of any population. The propagandist needs to identify particular groups and leaders that influence public opinion. Rather than rely on the old stimulus-response methods of individual psychology, the modern propagandist uses indirect association between group leaders and whatever the propagandist wishes to promote or sell. The utilization of groups and leaders is one of the best methods to disseminate propaganda in modern society. Hence, when planning an advertising campaign to sell a particular type of food product, Bernays would not direct that campaign to sell the product directly to individuals, but he would persuade doctors to recommend that product as being good for human health, or he would enlist celebrities or publicly known personalities. If trying to change fashion tastes, the propagandist should enroll celebrities and influential people to wear or use that fashion.

When the press mediates between members of groups and leaders, the press becomes the tool by which associations can be promoted and propaganda disseminated. Once particular rubber-stamps can be associated with group loyalty and identity, the members of the group will not only identify with the propaganda but will also disseminate it. By manipulating group leadership and identity, the propagandist will put the members of the group to work for him, whether they know it or not. Leaders can be made to lend the authority to any propaganda campaign *if and only if* doing so coincides win their interests. The task of the "public relations counsel" is to discover how to coincide the interests of his clients with the interests of leaders and groups. By coinciding and overlapping interests, the propagandist interlaces group formations and creates alliances. In the case of commercial advertising, for Bernays it was important that the relationship between business and the public

"…is not confined to the manufacture and sale of a given product, but includes at the same time the selling of itself and of those things for which it stands in the public mind." (Bernays, p. 46)

The public is not an amorphous mess which can be molded at will, or directed; the skillful leader and propagandist must be familiar with the structure, the prejudices, and the wishes of the public, and use this knowledge to manipulate and modify public perceptions of people's own needs in accordance with their cultural standards, habits, and ideals. These cultural norms can be changed, but the propagandist cannot ignore them or run counter to them. Both business and politics must create mutually beneficial partnerships between themselves and the public by using propaganda to explain themselves, their aims and objectives, to the public in terms which the public can understand, accept, and rally behind. No longer can business rest content with supplying the means to meet organically evolving demand. It must create the demand for its products. The same applies to the political sphere. Politicians must use already existing cultural attitudes and perceptions to create the needs that the politician can supply the means to satisfy. In other words, politicians must create the public awareness of a "problem" that the politicians have a "solution" for, and supply that "solution" after creating the public demand for it. Mass media is essential for this task. Just as modern manufacturers cannot wait until the public wants their products and must create new customers through advertising and propaganda, so the modern politician must understand and manipulate the group structure, the personalities, and the prejudices of the public to get them to recognize the politician as their leader. Just as business needs to insert itself into consumers' lives, through generating needs, life style choices, and patterns of consumption, thereby changing customs and culture, so politicians need to insert themselves into the voters' lives, through associating themselves with personal identities, group membership, and a particular worldview, thereby representing customs and culture. It is *who* the politician is perceived *to stand for* that matters most.

Based on carefully acquired knowledge of public opinion, the public relations expert can explain to the client either how best to take advantage of public opinion, by either appealing to it or manipulating it, or how the client can adapt to it, by either changing their practices or products. Bernays presented two methods to achieve this goal: *continuous interpretation* and

16

dramatization. While the propagandist needs to pay attention to individual circumstances, these general methods can be employed to good effect, either by alternating them or pursuing them concurrently. The *continuous interpretation* method works through all-pervasive media control and manipulation, whereby the public receives the desired impressions and impulses from every conceivable source continuously, without being conscious of it. *Dramatization* works by vividly seizing the attention of the public to some event or problem in order to fix the public mind on demanding some particular solution. For both these methods, mass media is essential and it is necessary to either control media sources directly or to have allies or influence through media. Clearly, mass media consolidation of media sources into fewer hands makes this problem easier to solve.[9]

For Bernays, in order for propaganda to be successful in the long term at reaching a large population and changing their habits and opinions, propaganda must be based on the truth. Deceit will be exposed eventually and it will backfire when it does. Modern business and politics must maintain sound knowledge of public opinion and understand how to interpret and change the public mind, and when necessary adapt to it and change policies and products accordingly.

"The great political problem in our modern democracy is how to induce our leaders to lead... The voice of the people expresses the mind of the people, and that mind is made up for it by the group leaders in whom it believes and by those persons who understand the manipulation of public opinion. It is composed of inherited prejudices and symbols and clichés and verbal formulas supplied to them by leaders."

Propaganda is the instrument by which political leaders can mold and form the will of the people by telling people what that "will" is. Politicians need to dramatize themselves and their platform, if they are to have any real meaning to the public. In order to be successful, political campaigns must be based on a scientific study of the public and how to sell the party, the candidates, the platform, and the ideas. Otherwise political campaigns are nothing more than "sideshows bombast, glitter, and speeches." (Bernays, p.75) Bernays criticized the political campaigns of his day for being based on antiquated methods and he urged them to take up modern public relations methods to

---

[9] Karl Rogers, *Media Consolidation and Net Neutrality in the U.S.* (Los Angeles, CA: Trébol Press, 2017)

secure the mass distribution of their ideas and adapt their communication strategy to the prejudices of the public via the use of mass media. Politician campaigns need to focus their recourses on using media to manipulate and raise emotions among the public, create a frenzied public interest in the campaign, and emphasize personality. With the benefit of hindsight, we can see that modern politics took Bernays' advice to heart.

It is essential that the messages of the political campaign are disseminated through diverse media; to present themselves through all-pervasive media to people acting through interlocking groups: economic, social, religious, education, cultural, rural, collegiate, sports, local, national, and political parties and associations.

"It is understood that the methods of propaganda can be effective only with the voter who makes up his own mind on the basis of group prejudices and desires. Where specific allegiances and loyalties exist, as in the case of political leadership, those loyalties will operate to mollify the free will of the voter. In this close relation between the [incumbent] and his constituents lies, of course, the strength of his position in politics." (Bernays, p. 72)

The successful politician *sways* the public by manipulating their prejudices, rather than merely pandering to truth, via the dramatization of his personality and close contact with the leaders of the groups of which the public is comprised.

"Good government can be sold to a community just as any other commodity can be sold... The newspapermen look to [political leaders] for news. And by his power of giving or withholding information the politician can often effectively censor political news. But being dependent, every day of the year and for year after year, upon certain politicians for news, the newspaper reports are obligated to work in harmony with their news sources." (Bernays, p.83)

As well as utilizing rubber-stamping and stereotyping, emotions and personality, and manipulating public prejudices through propaganda, the successful political leader will create the circumstances through which he can offer solutions and lead. By doing this

"when he spoke to his millions of listeners on the radio, he would not be seeking to force an argument down the throats of a public thinking of other things and annoyed by another demand on its attention; on the contrary, he would be answering the

18

spontaneous questions and expressing the emotional demands of a public already keyed to a certain pitch of interest in the subject." (Bernays, p. 84)

Politicians must have something to say that the public want to hear, and untrue or anti-social claims will ultimately backfire, but whether a politician is heard and his claims believed to be true or in the public good all depend on the skillful use of propaganda. Bernays saw no problem in "the cult of personality" or "hero worship" that surrounds the President of the United States, which has been created through propaganda, providing that reflects the cultural relation between the public and the office of the Presidency. Herein lies the rub: the propagandist does not seek to improve the public and help them become better informed; instead the propagandist takes advantage of the way the public is, exploits their prejudices and irrationality, and gives them what they want. In this respect, propaganda has become a fundamental component of democratic governance, without improving the public's understanding of governance.

While the public actions of the President are carefully staged-managed, chosen to dramatize the personality and office of the president, they are also used to sound-out the public, like a trial balloon of public policy, as well as used to sell the policies devised by the party machine, technical experts, and professional advisors,. Thus the behavior and words of the President have an inherent propaganda function for government and the political parties in general for the purpose of testing and selling domestic and foreign policy. In a democracy "in which the herd and the group follow those they recognize as leaders," (Bernays, p. 115) and the President is presented to the public as a personality, it is more important, according to Bernays, that candidates for the Presidency are selected on the basis of their knowledge of the methods of propaganda and public relations than on their knowledge of civics or political economy. Through propaganda, the statesman governs in a democracy by bringing the public mind to focus on specific events and policies that are used to regiment the public and gain support for particular courses of action.

Bernays argued that propaganda could also be of great service to the civil rights movement, education, and social services, but there is no guarantee against its misuse. It is a tool. It is value-neutral, or to put it another way, *value-promiscuous*.

"The great enemy of any attempt to change men's habits is inertia. Civilization is limited by inertia… Our attitude towards social relations, toward economics, toward national and international politics, continues past attitudes and strengthens them under the force of tradition… Opposing this traditional acceptance of existing ideas is an active public opinion that has been directed consciously into movements against inertia. Public opinion was made or changed formerly by tribal chiefs, by kings, by religions leaders. Today the privilege of attempting to sway public opinion is everyone's. If is one of the manifestations of democracy that any one may try to convince others and to assume leadership on behalf of his own thesis." (Bernays, p.111)

Progressive critics of the use of propaganda in democracies have presupposed that citizens are capable of thinking for themselves, possess a faculty to reason and achieve rational communication, and are open to learning about how to critically evaluate information. Since John Dewey advocated a public education system developed to teach children how to think critically and reason for themselves—as being essential for the possibility of the growth of an enlightened and democratic citizenry—progressive critics of mass communication have simultaneously worked to expose the uses of propaganda, censorship, and other forms of public manipulation and advocated a progressive education as the silver bullet.[10] By developing critical thinking, analytical skills, and the knowledge of propaganda techniques, it was hoped that an enlightened citizenry would emerge, which would be capable of making and articulating intelligent and reasoned decisions about the alternatives presented to them in the public sphere. It was also hoped that such a citizenry would be better placed to deal reasonably with societal pluralism and diversity, and respond and adapt to a changing world. However, increasingly, a more pessimistic view about public communication has come to dominate propaganda studies. This shift between the optimistic to the pessimistic view began after the 1950s. In the early 1930s, progressive critics, such as Frederick Lumley, warned that propaganda was not only used to disseminate and manipulate public opinion, but also reinforced and concealed irrational prejudices and selfish interests and, by doing so, distorts or prevents the possibility of rational communication.[11]

---

[10] John Dewey, *Democracy and Education* (Macmillan, 1916)
[11] Frederick E. Lumley, *The Propaganda Menace* (New York: Century, 1933)

After the 1950s, emboldened by the successes of Skinner's and Pavlov's behaviorism, Lumley's warning was taken as the basic insight behind the deliberate developments of strategies and techniques to manipulate irrational prejudices and selfish interests, and intensify them, in order to manipulate the public. Social researchers have become more concerned with the efficient and harmonious implementation and development of social policy and administrative methods than with nurturing the conditions for deliberative and participatory democracy. This positivistic approach tended to represent the public as an essentially irrational mass that is incapable of resisting being manipulated through propaganda and media control. From this view, it is the public that undermines the possibility of enlightened democracy, rather than some manipulative elite, and the best one can hope for is diversity and competition between sources of propaganda and ownership of media. This form of propaganda becomes self-fulfilling because it threatens to subvert the possibility of an enlightened citizenry that it presupposes is impossible and thereby reinforces the prejudices of the intellectuals and scientists who are developing propaganda techniques. The possibility of the existence of socially conscious, critically thinking, informed, and rational individuals is denied, and the use of propaganda in this manner threatens to drive societal development towards the creation of an irrational and totalitarian mass society. By successfully doing so, the self-justifications of the people who developed the means to create such a society would be confirmed by having done so.

During the 1950s and 1960s, social research became dominated by positivistic methods and data gathering rather than historical interpretation or grand theorizing.[12] With the growth of behaviorism and positivistic psychology, by the end of the 1950s, the dominant representation of the citizen was that of a politically disinterested individual, highly susceptible to propaganda, and largely incapable of rational communication or critical reflection, for whom only his or her selfish interests and subjective preferences were of immediate concern. The shift from political philosophy, with its normative and critical content, to political science, with its positivistic pretensions of being a quantitative science akin to the natural sciences, was the result of growing skepticism about the possibility of developing a critically

---

[12] R.K. Merton and P.F. Lazarsfeld, *Continuities in Social Research* (Glencoe, IL: Free Press, 1950)

engaged and rationally motivated democratic citizenry.[13] Despite the efforts of the advocates of critical thinking to expose the use of fallacies and slogans in propaganda, by the end of the 1950s the mainstream academic study and analysis of propaganda had moved from advancing critical exposés to analyzing and providing "scientific" techniques of marketing and other forms of mass persuasion.[14] The intellectual community moved from trying to liberate the common man to putting themselves at the service of political parties, advertisers, and marketing agencies. Rather than develop social theories of propaganda and educate the public in critical thinking and reflection, academics and political scientists have increasing applied and developed methodologies and specific techniques of empirical research sociology and psychology to the further development of propaganda.

These new methodologies and techniques brought new problems. Statisticians and social scientists had to develop quantitative methods to measure public opinion, track changes in public opinion, and determine whether any particular technique to manipulate public opinion was successful or not. The Gallup Poll was developed to provide such a method.[15] However, like advertising, which bypasses intellect and appeals to desires and emotions, political propaganda is most effective among an irrational, isolated, and poorly educated population. The conditions for the emergence of a critical, engaged, and informed citizenry, such as a good public education system and opportunities for democratic participation in public deliberations and decision-making processes, are anathema to those conditions needed for propaganda methods to saturate the public with information in a way that manipulates public consent or disapproval of a policy or proposal.[16] Media manipulation of public opinion is antithetical to the democratic development

---

[13] William Albig "Two Decades of Opinion Study: 1938-1956" *Public Opinion Quarterly*, 21, 1957

[14] Max Black, *Critical Thinking* (New York: Prentice Hall, 2nd. Edition, 1952). See also Sproule, *Democracy and Propaganda*, pp. 62-78 and pp. 249-61.

[15] George Gallup, *The Pulse of Democracy* (Simon and Schuster, 1940)

[16] A. McClung Lee and E. Briant Lee, *The Fine Art of Propaganda* (Harcourt & Brace, 1939); Terrance Qualter, *Opinion Control in the Democracies* (New York: St. Martins, 1985); Benjamin Ginsberg, *The Captive Public* (New York: Basic Books, 1986); R.A. Nelson, *A Chronology and Glossary of Propaganda in the United States* (Greenwood, 1996); W. Lance Bennett, *News: The Politics of Illusion* (New York: Longman, 2011), first published 1988; David Barsamian and Noam Chomsky, *Propaganda and the Public Mind: Conversations with Noam Chomsky* (Southend Press, 2003);

of an enlightened and engaged public capable of exercising freedom of choice and rational decision-making. The urbanization of society and the development of mass media have resulted in heavily mediated communications between people and political leaders, and have created the conditions for these political leaders to use propaganda to manipulate or distract the public.

Due to its pejorative connotations, propaganda works best when it is concealed as such, say by using terms like "educational movies" or "documentaries," or "issue advocacy ads," rather than "propaganda films." Henceforth, "propaganda" is what "they" do, while "we" don't use propaganda but instead use "information," "opinion," "documentary," "news," "advertising," or "issue advocacy." In 1914 and 1939, propaganda was what the Germans did. In 1953, propaganda was what the communists did. So it follows that, in 1953, when Bernays was hired by the United Fruit Company to whip up public anti-communist fears in order to compel the congressmen to pressure U.S. government to use the CIA to overthrow the Guatemalan democratically elected government of Jacobo Arbenz, replacing it with a military junta favorable to United Fruit and opposed to any land reforms, and begin the task of "democracy promotion" through military aid and covert interventions, this did not involve propaganda.[17] It was informing the democratic American public. Just as this approach was developed through the CPI and OPI to create an all-pervasive propaganda machine to sell America's intervention in the First World War as being necessary "to make the world safe for democracy," so the interventions in Latin America became sold as necessary for the sake of democracy. The CPI propaganda model has formed the basis for the marketing strategies used to sell each and every subsequent war to the American public, be it the Korean War, the Vietnam War, the invasion of Panama and Grenada, the war in Afghanistan, and both Iraq Wars, or "the Cold War," "the War on Drugs," and "the War on Terror." Modern propaganda focuses on the constitution of society as a whole, to articulate, disseminate, and organize some demand or solution through the enrolment and organization of groups and associations, repeated and reinforced in mass media, and politicians position themselves as listening

---

[17] Stephen C. Schlesinger, Stephen Schlesinger, and Stephen Kinzer, *Bitter Fruit: The Story Of The American Camp in Guatemala* (Cambridge, Mass Harvard University Press, 1999). See also Chomsky.

to the public and responding to their demands. Individual choice between rubber-stamps will not only reflect their membership of those groups and associations, but also how the individual understands "democracy" itself.

Media and the Manufacture of Consent:

Mass media has provided politicians with the means to manufacture both consent and discontent, while legislation has become so complex that elected lawmakers do not even read, let alone understand the laws they agree upon. Increasingly politicians are dependent upon bureaucrats, lawyers, and technical experts for précis and explanations, while hiring public relations firms to produce and run their propaganda campaigns for their re-election. Since the dawn of civilization, politicians have always resorted to abstractions and value statements, stereotypes and slogans, along with scapegoating and promising glorious victories, but nowadays propaganda can reach hundreds of millions of people, 24 hours a day. Rather than providing citizens with an impartial and critical analysis of any of public policy, giving good reasons, or simply raising public questions and concerns, politicians have intertwined facts and propaganda with the construction and reinforcement of a pseudo-reality through all-pervasive propaganda—*the hologram*—designed largely to distract the population or garner popular support along ideological lines, and this pseudo-reality may well have very little relation to the facts of experience about real events.

As early as 1911, Will Irwin warned us that the commercial interests of privately owned newspapers had created an intrinsic editorial selection bias in favor of news stories that either benefited advertisers or avoided offending them.[18] This created an editorial bias against covering stories that might offend advertisers and the interests of the owners. It also extended this editorial bias against any story that might result in withdrawn access to government sources, which have become the main information source for corporate media. Editors also avoid any story that might result in lawsuits or legal consequences. Reporters are pressured to support the opinions and

---

[18] Will Irwin, *The American Newspaper* (Iowa State University Press, 1969, first published in 1911); see also *Propaganda and the News* (New York: Whittlesey House, 1936)

24

prejudices of media owners, investors, and advertisers to favor the ideals and norms of the economic and political elite. If access to political leaders is cut off to media sources that do not play ball, this leads to a culture of "self-censorship" within corporate media, wherein criticisms of the government's policies are either silenced or marginalized, or channeled into the two-party political game.

In his 1920s exposé, *You Can't Print That!*, George Seldes, correspondent for the *Chicago Tribune*, wrote that journalists were constantly pressured to act as propagandists when governments snubbed critics and only cooperated with complicit reporters.[19] This created an intrinsic pressure on journalists to maintain friendly relations with government officials, alongside the internal editorial pressures for reporters to support the opinions and prejudices of newspaper owners. When the media supports and repeats governmental statements persistently and uncritically, irrespective of the facts or their inconsistency with previous statements, there is strong evidence for the case that media is engaged systematically in the dissemination of propaganda in support of governmental policies and agendas. Once the government is the major source of information and provides the framework of analysis, the media become the means of disseminating governmental information and the official line, masked as impartial investigative journalism based on relevant facts. Once the primary role of media is one of making sure that the governmental agenda remains unchallenged then we see the propaganda machine at work. Also, the operations of this machine should be evident when journalists and editors apply a double standard of criticism and rigor depending upon whether the news or facts are favorable or unfavorable to government claims or statements. Divisions and dissent within the media (including criticisms of the government) only tend to occur when the economic elite disagree with each other about policies or see an opportunity to further their own agenda by changing government personnel or public policy.

In his 1922 book *Public Opinion*, Walter Lippmann described how "the manufacture of consent" was central to governance.[20] Lippmann argued that

---

[19] George Seldes, *You Can't Print That!* (Garden City, 1929); see also *Freedom of the Press* (Bobbs-Merrill, 1935)
[20] Walter Lippmann *Public Opinion* (New York: Free Press, 1977), first published in 1922

direct or classical democracy was impossible in a modern society in which the majority of people were too ill-informed and irrational to be capable of anything other from being herded like sheep. He maintained that "democracy" was only possible as a *representative democracy* in which the majority of led by a political elite of professional politicians, bureaucrats, and technical experts. This political elite manufactures consent in order to shape public opinion to follow rational, intelligent, and sane courses of action. Propaganda is an essential instrument for the responsible and stable administration of society. There are not any wise philosopher kings to guide society. Instead, there is a competition the leaders of society and that competition is waged through disseminating propaganda. While we may criticize particular methods to manipulate news, public opinion, or the reception of personalities within society, propaganda is itself necessary for the stable operation of modern representative democracy. Harold Lasswell, one of the founders of the field of communications theory, wrote in his 1933 *Encyclopedia of Social Science* that the triumph of modern propaganda techniques is their success in keeping the public in line, allowing the ruling elite to overcome "the ignorance and stupidity of the masses." He asserted that we need to forget the "democratic dogmatism" that considers human beings to be the best judge of their own interests.

Noam Chomsky critiqued the invisible government and the role of media in manufacturing consent in his seminal work on propaganda *Manufacturing Consent*, co-authored with Edward Herman.[21] As Chomsky and Herman observed,

"In contrast to the standard conception of the media as cantankerous, obstinate, and ubiquitous in their search for truth and their independence of authority… the "societal purpose" of the media is to inculcate and defend the economic, social, and

---

[21] *Manufacturing Consent: The Political Economy of Mass Media* (New York: Pantheon, 1988), co-authored by Noam Chomsky and Edward Herman. See also the documentary *Manufacturing Consent: Noam Chomsky and the Media* (1992). For further discussions, see Chomsky's books *Media Control: The Spectacular Achievements of Propaganda* (Seven Stories Press, 1997); *Propaganda and the Public Mind* (South End Press, 2001) and also *Chomsky on Mis-education* (Macedo, ed., Rowman & Littlefield, 2004). See also Mark Achbar and Peter Wintonick's 1992 documentary *Manufacturing Consent: Noam Chomsky and the Media* and Rise Up Film's 2010 documentary *Psywar: The Real Battle is the Mind* http://www.riseupfilms.com/1/post/2012/03/psywar-the-real-battlefield-is-the-mind-rise-up-films.html

political agenda of privileged groups that dominate the domestic society and the state. The media serves this purpose in many ways: through selection of topics, distribution of concerns, framing of issues, filtering of information, emphasis and tone, and by keeping debate within the bounds of acceptable premises... the U.S. media do not function in the manner of a totalitarian state. Rather, they permit—indeed, encourage—spirited debate, criticism, and dissent, as long as these remain faithfully within the system of presuppositions and principles that constitute elite consensus, a system so powerful as to be internalized without awareness." (Chomsky and Herman, pp. 298-302)

Censorship and propaganda are dual aspects of the media collusion with government and this collusion has caused a crisis in democracy by manipulating or preventing public participation in decision-making processes. In this way, so-called representative governments are the product of market mechanisms to establish media conformity, silence critics, and marginalize opposition.[22] At the heart of this political model is an elitist approach to representative democracy, which asserts that the general public is either too ignorant or stupid to understand and decide matters of policy; therefore, propaganda is an essential method for the elite to gather public support and "educate" the population about what is in their best interest. Public manipulation through the use of propaganda has become a fundamental method of governance in Western societies, but also, through narrowcasting, political parties prevent any open public discussion of what is in the public interest and reduce the ability of society to develop. We should not be fooled by the subtle forms of propaganda used in Western media (in comparison to the cruder propaganda campaigns of Nazi and Soviet dictatorships), and we need to pay close attention to how the consolidated partnership between the government and mass media corporations has resulted in an increasingly refined and embedded system of information control and manipulation designed to achieve public consensus in favor of government policy and maintaining the status quo, while maintaining the illusion of the existence of a free press, for the benefit of politicians and the owners of media corporations. As Chomsky put it in *Necessary Illusions*,

"To confront power is costly and difficult; high standards of evidence and argument are imposed, and critical analysis is naturally not welcomed by those who are in a

---

[22] W. Preston, Jr., J.S. Herman, and J. Schiller, *Hope and Folly: The United States and UNESCO, 1945-1985* (University of Minnesota Press, 1989)

27

position to react vigorously and to determine the array of rewards and punishments. Conformity to a "patriotic agenda," in contrast, imposes no such costs. Charges against official enemies barely require substantiation; they are, furthermore, protected from correction, which can be dismissed as apologetics for the criminals or as missing the forest for the trees. The system protects itself with indignation against a challenge to the right of deceit in the service of power, and the very idea of subjecting the ideological system to rational inquiry elicits incomprehension or outrage, though it is often masked in other terms." (Chomsky, p.9)

Chomsky provided us with many examples of American newspapers, like the *New York Times* and *Washington Post*, misrepresenting the facts or flatly lying about them in order to serve a governmental or ideological agenda.[23] Using the example of Nicaragua, which was an "official enemy" of the Reagan administration, in comparison with "U.S. client states" such as Guatemala, El Salvador, and Honduras, Chomsky shows, citing example after example, the double-standards and hypocrisy in mainstream media reporting in the United States. A selective filter designed for the needs of government propaganda is imposed on newspaper and television reporting, for which state terrorism, death squads, police oppression, torture, rape, and murder are deemed to be irrelevant and not newsworthy when they do not serve those needs. Moreover, the mainstream media censorship of peace protests is nothing new. Millions of people worldwide took to the streets of capital cities to protest build-up for the war in Iraq. These largely went unreported. During the first Gulf War, the protests throughout America went unreported, as they did during the Reagan Administration's reckless nuclear arms build-up and escalation of the arms race with the Soviet Union. Not only do we see the uncritical citation of government press releases and official statements, but unwelcomed facts or contradictory reports go unreported.

"The constant barrage of properly selected material, with hardly a critical word or analytic passage, firmly instills the presuppositions that we behind it, shaping the

---

[23] Noam Chomsky, "The Craft of 'Historical Engineering'," *Chomsky on Mis-Education*, pp.57-134; reprinted in Chomsky, *Necessary Illusions, Thought Control in Democratic Societies* (Boston: South End Press, 1989) pp. 197-261; Cf. *Deterring Democracy* (Hill & Wang, 1992); *Hegemony or Survival: America's Quest for Global Dominance (American Empire Project)* (Holt, 2004); *Failed States: The Abuse of Power and the Assault on Democracy* (Holt, 2007). See also, James Aronson, *The Press and the Cold War* (Indianapolis: Bobbs-Merril, 1970)

perceptions of the audience within the framework of acceptable doctrines more effectively than the productions of any Ministry of Truth." (Chomsky, p. 123)

Chomsky paints a bleak and terrible picture of the realities of "democracy promotion." Indeed, we can see how "democracy promotion" by the United States in Latin America, especially in countries such as Guatemala and Colombia, two of the most violent countries in South America, and the Middle East, have utilized propaganda and are themselves forms of "propaganda by the deed." Nowadays, instead of anti-communism it has taken the form of anti-terrorism and anti-narcotics. On one hand, it is domestic propaganda used to justify military intervention and aid, including covert operations under the guise of anti-narcotic or anti-terrorist operations, to justify the continued funding and backing of authoritarian and corrupt regimes, in order to gain access to natural resources and cheap labor, and protect American interests in those countries. On the other hand, it is a psychological weapon used against democratic movements within Latin America and Latin America, to justify a myth of democracy that can never be achieved in practice, while simultaneously suppressing those movements using violent methods, and thereby portraying genuine democracy as "communism" or "mob rule," or even unthinkable, except in terms of supporting whatever puppet "democracy" that is in place. It is not a coincidence that the same countries in which "democracy promotion" occurs are the same countries that have been ravaged by civil war, terrorism, criminality, juntas, and occupying forces for decades. "Democracy promotion" is itself a propaganda campaign designed to conceal anti-democratic state-terrorism and corporate plunder, all under the guise of "elections" and "constitutional reforms," while demoralizing the oppressed people's ability even to think of democracy as a framework for resistance, governance, and rebuilding their country. It should be of little surprise that communism and religious fundamentalism became the frameworks for popular resistance in those countries, in response to militaristic interventions to suppress "communism" and "extremism." Violent and terroristic groups such as ISIL or FARC are the *consequence* of "democracy promotion" and not the reason for it. Of course this plays into the hands of the oppressor, given that in the propaganda framework of "democracy promotion," as both religious fundamentalism and communism are anti-democratic and oppressive by definition, associated with atrocities and terrorism, and their existence justifies further military interventions, emergency measures, and the "deferment of democracy" until a time when "the rule of law" has been "restored." This allows military operations to be classified under as state secrets, as a matter of military necessity, while at the same time portrayed as "police actions" or "nation building." It allows indefinite detention and the suspension of due process and legal rights, and even torture and assassinations, all under the guise of "democracy promotion."

The negative consequences of Western military interventions in the so-called developing and underdeveloped worlds, for example, must be kept secret from the public for as long as possible, or limited to the repetition of a handful of isolated atrocities or tragedies. Pundits will talk about blunders, misinterpretation, errors of judgment, friendly fire, collateral damage, the fog of war, or faulty intelligence, but these will be either explained away as "human failing," or as corruption and deceit on the part of an individual leader or official. The hologram is maintained by presenting the negative consequences of the regime's policies as isolated events, which the regime— and only the regime—can correct by further rationalizing its policies. It is essential that critics are marginalized as "conspiracy theorists" or "muckrakers." At all times a one-sided presentation of events is made that never allows questions to be raised by people about the overarching strategy of military intervention and its goals; the irrationality and unsustainability of the system itself is kept out of view. Even when popular movies or documentaries criticize the war, they will do so in a sentimentalized fashion and focus on how the war was conducted badly, and only gloss over the causes behind the war, if they touch on them at all, as if forces beyond anyone's control were to blame. Like Colonel Kurtz in *Apocalypse Now*, the propagandist/propagandee can denounce the hypocrisy of the American military high command for declaring the act of writing the word "fuck" on bombs as being obscene, while he also praised "the will" of the Viet Cong for hacking off the arms off inoculated babies, thereby emulating that "clarity of will" in his own "methods" to fight Viet Cong, acting without moral restraint and hypocrisy, without ever questioning why he should fight them all. At no point will any solidarity with "the enemy" against the architects of the war be thinkable. The demarcation between the two sides will still be maintained, even when "the horror" of the war is highlighted, and peace is to be established through one final act of meaningless murder before leaving. That is, until the elite no longer wish to continue the war; after which time, the media become champions of armistice and peace—and forgetting the war and its causes—until a new "enemy" and a new war becomes the new cause célèbre. No further debate of the causes or consequences of the war will occur. The focus moves on to other things—any other things—as if the war never happened at all. Or, if it did happen, it really only happened to "us." "The North Vietnamese did not win the war. America lost the war." "The Peace Movement and critical press won the peace!" The war ends when the owners and controllers of media end it. In this way, even a military loss can be represented a victory for democracy. As soon as the elite need to end the war, the once-jingoistic and belligerent media becomes "the watchdog", "the critic," and 'the Fourth Estate" in its criticisms of the war and its demand for peace, until it is needed to beat the drums of a new war and point out the follies of pacifism and non-intervention once again.

While arguably the potential for real democracy is being suppressed and stifled worldwide, especially in the industrialized nations, in favor of the interests of the economic elite of the owners of multinational corporations, banks, and major industries, through propaganda this has been largely achieved with the consent of the public.

"The importance of 'controlling the public mind' has been recognized with increasing clarity as popular struggles succeeded in extending the modalities of democracy, thus giving rise to what liberal elites call 'the crisis of democracy' as when normally passive and apathetic populations become organized and seek to enter the political arena to pursue their interests and demands, threatening stability and order." (Chomsky, p. 137)

Yet genuine democracy cannot be promoted through military intervention and propaganda, given that these are both anti-democratic methods. Democracy can only come from the people, in their own terms, as a grassroots form of political organization and social evolution. It is a cultural and historical transformation of a people that can only arise from within their culture, as a result of historical struggles, and cannot be imposed by external "liberators." Democracy promotion cannot occur at the end of the barrel of a gun. Without doubt, the contradictions inherent in "democracy promotion" through military methods and state-terrorism undermine propaganda's effectiveness in the long-term, but the damage is done. The effects of propaganda undermine the population's ability to think democratically and alienates them from the political process, or even its possibility. The result is that any resistance to the anti-democratic forces of the oppressor themselves take on anti-democratic forms, which of course can be used by the oppressor to justify the continued use of anti-democratic methods, especially a foreign oppressor that can use "insurgents" or "terrorists" to justify the expenditure and sacrifices imposed on its own people to continue the foreign intervention in the name of "national security." A created enemy (real or imagined) is a valuable propaganda tool that can be used against the domestic population to erode their rights and suppress democratic means of petitioning government, the free press, and democratic opposition and dissent. Perhaps it is even ironic that greater harms have been done by Western governments to liberal democracy than any terrorist organization could have ever achieved. The slogan "We fight them over there, so we don't have to fight them over here," is a lie in more ways than one. This is particularly effective when the domestic propaganda campaign is one of patriotism, national security, supporting the troops, and disseminating the myth that the aim of "the war on terrorism" is one of "defending freedom" through "democracy promotion."

To use one of Chomsky's often repeated examples: In the 1980s the U.S. corporate media and intellectual elite vigorously debated how best to deal with the Nicaraguan Sandinista threat to American national security and the US government's efforts to promote democracy in Central America, while there was hardly any debate or discussion about whether (or how) Nicaragua was a threat to American national security, or whether the US government was really attempting to promote democracy. Nor was there any corporate media discussion of why those "fledgling democracies" supported by the United States (such as Colombia, Guatemala, and El Salvador) have the worst records for human right abuses in Latin America. By serving the economic elite while sustaining the illusion of being an independent watchdog, corporate media has distorted and suppressed the public ability to learn about and understand public policy.[24]

Consider NAFTA, for example. This was pushed through Congress despite popular opposition and concerns raised by economists and the labor movement, given the failures of the U.S.-Canada Free Trade Agreement, while mainstream media remained silent about these concerns and failures,

---

[24] See also H.S. Rauschenbush and H.W. Laidler, *Power Control* (New Republic, 1928); E. Gruening, *The Public Pays* (Vanguard, 1931); and, B. Bagdikian, *Media Monopoly* (Beacon Press, 1987)

instead championing the official line that NAFTA would bring great economic benefits to America and help Mexico become a modern democracy. Of course few multinational corporations and investors have reaped huge profits as a result, while the predictable disastrous results for the American and Mexican people came to pass:

1. the destruction of the American unions and workers' protections through the treat and actuality of capital flight and outsourcing production;

2. the destruction of Mexican agriculture and economy, resulting in starvation, increased poverty, massive unemployment, and illegal immigration to the US;

3. the outsourcing of industry to China and the Third World.

Mainstream media, of course, dutifully suppressed any criticism of NAFTA, except those media by easily ridiculed extremists and alarmists like Ross Perot. If critics were permitted air time, it was essential that those critics appeared out of touch or extreme. The faired predictions of great economic benefits and flourishing democracy are quietly forgotten, as the disastrous consequences of NAFTA are concealed under the weight of mass media silence. Instead, the media treats these consequences as isolated and unconnected problems, such as unemployment and illegal immigration, or blames the former on the later to present a false causality for which "something must be done." The financial burden for dealing with the social costs of NAFTA are shifted on to tax payers or simply left neglected. Meanwhile Congress weights new legislation and reforms within carefully proscribed limits, such as whether to grant amnesty and a path to citizenship for illegal emigrants, or whether to build a multibillion dollars wall across the Southern border, increase the military presence on the border, and shift the burden on to law enforcement. At no point will NAFTA be questioned in either mainstream media or Congress. It is as if it never happened; its failures are the result of natural forces. If a critic does manage to mention NAFTA during an interview and it is not edited out, 'well, it is always easy to be wise in hindsight.'

Throughout the Americas, neoliberal economic "reforms" have generally been disastrous for the general population and the environment, and have largely only benefited the economic elite, which, of course, owns mainstream media and thereby imposes censorship and prevents the facts and realities of globalization and "free market" trade agreements, like NAFTA and CAFTA, from being widely known. They aim to prevent people from being able to connect the realities of their own experiences of their economic conditions with "the bigger picture" of U.S. foreign policy, neoliberal globalization, and the international accumulation of capital and power by multinational corporations. The reduction in real wages experienced by workers in America and Mexico have even been ignored in mainstream media or championed as "reduced labor costs" leading to "increased profitability." The debate in mainstream media and Congress is limited to whether America can afford to spend tax payers' money on Food Stamps and welfare for low paid workers or whether the money should be used to further reduce the deficit and taxes for corporations and the wealthiest Americans. Despite all the evidence to the contrary, the debate remains framed by the assumptions of "trickle-down" economics and corporations as "job creators," even by NAFTA's critics in mainstream media. The debate becomes reduced to whether or not corporations and wealthy investors should pay higher or lower taxes on their profits and capital gains. Meanwhile the majority of the Mexican population sink into poverty and misery, and the American working class faces lower wages, longer hours, and the constant threat of unemployment, homelessness, and "austerity measures." Even under the sway of so-called "populist" movements, where the promise of "tearing-up" or "renegotiating" NAFTA is made by political leaders or personalities, the reality is that NAFTA remains off the table and barely discussed.

However, it needs to be pointed out that the term "neoliberalism" is itself misleading, as is the term "free market" and are themselves the products of propaganda. The reality is a corporate-governmental system that creates, through regulation, contracting, loans, tax codes, and trade agreements, an environment that benefits powerful industries, bid businesses, and multinational corporations, *at the expenses* of small businesses, self-employed individuals, cooperatives, small farms, local economic self-determination, *and market competition.* The result in the creation of economic oligopolies and monopolies, backed up by the apparatus of the state, including police and military forces, and a legal and political framework that justifies oppressive measures against anyone who opposes corporate power as acting against "the national interest," thereby categorizing them as "terrorists" or "criminal elements," or…. "Socialists." As a result of this alliance between corporations and government, as popular resistance or organized labor opposes the inequalities and corruption that result from the alliance, the tendency is for the corporate state to degenerate into a fascist regime, capable of using a police-state apparatus and state-terrorism to crush organized labor and democratic opposition, but this is always combined with propaganda showing the government to be dealing with lawlessness or taking measures to deal with unrest and instability.

Internationally, "neoliberal reforms" and "free trade agreements" are used to destroy the development of local and national industries, agriculture, and independence, so as to place access to cheap natural resources, labor, and markets *exclusively* into the hands of cartels or multinational corporations, banks, and investors. Countries that oppose these reforms and agreements, instead preferring to adopt independent or nationalistic policies, face sanctions or coup d'états, or are designated as "rogue states" or "failed regimes" and are faced with the threat of military invasion or covert backing of terrorist groups that murder the civilian population, as has happened in Chile, Nicaragua, Bolivia, Cuba, Venezuela, Haiti, Iran, Lebanon and throughout the Third World. The aim is to destroy those economies and force the political system to adopt reactionary policies, thereby damaging or reversing and independent development, until such time that the civil order and government collapse and a corrupt puppet-government and internally repressive regime can be put in its place, as we can see in the case of regimes such as Iraq, Afghanistan, Guatemala, Haiti, El Salvador, Honduras, Panama, Indonesia, Nigeria, and Costa Rica. These serve as examples to any government that does not toe the line of U.S. foreign policy, and "neoliberal" reforms.

Of course, when these "free market trade agreements" result in "the wrong results," such as Mexican agricultural produce being cheaper and better that American produce, the U.S. government intervenes with impunity in favor of big agribusiness and either gives tax payers' money as subsidies or flat out bans of importation of the cheaper produce, even in contradiction to its own doctrines and the rules of the trade agreements it imposes on other countries. The deviation from the ideology of "free trade" and the double standard largely goes unreported in mainstream media, or if it is reported is framed in terms of whether protectionism for the benefit of American farmers is sometimes justified, despite the benefits of international free trade for American consumers.[25] The same IMF and WTO rules that prevent subsidized electricity and food for local population, on the grounds that these constitute illegal "price controls" and "government interference" into "the free market," are interpreted as allowing governmental subsidies, loans, non-bid contracts, and regulatory protections for big businesses. The press dutifully trots out its condemnation of "socialism" and its praise for "market liberalization."

While subsidies for big business and military spending are clear methods to funnel the wealth of nations back into the hands of the owners of the multinational corporations, this is insufficient for creating oligarchical or monopolistic control over the world's economies, and thereby its political systems. What is also needed, through the ideological doctrine of "privatization," is to destroy the public sector, thereby removing all competition, regardless of its cost to the population in general, and preventing local, state, or national governments from developing independent economic policies. The press fulfils its task of censoring any stories about corporate malfeasance or corruption, instead having the benefits of "free market discipline" and denouncing the "inefficiencies" of the public sector. If any discussion is permitted, it is framed in terms of whether, *in some cases*, it is necessary for the taxpayers to foot the bill of public sector jobs, or whether this creates dependency on government and a welfare culture of enlightenments. Hence, as Chomsky put it, the media does not see any contradiction or feel the need to explain the double-standards of politicians like

"Newt Gingrich, who sternly lectures seven-year-old children on the evils of welfare dependency while holding a national prize for directing public subsidies to his rich constituents. Or to the Heritage Foundation, which crafts the budget proposals for the congressional "conservatives" and therefore called for (an obtained) an increase in Pentagon spending beyond Clinton's increase to ensure that the "defense industrial base" remains solid, protected by state power, and offering dual-use technology to its beneficiaries to enable them to dominate commercial markets and enrich themselves as public expense." (Chomsky, p. 163)

---

[25] For example, David Sanger, "President Wins Tomato Accord for Floridians," the *New York Times*, Oct. 12, 1996.

The myth of "the free market" is propagated, while the public bears the costs and risks, and the owners of multinational corporations reap the profits. To put it as a slogan, it is a policy of socialized costs and privatized profits. Bank and corporate bailouts of 2008-9 provide us with a recent example.

The belief that elected political leaders control the administration of the State is itself an illusion based on the idea of a monolithic and unified government. The so-called political leaders are there to endorse decisions already made by bureaucrats, technical experts, lobbyists, industries, banks, corporations, pressure groups, political parties, and other politicians. Combined with mass media propaganda, the role of politicians and political parties is to maintain the illusion that the government speaks with one voice and is accountable to the people, while at the same time distracting people (by framing debates, promoting wedge-issues, and narrowcasting) from the real and complex operations of governmental agencies and institutions.

"The decision-making process consists of a complex mixture of personal judgements, traditions, conflicts among the state's many organs, and pressures from outside groups. Proliferation of decision-making centers has become the rule inside the political organism. This organism is not all that simple. When we talk of a president, ministers, or an assembly, we have not yet said anything, for the state has become a vast body, dealing with everything, possessing a multitude of centers, bureaus, services, and establishments." (Ellul, p. 139)

Ellul quite rightly talks of the technocracy as being the real government, but it needs to be understood (without any sugar coating) that the technocracy has itself become an instrument of corporate power. The administration is a means of the state, but that means has been exclusively put at the service of corporations, banks, and moneyed interests. The plutocracy of landed wealth has become transformed, via the corporate control over the technocracy of the state, into a corporate state, within which the operations of the state, including legislation, administration, along with the judiciary, police, and armed forces are organs of corporate power and domination, both politically and economically. The function of both integration and agitation propaganda is to conceal this face of contemporary governance.

Take General Electric and light bulbs as an example. Congress banned the incandescent light bulb, which took effect January 1st, 2014, and required only the manufacture of florescent light bulbs. Mainstream media frames this new law as either being good for the environment (the "liberal media" position) or an imposition by "a socialist nanny state" ("the conservative media" position) overtaken by "anti-capitalist greens." Either way, the new law is presented as anti-capitalist and pro-environment, regardless of whether the spin is for or against this law. However, what is completely ignored and remains undiscussed in mainstream media, is that the patent on incandescent light bulbs, held by General Electric, ran out on January 31st, 2013, after which time anyone could have made incandescent light bulbs if it were not for the ban, and General Electric holds the patent on florescent light bulbs, which after January 31st, 2013 became the only light bulbs available for manufacture and sale in the United States. Here we see how Congress and the law have become instruments to maintain a monopoly, while the media distract the public from reality.

In this respect, taking all of this into account, we can see that the political process has become not only meaningless, as a means of accountability to the governed, and is only meaningful as a means of maintaining the consent of the government. Changing politicians has no effect on the operations of the State (obviously with some exceptions, such as promoting or removing the rights of certain groups of people, or protecting or scapegoating other groups, or pushing through specific policy agendas) even if it promotes an illusion of "democracy" that conceals the fact that there is no democracy at all. It is little more than a form of catharsis and distraction, to present the illusion that public opinion matters and effects policy. Both technocracy and ideology have become instruments of corporate power, which is itself driven only by the imperatives to maximize profits and accumulate capital. The only competition within government or between political parties is between strategic differences between different cartels of corporations and industries. Sometimes the needs of the oil and energy companies gain dominance, other times the needs of the telecommunications and pharmaceutical giants gain ascendency, but as the markets have become increasingly dominated by monopolies and interrelated through a system of government-corporation dependencies, these differences became negligible and the division of political economy between cartels can be coordinated and negotiated, and it is this system that is concealed by corporate-owned media.

The whole political and bureaucratic system has become so thoroughly corrupted at every level and across all branches of government that any belief in reform, say electoral reform or amending the constitution to counter the

Citizens United v FEC ruling, for example, is itself naïve.[26] Nothing short of a political revolution can remedy this situation. This revolution can take the form of a massive democratic participation in the next elections to remove professional politicians from public office and replace them with citizens, thereby causing a constitutional crisis in which the sovereign body-politic is placed in opposition to the corporate controlled technocracy, forcing a struggle for political power to the fore. The only other alternative is a violent revolution to overthrow the corporate state, which, of course, the State will treat as an act of insurrection and respond accordingly. Within the current system of corporate domination and mass media distraction, "the government" is itself an illusionary abstraction that allows lobbyists, technocrats, and self-serving opportunists to act with autonomy and secrecy. There is no better example of this than the TTIP and TPP "negotiations" within which national sovereignty has been handed over to multinational corporations, which have granted themselves veto power over legislative bodies and the right to award themselves "compensation" for any "lost" profits due to "regulatory takings" caused by legislative restrictions that remain to be ironed out in the future. In effect, a coup d'état has taken place and the owners of these multinational corporations have asserted the right to use the State as an instrument for business operations, including police and armed forces to protect their "ownership" of the infrastructure and natural recourses of the signatory countries, as well as access to public funds and lands. When people talked of "the New World Order," this is what they referred to. It is unrestrained and internationally organized corporate hegemony and power over nations and the entire world, within which "governments" are nothing other than administrative instruments.

With public access to independent foreign media sources, it has proved impossible for the propaganda machine to maintain public ignorance indefinitely, but with increased consolidation of international media, it even becomes possible to control those sources as well, or at least anticipate them by disseminating damage-controlling spin and editorials. As long as the public have a ready-made set of off-the-peg opinions that can be used to counter any criticism or uncomfortable facts (such as numerous instances of the killing of children via air strikes or drone attacks,) often by bandying around "justifications" (such as "collateral damage" or "the enemy use human

---

[26] Karl Rogers, *Citizens United* (Los Angeles, CA: Trébol Press, 2016)

shields") or simply by joining-in the cult of infallibility of the leadership and demanding that others should unconditionally trust the leadership, the public themselves can disseminate propaganda and marginalize critics of the regime.

Chomsky highlighted the role of self-censorship in corporate media. Pressure is put on editors to avoid controversy that will upset corporate management, the owners of media corporations, and advertisers. Corporate media editors are also loathed to criticize any government policy if that will result in a loss of access. This has resulted in a tendency towards conservative news coverage and an over-reliance on official government sources (often concealed as "anonymous sources"). With increased media consolidation, mainstream media has marched lockstep towards the construction of an all-pervasive propaganda machine that serves corporate interests and for-profit business in general, rather than the wider public interest or democracy as a whole. When apparently independent media sources (radio, television, newspapers, publishers, Internet Service Providers, film studios, and Internet sites) are all owned by the same "parent companies," coordinated propaganda can be readily disseminated and seemingly corroborated through cross-media confirmation. Even apparently independent associations, such as the National Association of Broadcasters, which is one of the most powerful media advocacy groups in America, is funded by media corporations to lobby Congress for further media ownership deregulation and the defunding of public media (such as NPR and PBS). According to Bill Allison of the Center for Public Integrity, the NAB has over 300 professional lobbyists who spend tens of millions of dollars per year lobbying congressmen and the Federal Communications Commission, who lobby to suppress or vote against any proposal or legislation for free-air time for public media or political candidates, while simultaneously lobby the FCC for further deregulation and to relax the rules on media consolidation.

The self-proclaimed "liberal" or "conservative" media pundits on television, radio, and the Internet all read from the same pro-corporate script. This should be unsurprising, given the corporate ownership and control over media in America. Regardless of how well the pundits construct their narrative, interweaving carefully selected questions, facts, and jokes, they are all corporate employees. They frame their questions and commentary in ways that benefits their paymasters. They say whatever their paymasters want said. They ignore whatever their paymasters want ignored. They give to us the corporate message of the day. Instead of covering politics, media corporations cover personalities and the theater of politics, presenting a gloss of sound-bites and slogans, rather than delve into issues and the consequences of policy. There is little in the way of in-depth analysis of the facts. A recent Harvard study showed that during the primaries and election campaigns of the 2016 U.S. national election, only a tiny percentage of coverage focused on policies (less than 10%, with about 4% on the Democratic Party policies and 6% on Republican Party policies), with the rest (about 90%) focused on personality.[27] This study involved a detailed content analysis of the presidential election coverage on five television networks (ABC, CBS, CNN, Fox and NBC) and in five leading newspapers (Los Angeles Times, The New York Times, The Wall Street Journal, The Washington Post and USA Today). This is not simply giving the public what they want. It is a strategy of censorship and distraction. By pandering to their audience's prejudices and worldviews, the corporate media is able to distract their viewers, listeners, and readers from the corporate takeover of American politics, concealing the dominance of corporate control over elections and the three branches of government, as well as almost every facet of economic and technological activity. The "liberal" and "conservative" media do this by pretending to oppose each other—sneering at their distortion and misrepresentation of each other's sound-bites—while all the time focusing media attention on the scandalous, salacious, trivial, and divisive news and issues of the day, at all times keeping the focus shallow and short-term, and reinforcing the prejudices and worldview of their target audience. Everyone walks away vindicated and affirming their beliefs; no one learns anything new.

It is important to recognize that corporate media does not owe their allegiance to a political party or an ideology out of principle. Their allegiance us to shareholders and owners. But, as "gate-keepers" of the election process, the owners of mass media have considerable power over politicians. Ideology is merely a tool at their disposal. Politics allows them to color-code their discourse and focus their narrative on the hot-topics and divisive issues that result in predictable reactions from their target audience. The role of the media pundit and propagandist is to funnel their audience's dissatisfaction and alienation back into the political system by utilizing the techniques of

---

[27] http://theconversation.com/harvard-study-policy-issues-nearly-absent-in-presidential-campaign-coverage-65731

framing and scapegoating. No matter how seemingly paranoid or apocalyptic the message may be, it leaves the target audience reassured that they "have always known" what is going on—that they have insight—and they understand the clear demarcation between "them and us." The audience is provided with catharsis and hope. They are given new champions (who always are members of the political system) to support. They belong to "an inner circle" of truth-seers. Even the most seemingly "anti-government" or "seditious" message (talking of a government takeover, FEMA camps, CIA conspiracies, FBI raids, etc.) provides the audience with a sense of satisfaction and heightened sense of their own awareness, while at the same time leaving them further isolated and politically passive. The pundit allows the target audience to vent and expend its dissatisfaction and alienation, while channeling all their anger, resentment, and frustration away from the causes of these feelings (the political-economic system itself) towards scapegoats (such as "illegal immigrants," "liberals," "conservatives," or "them.") For even when "the government" is criticized, it is important that it is always against an aloof and unassailable totality, such as "the government," even when it is given a synonym, such as "the United Nations," "the Globalists," "the Illuminati," which presents the illusion of knowing something more, or all those feelings are projected against a single person—say whomever the current president is—as if one single person could really be the architect behind the policies of a whole nation.

The aim is straightforward. The corporate owners of government and media—the real architects of policy and laws—must remain above criticism and out of the limelight at all times. As well as using scapegoating, framing, and censorship to manipulate the public and advance a "divide and conquer" strategy, and sell advertising slots, the goal of corporate media punditry is to maintain the illusions of "a free press," market competition, political pluralism and criticism, and to channel the dissatisfaction and alienation of its target audience back into the status quo. The focus on divisive issues is set-up to distract people and also to divide them into camps which expend their political energies on each other, rather than towards the system of public manipulation that perpetuates these divisions and prevents any resolution to them. The aim of divisive discourse is to turn the attention of the working and middle classes against each other, and away from the corporate takeover of America, when in fact the main political parties—the Republican Party and Democratic Party—are two wings of the same Pro-Corporate Party, often receiving campaign donations and expenditures from the same corporations. Corporations, through using unlimited campaign expenditures to buy slots in corporate owned media, as well as through campaign donations and lobbying, and other pressures and influences over politicians, have corrupted the political system in their favor. They have become the gatekeepers of candidacy and public office. What is concealed is the fact that whomever you vote for serves the same interests, say the interests of Goldman Sachs, the Bank of America, Monsanto, Lockheed Martin, Boeing, General Electric, and Exxon Mobil, to name a few. Differences between candidates on hot-topics, such as gun control, abortion, and same sex marriage, are highlighted to present the illusion of opposition, whereas the real differences between the candidates is usually little more than the differences between the interests of two competing cartels of corporations. The real domestic policy difference is whether it is better to develop the customer base in America or whether it is better to shift market focus to Asia. The real foreign policy difference is how best to profit from war and the threat of war. And when the owners of corporate media stand to benefit from war, both "liberal" and "conservative" media pundits fall into line as its champions, "patriots," and cheerleaders.

The propaganda machine is a carefully orchestrated and coordinated system of control over a wide variety of media sources to give the appearance of independent corroboration and investigation. These media sources include radio and television, books, magazines, newspapers, and websites, all consolidated under the control of a small group of people who own mass media and telecommunications corporations. Owning the means to gather and disseminate news, entertainment, culture, and information, this cadre of individuals and their employees are able to censor people and disseminate propaganda. Through government license and market dominance, they are provided with the means to drown out everyone else and maintain monopoly control over mass media and communications across all media, providing that these media sources support the government and suppress news of any public opposition, especially during times of war. All of this is possible because of the implicit public trust that this partnership between private business and government operates in the public interest, even if done for profit and ambition.

In totalitarian regimes, propaganda is combined with the terrorist tactics of a police state to maintain control over the population. As Robert Chesney observed in *Orwell Rolls in his Grave*, the current system in the U.S. is very much like the Soviet system in the sense that the Soviet Union had hundreds of newspapers, TV stations, and radio stations, but they were all controlled by the elite and worked to maintain the system and the status quo.[28] While an isolated Communist Party member could be reprimanded in the press for some reported failure (or over-zealousness) or even treachery, just as the occasional capitalist or corporation is vilified in the American press for criminal acts or corruption, the system itself is off limits. The tendency in Western countries has been one of implementing close partnerships between government and private media, while using a variety of propaganda measures and censorship to frame public debates—making sure that certain questions are not asked—and to alienate the population from wanting to participate in the political process, thereby making democracy seem utopian or even undesirable. This is why stories of political corruption, deceit, and abuses of power are still published, providing that they remain isolated to specific individuals or a group, rather than being seen as a flaw in the system itself, and—at most—the discussion of "solutions" is limited to a discussion of whether some set of minor reforms should be implemented or not. As long as radical solutions are not discussed, the flaws in the political process can serve to foster public cynicism and apathy, which result in reducing the public role to one of being passive consumers of products and opinions that serve to maintain the status quo for lack of an alternative. As long as public frustrations and alienation can be channeled into scapegoating immigrants, homosexuals, promiscuity, or the political opposition, a political culture of "them vs. us" can be channeled into the two-party system. Any challenges to the system itself can be deflected and suppressed. Using techniques and strategies to dumb down and sufficiently distract the population so that the consent of the governed is achieved by default, propaganda has a disastrous effect on the health and cohesion of society by creating a political culture based on passivity, ignorance, fear, alienation, division, and irrationality.

If there is any truth to the above view, what we are witnessing is a shift away from a pluralistic, egalitarian, and inclusive ideal of participatory democracy, and towards an authoritarian and totalitarian corporate state,

---

[28] http://orwellrollsinhisgrave.com/

wherein corruption, secrecy, and the roles of media of those of entertainment, distraction, and operating a propaganda machine designed to turn a heavily divided population against each other. The failures of capitalism are either interpreted in the media as "an economic depression," largely without historical explanation as if they are the result of a failure of government policy, either the result of insufficient government spending on the private sector or the result of overly regulating and taxing the private sector. Big bailouts and the failures of neoliberal reforms are forgotten and written out of history, while the media "expert" mantra of neoliberalism and "free markets," and the call for further corporate tax cuts and deregulation, is repeated over and over, and over again. These are all rubber-stamps. Among the party faithful, rubber-stumps need no supporting evidence or argument if they correspond to or reinforce received opinion that tows the party line. Yet, if anyone uses statements or arguments to question or oppose the accepted orthodoxy, they require watertight documentary evidence, and, even if this is supplied, will be denounced as lies or part of some conspiracy. By definition, criticisms of the orthodoxy must be termed as "propaganda."

For example, the 1948 Smith-Mundt Act (repealed during the Bush Administration) prohibits government agencies from the domestic use of propaganda campaigns in America. However, it does contain provisions for "democracy promotion" propaganda campaigns abroad, which have taken the form of efforts to promote the neoliberal corporate ideology.[29] These overseas efforts for "democracy promotion" have been reported in the US media as confirmations of the global appeal of "the American way of life," and as a result of the close collusion between corporate media and the US government, are indirectly part of a sustained domestic propaganda program in favor of promoting both U.S. foreign policy and neoliberal ideology among the American population. As well as suppressing or falsifying facts, along with leaving the official version and assumptions unchallenged, the standard tactic of media conformity to government policy is to generate a "historical amnesia" that conceals failures and reversals of policy. This not only takes the form of media silence and self-censorship, but also takes the form of

---

[29] See Edward Bernays, *The Case for Reappraisal of U.S. Overseas Information Policies and Programs* (Praeger, 1970). See also See L. Bogart, *Premises for Propaganda* (New York: Free Press, 1976); M. Fishman, *Manufacturing the News* (University of Texas Press, 1980)

revisionism, falsification of records and testimonies, and the deliberate dissemination of misinformation. The double standards inherent in the use of propaganda (e.g., to vilify an enemy for performing the same kind of actions that are considered praiseworthy when performed by one's allies or oneself) reflect the excesses of partisan political rhetoric combined with a compliant press. These double standards are inherent to the political discourses that, by definition, hold any action against "us" to be evil and any act that "we" commit to be good (or, at least well-meaning). This dualism divests words of any universal meaning and, thereby, constitutes an Orwellian newspeak that becomes essential to the task of equating any rational criticism or even an alternative interpretation, analysis, and communication of reported events with being supportive of the enemy. It was for this reason that Herbert Marcuse considered it necessary for radical movements in opposition to the status quo of corporate capitalist society to create new political discourse capable of countering the double-speak of propagated by mass media.[30] Patriotism becomes synonymous with agreement and repetition.

Corporate media reliance on the use of double standards in developing interpretations (such as representing an act of military intervention and the establishment of a corrupt puppet regime as "democracy promotion") is more than blatant hypocrisy; it is inherent to the whole effort to present the illusion of freedom of the press while serving the propaganda needs of the government and its corporate partners. It is for this reason that "the War on Terror" concealed a permanent war not only against a shadow enemy, but against free speech, dissent, and criticism among the citizenry. When people were told by the Bush regime that "you are either with us or with the terrorists," the term "terrorist" became synonymous with anyone who damages, threatens, or even criticizes "national interests" (which are the interests of the government and its corporate partnerships). When this is combined with the threat and use of military force against citizens via the construction of a totalitarian police-state to preserve and pursue "national interests," then the rise of a corporate fascist state is concealed under the mask of "national security." For an example of this, we only need remember the corporate media support for the "War on Terror," the invasion of Iraq, and the passing of the Patriot Act after the attack on the World Trade Center,

---

[30] Cf. *An Essay on Liberation* (Boston: Beacon Press, 1969), pp. 74-7

September 11th, 2001.[31] Similarly, when leftist critics of the Obama Administration (for continuing or extending the policies of the Bush Administration) are labeled by the Democratic Party press and its supporters as supporting the Republican Party by creating dissent or "muddying the waters," the two-party system becomes totalitarian. For examples of this, we only need to look at how critics of "the war on terror" during the Bush Administration, including the use of drones, warrantless wiretapping, and indefinite detention, have become justifiers and apologists for these policies by the Obama Administration. The "them vs. us" attitude continues to indoctrinate people to oppose dissent, criticism, pluralism, and diversity, and even applaud undermining the conditions for democracy and the existence of a free press, while simultaneously representing their own suppressive actions as confirmations of the existence of their freedom of speech.

This explains why the educated elite are the prime targets of propaganda and also its main purveyors. Academics, journalists, and intellectuals consider themselves to be "opinion leaders" and, hence, are targeted by each other for being "mud rakers" and "aiding the enemy." The educated elite are used to keep debate within permissible bounds and establish a consensus that endorses the assertions underlying propaganda campaigns. Those who do not simply do not gain access to mainstream media and a large audience. When media attention and professional success are the rewards for championing the policies of the government and the opinions of the owners of media—or faithfully remaining within the framework of the two-party system in their criticisms of the policies of the government by adding credibility and intellectual justification for the slogans and memes of "the opposition"—and obscurity and marginalization are the outcomes of opposing the ruling system and its tactics, there are massive market pressures that select in favor of those that support the status quo and against those that challenge it. This acts as a safety-valve that channels the intellectual elite as being the means to stifle political dissent and independent thought among its own ranks. This is a form of self-censorship and cultural repression. In this way, political assertions and justifications can be publicly established as unchallenged truths—doctrines—

---

[31] Nancy Snow, *Information War: American Propaganda, Free Speech and Opinion Control since 9-11* (Seven Stories Press, 2003); Sheldon Rampton and John Stauber, *Weapons of Mass Deception: The Uses of Propaganda in Bush's War on Iraq* (Penguin, 2003); and, Arundhati Roy, *The Ordinary Person's Guide to Empire* (Southend Press, 2004)

and serve to limit what qualifies "intelligent debate" within "informed" intellectual circles. Anything outside these boundaries is immediately marginalized as being the irrational views of extremists, cranks, or conspiracy theorists—or the ill-informed—and, in this way, the intellectual elite both conform to the established agenda and promote it for the benefit of their own careers. The idea of media "self-censorship" was central to George Orwell's experience of the refusal of British publishers to publish his book *Animal Farm* during the Second World War because the publishers did not want to been seen to publish work that criticized the USSR, which was an ally of Britain.[32] Orwell observed that the censorship literary criticism was largely voluntary, without any need for government intervention, because of a tacit agreement between publishers that "it wouldn't do to mention a particular fact."

"Unpopular ideas can be silenced, and inconvenient facts kept dark, without the need for any official ban. Anyone who has lived long in a foreign country will know of instances of sensational items of news — things which on their own merits would get the big headlines-being kept right out of the British press, not because the Government intervened but because of a general tacit agreement that 'it wouldn't do' to mention that particular fact. So far as the daily newspapers go, this is easy to understand. The British press is extremely centralised, and most of it is owned by wealthy men who have every motive to be dishonest on certain important topics. But the same kind of veiled censorship also operates in books and periodicals, as well as in plays, films and radio. At any given moment there is an orthodoxy, a body of ideas which it is assumed that all right-thinking people will accept without question. It is not exactly forbidden to say this, that or the other, but it is 'not done' to say it, just as in mid-Victorian times it was 'not done' to mention trousers in the presence of a lady. Anyone who challenges the prevailing orthodoxy finds himself silenced with surprising effectiveness. A genuinely unfashionable opinion is almost never given a fair hearing, either in the popular press or in the highbrow periodicals." (Orwell, "Freedom of the Press")

---

[32] Michael Sheldon, *Orwell: the Authorized Biography* (New York: Harper Collins, 1991); Orwell's criticisms of censorship in the press can be found in his (unpublished) preface to Animal Farm, titled "The Freedom of the Press" http://orwell.ru/library/novels/Animal_Farm/english/efp_go

As Orwell quipped, "Circus dogs jump when the trainer cracks his whip, but the really well trained dog is the one that turns his somersault when there is no whip."[33]

Of course, this is nothing new. By 1922, the manipulation of public opinion and "the manufacture of consent" through the use of propaganda and mass media (radio and newspapers) had become central to governance in the United States and Great Britain.[34] The ideas of direct or classical democracy had largely fallen out of favor among political philosophers and scientists, and it was widely taken as a fact of political life that people were largely too ignorant and irrational to be capable of constituting an enlightened democracy, and instead were to be herded like sheep through the use of propaganda and regulations as methods of social engineering and the manufacture of consent. Direct democracy was considered to be something restricted to small communities, and in a modern society was an impossible ideal or a romantic fiction. Instead, liberal or representative democracy became the model for modern democracy in the United States and Britain. According to this model, decision-making should be left to experts (bureaucrats, technical experts, and political professionals) who act on behalf of the people. It was this change in how democracy was viewed that made "the manufacture of consent" into something central to the methods of democratic governance and the idea of the legitimacy of representative government. The idea was that the elite would use propaganda methods to shape public opinion to learn about policies, achieve a consent in favor of those policies, and understand and implement them in a "rational" manner, thereby achieving a stable society through the organization and manipulation of the masses. The elite assumed that propaganda was an essential instrument for the consensual and stable administration of society. The ideals of classical political philosophy was replaced with the positivistic idea that political science could be based on quantifiable factors and methods, such as polls and focus groups, and the insights of Freudian psychology into how drives and instincts could be subconsciously manipulated. Rather than place the emphasis on oration and the persuasiveness of individual speakers, as classical democracy does, the new method placed its emphasis on teams of

---

[33] Sheldon, *Orwell*, p. 367;
[34] Walter Lippmann, *Public Opinion* (New York: Free Press, 1977), first published in 1922, p. 158; Bernays *Propaganda* (1928) p. 14

researchers, writers, artists, photographers, film makers, psychologists, sociologists, and publicists. The rise in the new elite of bureaucrats, technical experts, and political professionals, who Chomsky later referred to as "the new Mandarins," led to an "invisible government" that used propaganda as the means by which the public or the majority could be educated for their own good and the good of society.[35] Echoing Bernays, Chomsky argues that the manipulation of the organized habits and opinions of the masses is an important element in American society, and those who manipulate this unseen mechanism of society constitute an invisible government and ruling power. Like it or not, whether in politics, finance, industry, agriculture, charity, politics, or education, propaganda has become the executive arm of the invisible government.

Party machines control and limit the choice of candidates on the ballot and the framework of public debate during the campaign. Within this limit, the electorate may vote for whomever they please. Beyond minor changes in personnel, the political elite remains unchanged. Events and opinions are already interpreted within the limits of the framework, and these limits allow candidates to appeal to public demands for leadership, policies, and reforms, which are themselves the products of successful propaganda campaigns. Politicians are able to sell ideas and policies by positioning themselves as responding to public demands, thereby maintaining the perception that this is done with the consent of the people (or at least the majority). Our political choices are all shaped by propaganda, just as our consumer choices are so shaped, especially when we are unaware of it and think that our choices are the outcome of our "rational" or "informed" decisions. The only real choices during political campaigns is between the propaganda campaigns of opposing political strategists to capture the minds of the public in the interest of some particular policy or candidate. In the absence of "rational agents" of classical political and economic philosophy, or "the philosopher kings" of ancient

---

[35] Noam Chomsky, *American Power and the New Mandarins* (New York: Pantheon Books, 1968). The idea of "the invisible government" by an elite of experts using propaganda for the good of society and the public was first discussed by Lippmann in his 1922 book *Public Opinion* (1977: p.1 and p. 158). See also the following books by Walter Lippmann: *A Preface to Politics* (Mitchell, 1913); *Liberty and the News* (Harcourt & Brace, 1920); *The Phantom Public* (Harcourt & Brace, 1925); *The Good Society* (Boston: Little & Brown, 1933); and *Drift and Mastery* (University of Wisconsin Press, 1985), first published in 1914

philosophy, society the only real competition is between propaganda techniques and teams of political experts. While we may well criticize any one example of propaganda taken in isolation, usually when used by "them" or whomever we consider to be "the opposition," propaganda itself remains quite invisible as it manipulates the selection and reception of news, opinions, and personalities. Thereby the ongoing and all-pervasive use of propaganda has become positioned as a necessary and seamless methodology to achieve a stable society and a legitimate representative democracy, even when it goes by other names, such as "getting the message out" and "educating the public." The propaganda industry becomes "the invisible government" under these conditions; by doing so, it presents itself as democracy and the marketplace of ideas, and unconsciously even the most zealous propagandist considers themselves to be a persuader and educator rather than a propagandist. Regardless of whether the propagandist works for a political party, an advertising agency, a trade association, a corporation or union, a charity, a special interest or pressure group, an NGO or non-profit educational organization, or a religious group, propaganda becomes the fundamental technique by which the interests and concerns of that group become known and promoted.

With the advancement of communication and mass media technologies, along with the overall complexity of society, the invisible government has developed incredibly sophisticated techniques to shape and control public opinion and attitudes. The ability to transmit ideas around the world and to any number of people at the push of a button has resulted in both the entrenched social integration of the public into the framework of political possibilities, which both establishes what constitutes which viewpoint or position qualifies as "mainstream," "moderate," or "centrist," thereby marginalizing other views as "radical" or "extreme," and thereby locks people into what on one side constitutes a totalitarian framework (which ridicules and dismisses alternatives) and on the other side intensifies factionalization and divisions within that framework of possibilities. Thus we end up with a very narrow set of possibilities constituting the totality of "left," "center," and "right" positions and viewpoints. Not only do people who live thousands of miles apart and have never met each other develop animosities and hostility towards each other, thereby fitting into the "them vs us" framework, but each and every person is left feeling themselves to be in control over what they learn and how they learn it, so their own position within the framework is the "informed" and "true" position while all the others are "propagandized." Such people can be readily manipulated and organized through both their associations with others via shared ideas and interests, as expressions of their personal identity in relation to a political group or party, and also by manipulating the many and complex divisions and differences that exist in any heterogeneous society like the United States of America. Thus ethnic, religious, racial, economic, ethical, social, and sexual differences all can be used to divide people along lines of political identity within the same and largely invisible framework, and these divisions and subdivisions can be used to intensify the level of hostility between groups and reduce the possibility of communication and compromise between them. The divisions within this invisible framework becomes the primary mechanism through which democracy is organized and expressed along party-lines, wherein each party attempts to collectivize its members into a "group mind," and thereby simplifying policy debate and political thinking into a choice between two possible positions: ours and theirs. Individual political speech and patterns of consumption are shaped by group influences, which shape the individual into a member of the group, and, by doing so, allow members of the group to identify each other as members, and therefore shape the habits and behavior of individuals. The individual may well think that they make their own decisions and choices, but these decisions and choices are shaped unconsciously by the groups to which individuals belong by systematically and technically manipulating the language and attitudes expressed by members of those groups. To understand how propaganda works, one needs to reveal and understand this mechanism.

It is for this reason that from the outset the founders of the public relations industry, such as Bernays, psychology and sociology were essential to provide a scientific footing for the understanding of the mechanisms by which propaganda is received. The study of mass psychology is essential to discover the best (most effective) propaganda techniques and methods through which the invisible government can manipulate the behavior of individuals within groups by using groups as the vehicle for propaganda. Even though psychology is not an exact science (in the way that physics and chemistry are exact sciences) because there remains irresolvable ambiguity when it comes to human interpretations and motivations, the basic psychological insight used by the modern propagandist is that human beings operate as political animals through group identity and behavior, and the group has mental influences and agency over and above those of the individual within the group. This idea of a "group mind" or "collective mind" captures and expresses the extent that individuals conform to group impulses and influences, and therefore the behavior of individuals within groups cannot be understood as the sum of individual choices and preferences. While individual human behavior is inherently unpredictable and ambiguous, and there are always unforeseen events to which individuals respond, the modern propagandist studies groups and how to influence the leaders of groups, with or without their cooperation, through the systematic and technical application of the study of the psychology of groups and the circumstances in which they exist. The propagandist uses their understanding of the mechanisms of cause and effect within the group mind to predict and change human speech and behavior in a consistent and reproducible manner. Propaganda influences the individual within groups and provides the group mind with ideas and motives without the individual necessarily being aware of them, and it is possible to predict with a high degree of accuracy the reception of propaganda within groups. Individuals do not actually need to gather together in assemblies or meetings to be influenced by the group mind. People remain social beings and continue to be influenced by their social groups even when they are alone.

While for the propagandist such a mechanism is essential for democracy, and its abuses should be constrained through the ethical practice of propaganda (i.e. that it does not promote falsehoods and that it is done for the public good), one of the greatest concerns is whether people can resist this mechanism and do without it. According to the classical view of democracy, people are only fit to govern themselves through education, knowledge, reason, and moral conscience. If the classical view is wrong, in any society people remain confused and chaotic without leadership, and therefore the use of propaganda is unavoidable (essential) if people are to remain connected to their leaders, which, along with technical and political experts, constitutes the ruling elite, and therefore propaganda becomes the means by which a stable and representative political system and culture become possible. By communicating with varied groups and leaders, shaping both the client's and public's understanding of their needs and how to satisfy them, the relations between the client and the public can be formulated in terms of propaganda strategies, tactics, and techniques that act as means for the understanding and articulation of the client's and public's interests. This may involve the client learning how better to listen to and interpret the public, and the public shifting in attitude towards its own needs and interests. For the "democratic" propagandist, people's goodwill, confidence, and understanding of their needs and how to satisfy them, are best achieved through the sharing of honest and frank information, and the function of propaganda is to aid this process rather than to deceive the public. A voter registration drive would be an example of this. Propaganda is used to emphasize the importance of voting and its relation with good citizenship and civic mindedness. False or misleading statements in this context are likely to backfire and do not serve any purpose other than risking public mistrust or even hostility.

Hence, even though the "democratic" public relations consultant uses propaganda, they must do so in a way that is already sensitive towards the public, and "democratic" propaganda campaigns are conducted in the spirit of inclusiveness (open to all citizens) and ethical conduct (using truthful information aimed at motivating citizens and best serving the interests of both the client and the citizenry), as well as dealing with the pragmatic concerns about how best to get the message across, whatever that message so happens to be. Professional and ethical concerns compel the "democratic" propagandist to choose their clients carefully and reject antisocial or fraudulent clients, and act in the best interest (however this is perceived) of both the client and the public. Should the public relations consultant get a reputation for being a propagandist this would bring their career to an end. Rather than deceive the public, the successful propagandist understands the content and structures of society, its social divisions, groups, leaders, and trends, and takes advantage of them by using them to disseminate the message and change cultural habits. The propagandist in this context can genuinely work towards helping political accountability and transparency of government, facilitate communication between the public and their representatives, inform the public about how the electoral process and legislature works, and raise public interest and participation in the political process, as well inform people about the problems facing the nation and possible methods to solve them. While this does not necessarily teach us much about the nature of good governance with the consent of the governed, it does teach us about the techniques required to gain that consent. For the "democratic" propagandist, the democratic function of propaganda is to facilitate communication between politicians and their constituents, between educators and the educated, governmental agencies and non-governmental organizations, and by providing citizens and their leaders with an awareness of "social needs" and "public consensus" (what classical political philosophers called the "the will of the people").

For the "democratic" propagandist, literacy, education, and communication are supposed to be the means by which citizens can learn how to make informed decisions and practical judgments, and thereby reach a democratic consensus in debate and deliberation with others, and, hopefully, recognize and choose good representatives and leaders. However, this has not worked to plan. Instead of reaching a consensus in accordance with a shared intellectual and moral conscience based on knowledge and reason, which are the hallmarks of rational thought and speech, citizens in a mass society passively receive "off-the-peg" opinions and positions within the narrow confines of the framework of mass media, through which the citizen identifies themselves in relation to those who share these opinions and positions, and against those who don't. Instead of political speech taking the form of enlightened deliberation and debate, whereby people learn how to govern themselves, the American public largely receives opinions and positions as a series of rubber stamps, a particular set of opinions and positions held by members of particular social groups, whereby the use and repetition of use confirms and reconfirms group membership and identity. Such rubber stamps are a shibboleth. Individuals will be hard pressed to explain why they hold to these opinions and positions, largely appealing to their own subjectivity ("it's my opinion" or "it's what I believe"), yet these opinions and positions are fundamental identifiers that guide how different people will interact with each other and relate to one another. Each rubber-stamp will find its "self-evident truth" confirmed and reinforced through usage in an all-pervasive cultural background of slogans and headlines, talking-points, criticisms and refutations in newspaper editorials, the opinions of celebrities and media pundits (TV and radio talk show hosts, etc.), carefully selected scientific data and historical interpretations, comedic stand-up routines and jokes, music lyrics and poetry, and in everyday conversation and humor shared by members of the same group. While the individual considers each rubber-stamp to be their own—a product of their own thought and experience—it is simply the case that the individual's rubber-stamps are duplicates of those held by millions of others, and confirmed and reinforced in the minds of individuals through such repetition when interacting with people who share the same opinions and positions. When under the same circumstances, and given the same stimuli, these individuals will speak with a collective voice and group mind, all the while thinking themselves to be the originators or discoverers of the opinion or belief, thereby finding "proof" of their correctness in their repetition throughout the members of the group, as they use rubber stamps to validate their membership of that group.

If there is merit in this view and the American public does receives most of their ideas and opinions in the form of rubber-stamps and mainstream media is primarily concerned with the production and distribution of these rubber-stamps, this is quite troubling for democracy. In the commercial section these take the form of advertisements and brand names, and integrating these into society through personal consumer preferences and lifestyle choices, often using celebrities and movie stars as leaders of fashion and consumer trends. In the political section, this takes the form of news and commentary, a framework of opinions and positions, often using media pundits, celebrities, and politicians as leaders of political discourse and calls for policy change. Through the coordinated organization of propaganda individuals are often unaware of it and consider rubber-stamps to be confirmed as self-evident truths when they are received from seemingly diverse and independent media sources. Of course when propaganda is used to spread a particular doctrine, and while the merits of that doctrine do depend on the cause to which it is directed and also the correctness of the information that are used in support of the doctrine in question. Without mass support and public approval, any campaign or movement to change culture or policy will fail, no matter how noble or laudable it may be. Efforts to make and sustain any changes in society will be unsuccessful unless the dissemination and use of rubber-stamps is sufficiently organized to regiment the framework public opinion and demands. If people support the cause and the information is repeated by a number of sources, they are quite unlikely to be aware of having received propaganda at all, and in this way they too can participate in the dissemination of propaganda without knowing that they are doing so, simply by repeating the rubber-stamp as if it is their own opinion or idea. When propaganda becomes "owned" by the individual through the use of rubber-stamps it becomes invisible and tacit to speech and thought.

Whether or not any particular communication is labelled as propaganda by its speaker depends on its function and the intention of the speaker, but in most part the disseminators of propaganda are unaware of it and consider themselves to be engaged in "free speech" and the sharing of opinions, all the while denouncing rival or opposing groups for using propaganda, given the sinister connotations associated with the word. This is as true when involved in political speech as it is when deciding between commercial goods and services. There seems little possibility of regaining any sense of neutrality to the term, given the intimate psychological connection between rubber-stamps and social identity, and once any opinion or interpretation has been established through propaganda, people within propagandized groups will continue to disseminate it as a series of rubber-stamps, each repeated and reinforced by the group members, and, as such, propaganda becomes not only the basis by which pressure can be brought to bear on politicians to act on the rubber-stamp and incorporate it into public discourse and policy. This also provides the vocabulary and associations used by people to take in everyday conversation about society and social problems and needs. When people associate with groups they learn and develop language by learning new expressions and ways of putting expressions together, inserted into everyday conversation and humor, this often takes the form of the repetition of slogans, talking-points, and sound bites.

Once stereotypes and prejudices are clothed in rubber-stamps, the propagandist can use them to establish the self-evident truth of the stereotypes and prejudices used to manipulate the public to demand specific changes in policy or new laws, taxes, and action. For examples, often without definition, and usually applied in an ad hoc and inconsistent manner, the term "free market" is one such rubber-stamp which will immediately be accepted and used by members of the group for which this is a self-evident value, while members of opposing groups or political parties will take this term as a sinister term that they associate with the opposing group or party, or sinister forces and conspiracies. It simply does not matter whether any particular rubber-stamp has any meaning or content outside its usage within the group for it to be continued to be used by that group. It has a social function in establishing group identity and coherence, and to challenge the term on the basis of its empirical or semantic truth (its factuality or meaning) is simply to talk at cross-purposes with members of that group, and any such challenge will be taken to be an attack on that group, or will result in the challenger being associated with an opposing group and dismissed as a result. In this way, challenges to the factuality or meaning of slogans like "the free market is democratic" will be taken that the challenger opposes "the free market" and "democracy," thereby showing themselves to be an opponent of the group and subject to further rubber-stamping (e.g. declaring challengers to be "communists" or "socialists," and therefore invalid by definition), which are used to deflect and suppress the challenge as being intrinsically suspect in virtue of being a challenge. In this way, when a particular rubber stamp is labelled as "conservative" or "liberal" by people who oppose members of that group, it is a way of silencing the user of that rubber stamp as having nothing of value to say, and compels all political speech to take the form of either confrontation or conformity. As such, rubber stamps are not merely clichés or platitudes, but serve an important role in cementing social group identity, deflecting criticisms and censoring alternative interpretations, forming and maintaining political factions, and providing political speech with content and structure, and thereby shaping public discourse and political culture. Rubber stamps are fundamental units of political speech within the so-called "Culture War" within America; they effectively allow the identification of allies and enemies, and providing a means by which proponents of one particular discourse can inoculate themselves against criticisms, inconvenient facts, and alternative ways of thinking.

The propagandist, whether consciously or unconsciously, has no need for consistency when using rubber stamps. In this way, the same propagandist or propaganda techniques can be used as equally well when selling cigarettes and tobacco products as they can be used in stop smoking campaigns. One simply invents new rubber stamps depending on one's purposes and attempts to insert these into peoples' everyday speech and conversations. Hence, despite having served the tobacco industry for decades, Bernays was able to use the same propaganda techniques and strategies to serve public health and anti-smoking campaigns, and thereby increase public awareness of the carcinogenic properties of tobacco smoke and the dangers of passive smoking. Bernays argued that charities, businesses, educators, churches, and politicians all use propaganda, and whether any particular speech is termed as "propaganda" or "information" depends on the propaganda-function of labelling it as such. The act of labelling is a matter of rubber stamping the speech as either being suspicious and sinister (deceptive or manipulative), or as truth and simply a statement of the facts. Just as when a group of citizens uses propaganda to promote an opinion or policy, they will label their own speech as "free speech," and denounce their opponents for using "propaganda," the use of propaganda is itself largely a fluid and invisible social effort by particular groups to create and shape public discourse and policy by inserting particular rubber stamps into public discourse and political debate, thereby promoting that particular group within society by promoting their enterprise, ideas, and language, and dismissing those of their opponents and critics. It is all-pervasive throughout society, and used to enroll public support for every important undertaking, whether it is a public works program, a new building, a movie, a college or university course, government bonds or gold, or electing a president. This is all achieved by inserting rubber stamps into public discourse. Once public discourse has been changed through the use of propaganda, not only will the proponents of particular rubber-stamps continue to disseminate and reinforce them as "truth" or "information" through the repeated use of those rubber stamps, but the terms of public debate react and responds, and therefore is shaped by those rubber stamps not only to maintain and reinforce stereotypes, prejudices, and assumptions, but more importantly to establish the terms through which the issue can be discussed and deliberated upon. Opponents and critics end up in a reactionary position as a result, and, even in opposition and criticism, end up repeating and reinforcing the same rubber stamps used by the people they oppose and criticize.

Propaganda shapes the worldview of people and regiments public discourse in newspapers, television, and radio, and also on the Internet and in everyday speech. Rubber-stamps become the currency of exchange within the marketplace of ideas and show one's allegiances and associations within that marketplace. The group mind does not think, at least not in the same way that an individual does, but through the social impulse to follow leaders and imitate the speech and attitudes of group members, the choice and use of rubber stamps provides the group with mental characteristics, motives, impulses, habits, and emotions, and a worldview. Having a shared worldview and language (patterns of speech and listening, as well as vocabulary and their implied meanings) are qualifying conditions for membership of any group. By manipulating these characteristics, and by manipulating leaders, the propagandist is able to effect the popularity of a song or a vacation resort, cause a run on a bank or panic in the stock exchange, create a best seller or box office success, or get politicians elected to public office. Clichés, stereotypes, memes, phrases, images, and slogans all form rubber stamps that are used to connect the beliefs of the members of the group and the identity of the individual within that group to larger units of discourse (talking points, arguments, opinions, reasons, etc.) and the shared worldview of the group, while presenting the individual with the illusion of choice and ownership of those ideas and meanings. Hence it remains possible to turn a group against a particular politician by exposing the groups that support and fund his or her campaign as "special interests," thereby connecting that support with the idea of corruption and deceit if those special interests are perceived as opposing the group's interests, yet the exact same circumstances can be celebrated as forms of "free speech" and "freedom of association" if the interests of the group and those of "the special interest" converge and support each other. Similarly, voters can be turned against any politicians or special interest group by connecting their agenda with some bogey man, for example opponents of a single-payer healthcare system simply need to declare it to be "socialism" to galvanize the opposition of conservative groups and there is no need to explain what "socialism" is or why a single-payer healthcare system would be an example of it.

The propaganda value of radio and film, alongside newspapers, within the so-called democratic countries has been recognized since before the Second World War.[36] Yet, within contemporary society, one of the primary functions of propaganda is to divide people against each other, acting within factions, and responding to an increasingly factionalized media, via the reinforcement of their prejudices and worldviews. This inoculates the target audience against any views or facts that challenge or problematize these prejudices and worldviews. It achieves this by generating skepticism and suspicion against any or all other media sources by rubber-stamping views and opinions as either belonging to "us" or "them." This in itself undermines the possibility of a frank exchange of views, opinions, and facts between different people. Yet democracy depends on this possibility. Within the corporate state, a two-party system is effectively two propaganda machines designed to keep the population divided against each other and distracted from the corporate control over government. By responding to each other and maintaining focus on wedge-issues, these two propaganda machines complement and enhance each other even though they seem opposed to one another. They achieve this by controlling the focus of political debate and

---

[36] Lazerfield, P.F., *Print, Radio and Film in a Democracy* (University of Chicago Press, 1942)

framing the media coverage of public opinion to the extent that sloganeering and rubber-stamping has replaced public debate. This simulacrum has replaced political discourse. This has created a form of political Newspeak that prevents new ideas and critical thinking from entering the public realm, which prevents the supporters from either party from being able to communicate with supporters of the other party, without simply slinging slogans and sound-bites at each other. Given that the measures of public opinion have been reduced to polls and votes, the degeneration and polarization of the political process has become completely concealed from the public. People are forced to be either "for" or "against," or "yes" or "no," without any possibility of democratic deliberation. There is no possibility of people debating or controlling the questions asked of them. They are simply herded into one of two corrals; all the while the illusion of choice is maintained. Pepsi or Coke?

Jacque Ellul and the Sociology of Propaganda:

Once we look at how group think and group identity are the mechanisms for the dissemination of propaganda, we need to analyze it as a sociological phenomenon. How can we do this? The French social theorist Jacque Ellul provided us with a starting point in his 1965 book *Propaganda*.[37] As a sociological phenomenon, modern propaganda is a product of the technological society.[38] The all-pervading efforts of modern propaganda holds the technological society together and affirms (motivates) its further development and expansion of technology and techniques to improve efficiency and power. Ellul was concerned with propaganda in terms of its effectiveness in obtaining results through techniques. His analyses took Harold Lasswell's 1939 definition of propaganda as its starting point: "To maximize the power at home by subordinating groups and individuals, while

---

[37] Jacque Ellul, *Propaganda: the Formation of Men's Attitudes* (New York: Alfred A. Knopf, 1965)

[38] J. Ellul, *The Technological Society* (New York: Knopf, 1964). Also, for its significance on the origin and development of science, see K. Rogers, *On the Metaphysics of Experimental Physics* (Basingstoke New York: Palgrave Macmillan, 2005); *The Fire of Hephaestus: Rethinking Science, Rethinking Nature* (Los Angeles, CA: Trébol Press, 2016).

reducing material cost of power."[39] As a technological phenomenon, propaganda is concerned with the application of efficient techniques. Ineffective propaganda is not propaganda at all.

"Not only is propaganda itself a technique, it is also an indispensable condition for the development of technical progress and the establishment of a technological civilization. And, as with all techniques, propaganda is subject to the law of efficiency." (Ellul, p. x)

Modern propaganda cannot exist without technologies of mass communication—mass media—including newspapers, radio, television, music recordings, art reproduction, motion pictures, and, today, the Internet. Billions of people worldwide are connected to the Internet via computers and mobile devices, such as phones, laptops, tablets, and a whole new generation of microelectronic based portable telecommunication transmitters and receivers that are becoming increasingly smaller. Already such devices take the form of goggles attached to an earpiece, and the physical implant of microelectronic communications technology is around the corner. Such devices will be invisible to outward inspection and simply part of their users' body and daily life. Modern propaganda is also based on a century of sociological and psychological research, for which millions of people around the world have unwillingly been the test subjects of its experiments, trials, successes and failures, through public relations, advertising, political campaign, psychological warfare, news reporting, opinion manipulation, public information, and education. The findings of social psychology, behaviorism, sociology, and mass communications research have informed and been informed by the propaganda techniques developed during the First World War, the Russian Revolution, the rise of Hitler and Nazi Germany, the Second World War, the Chinese Revolution, the Cold War, the "War on Drugs," and the "War on Terrorism." However, even though modern propaganda depends on developments in science and technology for its existence, it also requires specific sociological conditions to exist.

One of these sociological conditions is provided by a mass society comprised of isolated individuals who relate to each other and society itself

---

[39] Lasswell, H., and Blumenstock D., *World Revolutionary Propaganda* (New York: Alfred A. Knopf, 1939)

via mass communications technology and receive their knowledge and view of the world through mass media. The individual gains freedom and autonomy from the bonds of family, village, parish, guild, union, and community by becoming integrated into mass society via technology and economic relations (those of labor, production, exchange, and consumption). The individual can only escape the grip of mass society and modern propaganda by disconnecting completely from mass media and communications, and by returning to organic associations and community life based on shared experiences, meanings, and relationships which are unmediated by mass media and communications. It is only by returning to the immediacy of practical and intimate interpersonal relations, which are themselves conditioned by history and Nature through their consequences and horizon of possibilities, can human beings hope to explore and develop the kind of primitive and rational relations based on mindful care and attentiveness to reality that are antithetical to modern propaganda. However, except by disappearing into the woods or some other isolated place, this is hardly a viable option for the majority of people.

The urbanization, specialization, professionalization, *and technologization* of human life have provided the means by which the individual has been uprooted from community life and local contexts to become an individual within a mass society, dependent on that society to survive, and susceptible to propaganda. While the deconstruction of mass society and its reconstruction into a pluralistic and diverse society based on free associations and communities without being mediated by mass communications, runs the risk of degenerating into a feudal society based on one rule by elites, or barbarism and civil war, it also has the potential to evolve into a participatory, emancipatory, and egalitarian society, wherein local self-determination and self-sufficiency are both aspirations and practical possibilities against which the current state of affairs can be critically evaluated and judged. It is not just the material, spiritual, and emotional life of participatory democracy with communities, free associations, and unions that counter the influences of modern propaganda, but it is the immediacy of shared, practical concerns and experiences in a context of localized problem solving through communicative action based on interpersonal and mutually respectful relations. Without the importation of generalized abstractions, interpretations, and symbols—exchanged and disseminated as rubber-stamps within mass mediated groups—propaganda cannot occur, as one must deal with one's neighbors in their terms, developed in local contexts to relate immediate experiences and problems.

Under these circumstances, the individual in mass society needs propaganda in order to participate within that society as a citizen and autonomous agent. He must judge for himself. She must be informed. Whereas localized communities develop horizontal and organic relations between people—a web of interpersonal relations through which daily life is conducted without needing mass media or mass communications—in the mass society, the technological society, co-existence with others occurs via vertical and mediated relations, quite literally via technology and satellites, wherein mass media becomes the only shared public space. The individual human being is transformed into "the mass man" via the mass society.[40] Within such a society, propaganda becomes the glue that holds it together and gives it collective meaning as something the individual can grasp as a whole and communicate to other individuals. Propaganda mediates public discourse itself; language becomes reduced to the exchange of rubber-stamps, clichés, stereotypes, and reinforcements of each other's worldview, interpretations, and slogans. The individual remains quite isolated.

We need to qualify what is meant by isolated individual here. In modern society, the individual may belong to many groups simultaneously, whether political groups, work related, friends, financial interests, or entertainment, and the individual may well find overlapping concerns and interests with others within these groups. In modern society, individuals have families and sexual relationships. But the individual does not owe any allegiance to the group and is not bound to them. The individual is able to change groups. Families are small, nuclear rather than extended families, and divorce rates are high. The individual's primarily relation is to society itself, as an individual with social rights, given by law and the constitution, and secured by the legal and political institutions of society. Propaganda is the means by which the individual is informed of this. The individual's economic relations are mediated by money and time, through relations of exchange, secured by legal and political institutions, administration, regulatory bodies, and banking. The individual's relations are mediated by abstracts, as he or she measures his or her place within society in terms of these abstracts— like money, rights, the

---

[40] Cf. Ellul chapter 2 and José Ortega Y Gasset, *The Revolt of the Masses.*

State, and the law—and their exchange value and general currency within interactions as mechanisms of interaction. The individual finds themselves developing their identity in terms of their group identities, but these too are mediated by abstracts in relation to society. It is in this sense that the individual is isolated—wherein the totality of their relations with others are mediated by abstracts and exchange values; money for products and services, time and labor for money, money and time for friends and relations. Discourse and communication are also mediated by these abstracts, rubber-stamps and group relations, all in relation to society, rather than directly between persons bound to each other through the immediacy of place and common experiences. Through the technologies of mediation, exchange, and communication, the individual connects to others, and these technologies themselves give substance and meaning in relation to the whole society—the technological society—as a shared mass society comprised of isolated individuals, even when they lived in densely populated cities in close proximity to each other.

It is through these media that brings the isolated individual in new constant contact with propaganda, as both propagandee and propagandist, to the extent that propaganda fulfils a psychological need for being knowledgeable about political and current affairs, about events around the world, and belonging to groups, sharing their prejudices and worldview, and being able to express their opinion about the issues and problems of current and contemporary concerns and interest to other group members. At least, this explains the popularity of so-called "social media" sites like Facebook and Twitter.

"For propaganda to *succeed*, it must correspond to a need for propaganda on the individual's part... one cannot reach through propaganda those who do not need what it offers. The propagandee is by no means just on innocent victim. He provokes the psychological action of propaganda, and not merely leads himself to it, but even derives satisfaction from it. Without this previous, implicit consent, without this need for propaganda experienced by practically *every* citizen of the technical age, propaganda could not spread." (Ellul, p. 121)

Hence we need to understand propaganda in a two-fold sociological and psychological sense as providing the means by which the established social order can be reproduced and also by providing the individual with the means to feel that they both belong to and are participants in the established social order, even when they feel that they are critical of that social order. Propaganda is the means by which power is socially normalized and intellectually grasped by both mass society and the individuals within it. It provides unity within the totality, by those who seek to reform and transform the system from within, as well as by those who seek to enjoy the privileges and advantages afforded to them by the system.

In the technological society, itself constructed via techniques and inventions to make all facets of human life efficient, constantly driven to innovate new gadgets and powers, everything in the political and economic spheres is penetrated and molded by propaganda. By its nature, in order to be effective, propaganda operates without people being conscious of it at all. However, for Ellul, propaganda is only partly understandable in terms of psychology; it must also be analyzed as a sociological phenomenon, disseminated within and acting upon social groups and whole nations. Any adequate definition must include an understanding of propaganda is an effective technique applied to change human opinions and actions; psychological welfare to demoralize a population or the enemy; re-education and brainwashing of prisoners; and public relations and cultural change. In all its areas of application, propaganda is directed towards making people conform, and in this respect, it has general characteristics and effects regardless of whether it was used in Nazi Germany, the Soviet Union, or the United States of America. Propaganda operates in the technology society (whatever ideology its political regime declares itself to champion) by solving problems created by technology, integrating people into the technological world by providing the means of adapting themselves to that world and its development. While the level of advancement of propaganda depends on how developed the administrative techniques and political organization of the regime, it does not depend on the nature of its ideology. For Ellul, the power and necessity of propaganda in modern society reveals it as an anti-democratic force that suppressed human freedom and makes the democracy impossible. Propaganda is a danger to the human personality.

"When man will be fully adapted to this technological society, when he will end by obeying with enthusiasm, convinced of the excellence of what is he forced to do, the constraint of the organization will no longer be felt by him; the truth is, it will no longer be a constraint, and the police will have nothing to do. The civil and technological good-will and the enthusiasm for the right social myths—both created by propaganda—will have finally solved the problem of man." (Ellul, p. xviii)

Symbols, myths, abstracts, and stereotypes are not only the psychological elements of propaganda, but are the elements of its grammar and syntax. The individual in mass society may well be a materialist and they are certainly a worker and consumer, but through these elements of propaganda the individual is detached from objective reality. Instead, they interact with an abstract reality. The individual needs propaganda in order to consider themselves connected and informed, and hence is readily manipulated by propagandists to feel intensely about any particular issue, event, or personality, although fleetingly, and is easily distracted. Propaganda fills the need created by alienation and isolation, as the individual is increasingly detached from personal relations and the meaning of human existence, and, by interacting with an abstract reality, the individual is both given the sense of being involved and also shielded from reality. As alienation increases and attention spans decrease, the intense activity of absorbing and dissemination propaganda increases to fill the individual's time. This is particularly evident in the fast pace interactions of point and click social media. The individual becomes so lost to news cycles and media-centric opinion that the possibility of genuine public debate based on private reflection on matters of sincere concern and immediate experience become repressed, all the while the individual feels themselves to be well-informed and knowledgeable. The individual becomes propagandee and propagandist in order to participate in public opinion and allegiance, without being aware that this is happening at all. This allows the individual to feel that they know what public opinion is and how they stand in relation to it, while being submerged in a "for or against" relationship to "the news."

"The 'majority effect,' so essential as a means of propaganda, can be felt only in a mass society; for example, the argument that "all Frenchmen want peace in Algeria" or, on the other hand, "all Frenchmen want to hold on to Algeria" is valid only if "All Frenchmen" represents an immediate and massive reality. Thus the mass society was a primary condition for the emergence of propaganda; once formed, it evoked the power and functions of propaganda." (Ellul, p. 96)

The conditions of life in mass societies leads to individual alienation, isolation, and frustration; produce fragmentary and shallow relations between people; lead to a loss of feelings of intimacy and solidarity; increases feelings of insecurity and anxiety; and, intensifies the conditions in our environment. These conditions and their consequences lead to the development of a psychological need for propaganda, which acts as a substitute for knowledge, a sense of place and belonging, and a meaningful understanding of the world. Whether the individual communes with "the majority" or "the leader" through propaganda, the effects are the same: the individual feels connected with society as a totality. Even though it leaves the individual in an irrational relation with reality, propaganda forms a bridge between the individual and mass society, thereby allowing the individual to feel integrated with society, informed, and capable of grasping and communicating reality in the terms given by the propagandist. Thus the individual has an opinion on worldly events of which the individual has no firsthand knowledge or experience, while feeling themselves an expert or well-informed on the subject. The tendency will be towards self-affirmation and self-justification of the absolute correctness of one's "own" opinion, and the absolute incorrectness of the opposing view. Questions outside the frame given by the propagandists will be unaskable or dismissed as extremist (or naive) without a second thought. For example, individuals in America learning about Iran's nuclear program from American newspapers, television, radio, and the Internet will find the parameters of debate quite consumed by the limits of acceptable opinion. The individual may well consider diplomacy and sanctions to be the best and only way to dissuade Iran from pursuing the program. Or the individual may well parrot that this is naive and military action is the only realistic option; although there may well be some room for disagreements as to whether the military action should be conducted by the United Nations, Israel, or the United States. But what will be unaskable is whether Iran has a right to pursue a nuclear weapons program, given that the major opponents of Iran within the International Community all have nuclear weapons. And it almost goes without saying that the individual will not question the validity or sources of the evidence presented before them. It does not seem to matter how many times that the government lies and the media is complicit in these lies, the individual propagandee will take the news and facts at face value as being the facts, even if they disagree with the interpretation of the meaning of those "facts."

Someone always has to suffer the consequences of irrational and ideologically-motivated decisions, but in mass societies these consequences can be dumped on some underclass, such as the poorest people or people of the Third World, by using the powers of technology and economic leverage, in such a way as to leave the individual within mass society shielded from the consequences of these decisions. This shielding is necessary for propaganda to remain effective. When an increasing percentage of the population experiences the consequences of the decisions of the ruling elite, say during an economic crisis or depression, the effectiveness of the propaganda being used diminishes in direct proportion to the loss of shielding. When workers have jobs and can maintain a certain level of consumption and security, they will not question the propaganda in favor of the economic system, but should they lose their jobs, their security, and their level of consumption, it becomes harder to sustain the status quo through propaganda. Of course scapegoating can always be used to blame immigrants, minorities, or unions for unemployment, but even this becomes questionable when experience shows the ruling elite maintaining their own level of consumption and privileges while the lower classes suffer the consequences of the ruling elite's decisions.

Remember back to the media coverage of the aftermath of Hurricane Katrina in New Orleans in August 2005 when it soon became apparent that the portrayal of how the Bush Administration and FEMA were handling the disaster rapidly contradicted the reality of the disaster itself, when it was apparent that the only response made by the Bush Administration for the first few days was to handle media spin and reassure people that the government was doing a good job.[41] This contradiction was so evident that Anderson Cooper on CNN condemned the government response after Mayor Ray Nagin's expression of outrage at the government and plea for help on WWL-radio. The hologram was disrupted and people began to glimpse the reality. The flaws in society were revealed in the aftermath of the hurricane and the burst levees. Television audiences saw a starkly class-based society in which the private sector had failed to provide a means for poor Americans without their own transportation to escape the city, leaving them huddled in the New Orleans stadium or the roofs of their flooded houses. Footage of the Coastguard struggling alone to provide relief to these people shocked the nation. Yet, all the while, the Bush Administration had claimed that FEMA was working well. As television audiences saw a glimpse of societal collapse in the wake of a natural disaster, the media began to focus its attention on "looters" and demanded that the National Guard be brought in to restore order. FEMA was not working well. This grew increasingly

---

[41] See Douglas Brinkley, *The Great Deluge: Hurricane Katrina, New Orleans, and the Mississippi Gulf Coast* (Harper, 2007); and *When the Levees Broke: A Requiem In Four Acts* (2006) directed by Spike Lee and Sam Pollard.

apparent regardless of all the efforts to blame "looters." Where was the federal government? Why were the news helicopters there but not FEMA? When footage of dying and dead elderly Americans were broadcast around the country and the unsanitary conditions of shelters and hospitals, along with the pleas of children and their parents, and still nothing was being done by the authorities, except to protect stores and buildings from "looters," the hologram could not be sustained. The government was not working well. America was not working well. Finally, after widespread criticism and condemnation from all quarters, the federal government began to act. Food, water, blankets, and medical supplies were brought in. The National Guard started helping, rather than guarding. People were evacuated. Everyone breathed a sigh of relief. Despite the Bush Administration's insistence that Americans should not play "the blame game" and now was the time to get on with the business of allocating the lucrative reconstruction contracts, it was clear that "the blame game" was going to be played. The Bush Administration had to act quickly to control the spin... accusations of racism... deny, deny, deny... change the story... business as usual, and leave the talking heads on television and opinion spinners in the newspapers to argue back and forth whether the Bush Administration was racist or not. The system itself was no longer questioned. The hologram was restored.

Hence, we can see that immediate first-hand and immediate experience of the facts and problems of life, understood through personal reflection and interpersonal communication, problematizes propaganda and strains it to the point of exposing its limits, inconsistencies, and contradictions. Propaganda is simply most effective when individuals rely on second-hand and mediated experiences of others in order to remain informed about current events and society in general. In order to be most effective (and invisible), propaganda must utilize symbols and abstracts without them being contradicted by immediate problems and experiences. In order for modern propaganda to exist within a society and effectively manipulate public opinion (or distract it) the following conditions must be met:

1. individuals exist as isolated individuals within a mass society;

2. experiences of current events and social problems are second-hand and mediated;

3. mass media is established and disseminated through mass communications technologies;

4. mass communications technologies are controlled by a political or economic elite;

5. controlled mass media have diverse forms (newspapers, television, radio, books, movies, websites, etc.), are seemingly independent (but are not), and are all-pervasive.

Often when we think of propaganda, we think of it coming from a cabal of professional propagandists, on behalf of a leader, a political party, a corporation, a ruling elite, etc. This is what has been termed as *vertical propaganda*. It comes from above, developed behind the scenes, and disseminated through mass multimedia and official channels, posters, literature, film, etc. The relationship between the individual and their leader is mediated by propaganda, which they receive passively and make their own to demonstrate their loyalty and political affiliation. However, there is another form of propaganda that is of particular interest to sociological analysis. This propaganda is disseminated and developed by members of groups, shared between each other and used to enroll others into their group. This form of propaganda is termed as *horizontal propaganda*. Individuals within the group are active receivers and disseminators of propaganda— simultaneously propagandists and propagandees—through which they develop and demonstrate their political consciousness. Through both vertical and horizontal propaganda, the individual maintains an unconscious and irrational relation with the group identity, but feels passionately that they belong to the group and some higher purpose through vertical propaganda, which mediates their relation to the political superstructure, and actively and intellectually participate in propaganda within the group through horizontal propaganda, which mediates their relation to the political superstructure via their social group identity.

The individual participates actively in the life of this group, in a genuine and lively dialogue, but the hallmark of horizontal propaganda is when the group polices itself for "correct views and opinions" as a condition for continued group membership. In China, during the early 1960s, the group watched carefully to see that each member speaks, expresses itself, and gives correct opinions. Only by speaking the correct opinions could the individual gradually discover his own convictions (which also will be those of the group), become irrevocably involved, and help others to form the opinions of the group, which helps each individual to discover the correct line. The individual feels that they are discovering or expressing the truth in their own terms, while simultaneously embodying the prejudices, rubber-stamps, and worldview of the group and the political superstructure. In this way, vertical and horizontal propaganda can become intertwined and developed in relation to each other.

Of course, this means that one of the fundamental problems facing the propagandist is how to maintain group homogeneity. In Mao's China this was solved by destroying traditional groups, like the family, and by dividing society up into new political units, the communes, in which horizontal propaganda could work, that could maintain their connection with the Communist Party and leadership through vertical propaganda. However, in a modern heterogeneous society like contemporary America, this problem is solved through partitioned and factionalized mass media. By dividing society into political factions that distrust each other—declaring each other to be liars and propagandists—and are incapable of communicating with each other in a spirit of mutual respect and understanding, society can be broken up into homogenous bubbles (holograms) in which micro-totalitarianism can be achieved while maintaining the illusion of democracy and pluralism in political debate.

The most pernicious aspect of vertical and horizontal propaganda is that the former maintains the individual in a state of irrational passivity, while the latter intensifies that state of irrationality through active participation under the guise of becoming informed and educated, while informing and educating others through the dissemination of propaganda. Even when considering themselves to be social critics and dissenters exercising their right to free speech, group members conform to the myths, expectations, formulas, norms, and rubber-stamps of the group. Deviation from the group's shared prejudices and worldview will not be tolerated. People who deviate from these norms rapidly become excluded and treated with suspicion, and therefore members of the group actively police and correct themselves in relation to the approval of other group members. The individual becomes encircled by self-reinforcing discourse and behavior in relation to the propaganda disseminated by the group. Propaganda develops a pathological resistance to reason, learning, and persuasion, and undermines the human ability for intelligent and imaginative thought.[42] It leads to an increasingly irrational and reactionary population. This is deeply disturbing because it means that strategies of social engineering and the engineering of consent require and utilize an antidemocratic divide and conquer tactic—dividing society into mutually antagonistic factions—by not only exploiting ignorance, fear, resentment, and irrationally, but also fostering them and embedding them deeper in people by exploiting and reinforcing the worst of human nature.[43] If the population is continually assaulted by propaganda to divide people against each other and place irrational human desires and fears over human needs and reasoned deliberation, this undermines the foundation for a good society

The damaging effect of propaganda is that is requires and intensifies the irrationality of the individual acting within groups. It erodes and destroys the ability of human beings to think critically and reflect rationally on the information they receive, what they truly know, and how to discover the truth about the world. It is accepted without understanding providing it agrees with the preconceptions and assumptions of group identity. Its origins and foundations, and its premises and preconditions, as well as its entailments, are left unquestioned and unknown by the individual for whom it is a "self-evident truth." This is the consequence of propaganda's appeal to psychological needs, fears, vanity, social instincts, and feelings and passions in general, even if its details and development we made logically in relation to the facts. Propaganda can be rationally developed—with careful attention to its tactics, methods, and strategy—but it retains an irrational relation with the individual. If the mask that it creates for the individual—with which they identify themselves—was to be removed, the individual would be left with a void and the inevitable descent into nihilism. The intellectual capacity and reflective core of the individual is eroded to nothing at all—and this intensifies the individual's need for propaganda to fill that void. In this sense, we can describe, without irony, propaganda as addictive.

Propaganda integrates all the forces that act on the individual within modern society, and gives them significance in such a way that fully justifies

---

[42] See Lewis Mumford, *Values for Survival* (Harcourt & Brace, 1946).
[43] Graham Wallas, *Human Nature in Politics* (London: Constable, 1948), first published 1920

the individual's conformity or leaves the individual isolated and impotent in their dissent. The individual can stockpile guns and ammunition, put anti-government posters in their windows, and talk of rebellion and sedition, all in response to videos they see on YouTube (or something they saw on any of the many "conspiracy theory" sites on the Internet, such as Infowars.com), but they either conform to the demands and expectations of society, in contradiction to their discourse, or they remain impotent and isolated n their private realm, incapable of engaging in coordinated and organized political action that will change the social order. The dissenting individual is forced to choose between being a conformist and hypocrite, or an isolated and alienated individual lost impotently in the privacy of their own thoughts and inaction. Their stockpiles become simply a consumer fetish and an expensive form of hoarding. Either way, the trends and courses of action that develop society remain unaltered and all-pervasive, and the individual is driven deeper into paranoia, alienation, and pathology. What is the aim of conspiracy theories and anti-government and anti-democratic rhetoric within corporate media? The aim is to alienate the audience from politics; to make people feel a sense of disgust and anger at the political process and institutions, but feel largely helpless to do anything about it, except to retreat into the private sphere. Its aim is to generate a hatred of politics and government, a distain for political parties, and a disinclination for democratic participation. The consequence of this media-generated public alienation, apathy, and cynicism is that the public retreats into its allotted role of passive spectator, leaving political participation to professional politicians, bureaucrats, lobbyists, and their corporate paymasters. As a result of anti-government propaganda and the cult of personality that surrounds a figure-head like the President of the United States, with both parties playing the political games of faux opposition and collecting campaign donations by stirring up passions over the perennial "wedge issues," the population remains largely distracted from and oblivious to the operations of "the invisible government" of cartels of corporations, powerful industries, and moneyed interests. All of this, allows the construction of the corporate state to continue unnoticed.

Following on from Bernays' application of mass psychology, Ellul made an important point that needs to be understood, if we wish to understand modern propaganda. It is a mistake to think that modern propaganda is based in lies and fictions, and, as a result believe that propaganda cannot be true and be propaganda at the same time. All successful propaganda is based in truth, even if it also uses lies and fictions to deceive its target audience. Otherwise it would be easily exposed and its effectiveness would be limited and short-lived. Propaganda operates by telling the truth, but only as a particular version of the truth that is based in carefully selected interpretations and representations (cartoons, movies, slogans, memes, etc.) based on half-truths, limited truth, and truth out of context. Propaganda is based on a particular relationship with the truth, and we remain vulnerable to it as long as we believe that propaganda is based only in lies and fictions. Modern propaganda is based on scientific analyses of psychology and sociology—based on an understanding of human tendencies, desires, needs and conditioning—and how to develop these analyses into techniques to manipulate people and further erode their capacity for thought. The propagandist creates mechanisms that operate whenever human beings act in society, whether alone or in a group, based on the information they encounter within mass media. The propagandist has increasingly a scientific understanding of human nature and behavior, and, after proper training, tests his knowledge by refining how he controls its use, measures its results, and defines its effects, the propagandist deals with individuals acting with a mass or crowd of people, therein the effects of propaganda can be measured, and the resistance of the individual can be overcome. It is the general ignorance of the population about the methods of propaganda that leave them most vulnerable to it.

Ellul pointed out another common error that leaves many people vulnerable to propaganda: the belief that the main purpose of propaganda is to change peoples' opinions. Ellul accepted that this is one of the aims of propaganda, but he argued that it is a limited, subordinate aim. Modern propaganda has evolved beyond Bernays' conception of it. Frankenstein's monster has developed a life of its own. It not only shapes opinions and consumer choices, thereby changing culture and leading people to take up certain habits and lifestyles, identifying with particular groups, classes, and political parties, but it also creates a cultural inertia, intensifying existing trends and courses of action of society as a whole to which most individuals conform. Its prime aim is to intensify the irrationality and alienation of the individual. Indeed, it continues to sharpen and focus human action into particular trends or courses, or prevents interference and opposition by creating inaction or non-action among groups or classes or people who would otherwise resist or oppose those trends or courses of action, but its main goal is to leave the individual isolated and impotent. Among already dissenting and rebellions groups and classes, propaganda can be used to lead people to defeatism, resignation, and a sense of hopelessness, alienating them individually from their common cause. Even if the propaganda generates dissent and opposition, it replaces it with nothing else, leaving the individual raging against the machine but having nothing to replace it with. Nihilism is the inevitable result.

Propaganda works both by *agitation* and *integration*, and also by generating *self-censorship* and *self-repression* among particular groups and classes of people. Propaganda of integration molds the personality of the individual. This personality is completely irrational and based on nothing more than conformity to the group identity and rubber-stamps, norms, and behavior, as the means of satisfying psychological needs, which are often not even consciously understood by the individual. Integration propaganda leads people to adjust to desired patterns. Modern public relations would be a good example of this. It is a mask, even though the individual may well completely identify themselves with it. Agitation propaganda leads people to dissent and rebellion—and nothing else. This kind of propaganda is well-known. Early Bolshevik propaganda would be a good example. Agitation propaganda is subversive—in opposition to the integration propaganda of the incumbent government or social order—it seeks to disrupt or overthrow the system, to create dissent and conflict, war, rebellion, and revolution.

"It has always had a place in the course of the history. All revolutionary movements, all popular wars have been nourished by such propaganda of agitation. Spartacus relied on this kind of propaganda, as did the communes, the crusades, the French Revolution of 1793, and so on. But it reached its height with Lenin, which leads us to note that, though it is most often in opposition's propaganda, the propaganda of agitation can also be made by government. For example, when a government wants to galvanize energies to mobilize the entire nation for war, it will use a propaganda of agitation. At the moment the subversion is aimed at the enemy, whose strength must be destroyed by psychological as well as physical means, and whose force must be overcome by the vigor of one's own nation." (Ellul, p. 71)

When developed and disseminated to cause dissent (or mass opposition to an "internal enemy") agitation propaganda is aimed carefully at a class, ethnic group, or segment of the population. Partitioned and factionalized mass media is particularly important for the establishment and dissemination of agitation propaganda.

Of course it needs to be pointed out that the aim of agitation propaganda is not always to galvanize action; it is also used to maintain inaction or non-action among a section of the population. It is to leave them feeling hopeless and defeated. The effect of this strategy is to alienate the target population from government or their fellow citizens, leaving them in a state of distrust and isolation, with no other cause of action but to remove themselves from public life and retreat into the private realm. This often comes in the form of conspiracy theories. Such a form of agitation propaganda manipulates paranoia and fear—generating a state of neurosis—while leaving the target individuals with a cathartic sense of having what they "knew all along" confirmed, but without any idea what to do, except perhaps to fall into the surrealist mode of storing food, water, ammunition, guns, and a flashlight for the "inevitable" government crackdown or collapse of society. This kind of propaganda relies on the idea of some "them"—e.g. some government conspiracy, some international conspiracy, or even a mysterious organization (i.e. the Illuminati) that remains out of reach and beyond experience, but used to explain the conditions under which the target demographic finds themselves. In this way, the disintegration and obsolescence of certain institutions, say the Church, marriage, gender roles, or racial segregation, etc., which are often the result of protracted historical struggles and their own internal contradictions that arise in a heterogeneous society, can be *blamed* on some deliberate policy or strategy by a group or "internal enemy." The failures of "traditional family values" can be blamed on liberals, feminists, homosexuals, communists, atheists, etc., and thereby avoid any reflection on the forces of repression and control at work in maintaining those institutions, and how they privilege a particular class or group of people.

This kind of strategy results in maintaining divisions within society—turning people against each other—and, rather than teaching people how to adapt to social changes and evolve, agitation propaganda reinforces bigotry, misogyny, racism, and resentment, which can be used to distract the target demographic from or motivate their support for political policies and strategies. Whether we are analyzing Stalin's campaign against the Kulaks in the late 1920s, Hitler's campaign against Jews and Bolsheviks, Mao's campaign against traditional Chinese habits and customs, or American conservative campaigns against abortion and same-sex marriage, or the campaigns of the Left in America in against "Wall Street," or Alt-Right campaigns against "the Globalist conspiracy," the methods and results are comparable. Remember that all of these campaigns have some truth to them, but they primarily involve distortions and carefully selected interpretations and facts. They are not about changing the system, but about invoking and directing anger against specific people. They are never directed towards the system itself—as this always continues unchanged or is even intensified—but to a class of people within the system. In all these cases, agitation propaganda works by creating a sense of crisis or threat, mass hysteria and zeal, and always involves hostility towards a specific group or class. However, instead of motivating individuals to learn the truth about their conditions and work to making real and genuine changes to society, their call to condemn and exert energies are primarily about maintaining inertia and opposition to change. The aim is to keep the individual perpetually agitated, angry, and oppositional, but incapable of constructive or creative action. There is no vision behind agitation propaganda. Hence, Bolshevik (and Marxist) visions of the post-revolutionary society were always vague and unspecified, except by appeals to abstractions such as "equality," "freedom from exploitation," and "post-scarcity," without any detailed vision of the kind of society this would involve or how it could actually be built. It is never questioned whether their avowed goals can actually be achieved, except by removing or even killing a group of people, destroying the social order, or rioting in the streets. It is tantamount to magical thinking, but, most importantly, functions to dissipate frustration and anger about genuine inequalities and injustices.

"This subversive propaganda of agitation is obviously the flashiest: it attracts attention because of its explosive and revolutionary character. It is also the easiest to make; in order to succeed, it need only be addressed to the most simple and violent sentiments through the most elementary means. Hate is generally its most profitable recourse. It is extremely easy to launch a revolutionary movement based on hatred of a particular enemy. Hatred is probably the most spontaneous and common sentiment; it consists of attributing one's misfortunes and sins to 'another,' who be killed in order to assure the disappearance of those misfortunes and sins. Whether the object of hatred is the bourgeois, the Communists, the Jew, the colonialists, or the saboteur makes no difference. Propaganda of agitation succeeds each time it designates someone as the source of all misery, provided that he is not too powerful." (Ellul, p. 73)

Just as "the Left" use propaganda of agitation against capitalism, "the Right" use propaganda of agitation against immigrants, homosexuals, feminists, Jews, Mexicans, Muslims, some mysterious "Globalist" conspiracy, or "the Left." Propaganda of agitation works by creating "victims" and "enemies." It does not matter whether the designated "enemy" (who may well be responsible for injustices) is actually the cause of the harms or evils that have befallen the "victims." It is simply the case that the "victims" have now someone to project their resentments upon and blame for their conditions. It is easy enough for skillful propagandist to provide the "victims" with a strategy to obtain their "liberty" from their "enemies." Each propagandee readily becomes a propagandist, and anyone who questions the propaganda becomes "the enemy" or "a fellow traveler." Black or white—dualistic—thinking is not only the hallmark of agitation propaganda, but becomes the shibboleth by which the individual can declare their allegiance with the group identity and their opposition to "them," whoever that might be. It is at this level of "us v. them" thinking that agitation propaganda and integration propaganda become closely related through factionalized mass media. Not only does the individual need to share the same "enemies" and rubber-stamps to explain their conflict—"national independence," "liberty," "democracy," "religious freedom," "faith," "a return to traditional values," "law and order," "equality," etc.—but they need to conform to the myths, truths, and behavior of the group (and even styles of clothing, music, and speech) to show that they are one of "us" and not one of "them." The more intensified the struggle against "the enemy," the more dissent from norms and stereotypes will be treated with suspicion and hostility. Even though a society may well be heterogeneous, factionalized, or divided—perhaps to the intensity of a civil war—through the combined actions or agitation and integration propaganda, each and all factions, no matter how small, tend towards conformity and totalitarianism.

Another mistake is to believe that propaganda only works on the uneducated sector of the population. Ellul's thesis on integration propaganda provided us with a valuable insight: modern propaganda requires a modern education if it is to be effective. This insight contradicts the common belief that education is the best prophylactic against propaganda, as if propaganda only effects uneducated, ignorant, stupid, or gullible people. Modern education is a form of "pre-propaganda," as Ellul termed it, which is designed to condition the minds of children to accept propaganda by filling their needs with vast amounts of incoherent information and rules, leaving them disposed to receiving passively propaganda and manipulation in accordance with ulterior motives, posing as facts and techniques. Rote learning and examinations tend to pre-condition the mind of children to learn to regurgitate, without thought, without reflection, and without criticality, massive amounts of information. Ellul's model of propaganda is that through education (pre-propaganda) pseudo-needs are generated, and propaganda provides the pseudo-satisfaction of these pseudo-needs. It is highly pernicious and, once fully launched is irreversible. Ellul traced how this model works in various political systems—Communist, Nazi, and Democratic—and showed how education as pre-propaganda transforms society and people in pernicious and irreversible ways, leading to an increasingly acquiescent and conformist population within a totalitarian society, whatever political form it so happens to have. In order to be effective, propaganda requires that its target population are properly prepared through pre-propaganda techniques. Pre-propaganda requires control over the education of children, if propaganda is to achieve its optimum effectiveness. It is essential that children are already predisposed towards a particular worldview, which propaganda can then reinforce and confirm its correctness and truth. At that point, they are ready for indoctrination through propaganda. It is much easier to indoctrinate a population to believe in the manifest destiny of the United States of America to be a force for human progress and liberation in the world, if its target population have already seen seemingly independent movies and school books showing them how early pioneers tamed the wilderness, now American soldiers saved Europe from Nazi Germany, how Americans modernized agriculture and industry, or the American automobile are aerospace industry, how Americans went to the Moon, and how Americans won the Cold War. Once schoolchildren recite the platitudes that America is the greatest and freest country in the world, without much knowledge of other countries, and accept these truths as axiomatic, they are ready to receive whatever propaganda promotes American freedom and greatness. Similar myths and narratives were found in the Soviet Union and its educational programs and curricula.

As Joel Spring argued in *Education and the Rise of the Corporate State*, the development of a factory-like schoolroom in the nineteenth century was not an accident. Public school education was developed to teach the literacy and mathematical skills needed to provide industry with skilled and semi-skilled workers, as well as indoctrinate children into patriotism and nationalism. States and public officials began to control and censor textbooks and the content of school libraries. The idea being to create generations of obedient workers. Although the idea of the public school in America was first implemented by Methodists, Baptists, and Anabaptists to teach children how to read the Bible, even the Bible was ultimately removed from the classroom and school library. The task of pre-propaganda is not that of indoctrinating children into any particular ideology. Its task is more fundamental. Through discipline, mindless tasks, testing, punishment and rewards, and repetition— throughout the organization of the classroom and the school day—the partition between private thoughts and public action is created to teach the child the necessity of conforming to group action and being obedient to authority, regardless of their personal feelings, beliefs, or desires. The task of pre-propaganda is to normalize irrationality and conformity by modifying the children's behavior and motivations. When a child conforms, regardless of the pointlessness of the behavior, and its properly motivated in relation to the system of rewards and punishments, whatever that system may be, to behave in an inappropriate manner within the group, that child is considered to be educated, within the terms of pre-propaganda conditioning, and is now ready to receive propaganda and make it their own. Of course the myths taught during childhood may well prove the propagandist's useful starting points for establishing prejudices and a worldview as truths and motives for action, but if those particular myths are not useful, the effective propagandist can readily dismiss them as lies, in order to replace them with a new set. In fact, the resentments and alienation a person may well feel as an adult towards their own childhood, education can be used by the propagandist to affirm the prejudices and worldview of the group—negating that childhood education as worthless indoctrination—while retaining all the pre-propaganda conditioning that education provided.

In this way, certain questions will not be asked and doubts will not be felt. Propaganda can then take the form of corroborating evidence and even critique carefully framed interpretations to make some questions necessary and others unthinkable, or at least unaskable. It is always essential that, whatever their private doubts, the target audience has nowhere else to go but to the worldview promoted through the efforts of educators and propagandists. It is for this reason that the ideological demand of "market discipline" is imposed on schools and universities in a capitalist society. It is imperative that children and young adults learn that an education is *for the needs or the market*; to prepare them for propaganda techniques that equate success and freedom with profit and consumption, and nothing else. There are three main reasons why educated people are susceptible to modern propaganda:

1. they absorb the largest amount of second hand, unverifiable information;

2. they feel compelled to have an opinion on every important question of our time, and easily succumb to opinions offered to them as the basis for their own opinion;

3. they consider themselves as capable of independent thought and therefore invulnerable to propaganda.

For these people, they not only are effected by propaganda without knowing it, but they disseminate it unconsciously as their own opinion, and they have a psychological need for propaganda.

The nearer propaganda approximates a totalitarian and all-pervasive worldview, the more invisible it becomes, the harder it is to resist, and dissenters have nowhere else to go, no acceptable linguistic resources by which to oppose and contradict the totalitarian worldview, and thereby seem insane, ridiculous, or idiotic. Even history must be rewritten to remove any uncomfortable contradictions or inconsistencies in the myths underlying the totalitarian worldview. It is essential that those who accept the worldview *are absolutely correct at all times*, and those who challenge or criticize it are *absolutely wrong without question*. Opponents must be shown to be idiots or liars, simply because they are opponents. As Ellul warned, let's not make the mistake of believing that only authoritarian dictatorships will use propaganda to rewrite history. The substitution of propaganda for history (and literature) is the result of propaganda itself. Anything else prevents propaganda from being total, which reduces its effectiveness. The intrinsic necessity of propaganda to be all-pervasive and total is itself a consequence of the technological imperative to achieve efficiency of means. It is a consequence of the technological society and quite independent of the ideological form of the political superstructure of that society. The aim of modern propaganda is the complete and total societal indoctrination—it is irrelevant what is the particular ideology, worldview, or *Weltanschauung*, the only requirement and necessity is that it is total. It is this technological imperative that makes propaganda totalitarian. Hence, propaganda must be psychological, sociological, and technological in its nature.

Through appealing to individuals within groups, via propaganda of the word and deed, that particular thoughts and actions are normalized—idealized through myths and exemplary individuals—as representations of societal expectations and demands to which the individual must conform, if they seek to be successful as a member of society, or as a patriot, or as a real man, or as a good mother, or as a role model for the next generation. Propaganda works by promoting virtues and ideals, and juxtaposing casual connections and semantic content with whatever totalitarian worldview is being promoted in that particular society by its organized and coordinated propagandists. In this respect, we can see Ellul's model of propaganda as offering us a more general theory of propaganda than Bernays did, but Bernays' theory remains consistent with Ellul's, as a limited and special case, with a more restricted degree of applicability. While Bernays saw how propaganda worked within established groups, with their leaders and opinion-makers, Ellul took this for granted and extended it to show how modern propaganda is effective upon and needed by alienated and isolated individuals within a modern society for which family, church, and community are eroded and obsolete, to create a sense of belonging, membership, identity, and social purpose, via a shared set of beliefs and expectations about society and the individual's place within it. For those individuals who dissent or reject these beliefs and expectations, the aim of propaganda is to leave them alienated and isolated, without the intellectual or social resources to resist and change things, other than through individual, subjective, and private acts. We could also add criminal, self-destructive, violent, and perverse actions. These are all actions that have dramatic effects in the private realm but have no impact on the social order—if anything, they reinforce or justify the social order. None of this matters to the propagandist. All that matters is that the individual is forced to conform to the status quo, or de-politicized and isolated.

Without propaganda, the individual is left feeling helpless and alone in modern society. Propaganda gives the individual a vision of themselves as being a part of something greater and important, with meaning and significance. Propaganda gives people a *raison d'être* and a need for more propaganda; to constantly renew and reinforce the feeling of doing something important and valuable, of having important things to say, and having something to contribute to the development of society and humanity in general. Of course, this is all illusionary and simply conditions the individual to conform to the demands and expectations given to them by the propagandist, who in turn is conforming to the demands and expectations given to him or her. The propagandist is a susceptible to propaganda as anyone else. Perhaps more so. It is important that the propagandist is seen to believe in their cause. This gives the audience a direct incitement, someone to identify with, and a sense of involvement. It does not matter whether the propagandist really believes in the cause, but more often than not, given that they are members of the same society, the propagandist is also a propagandee, influenced by propaganda, sharing the same worldview, prejudices, ideals, and attitudes as the target population. In this respect, the propagandist promotes an indirect incitement by being an unconscious channel of covert propaganda, alongside the overt propaganda they are consciously promoting and the covert propaganda they are deliberately disseminating.

Propaganda must be continuous—it must came from all-pervasive sources and cannot leave any gaps that could be filled with contrary viewpoints or questions for which it does not already provide counter-responses or answers. It needs also to be long-lasting; the target audience will see or hear it repeated over a long-period of time, often from many sources, and different versions will appear periodically, each designated to reinforce the same certainties and accepted assumptions by corroborating the other versions. As Ellul put it, "Propaganda tends to make the individual exist in a separate world; he must not have outside points of reference." (p. 17) It is for this reason that it can be said that the propagandee inhabits an ersatz reality—the hologram, as I call it. Its effectiveness depends on its slow and constant impregnation of thought, speech, and action, creating convictions and compliance, and distancing the individual from any contrary views (unless the individual has been provided with the rubber-stamps required to counter, explain away, or dismiss that contrary view) or external points of reference. By reinforcing prejudices and myths, the individual feels that they own the propaganda as their truth—and they have a right to their own opinion; a right to free speech. When the alternative is to remain in silence and ignorance—to admit that one has succumbed to propaganda and has no basis for one's beliefs—and lose one's identity within a group, the psychological risks and costs involved in resisting propaganda are high. After continuous and lasting bombardment, resistance is weakened; adaptation and acceptance is easier, especially when one is preoccupied with the demands of everyday life. Hence, the success of propaganda requires three conditions: continuity, an all-pervasive combination of different media, and stark consequences for non-conformity.

This returns us to Ellul's point about how modern propaganda is a fundamental characteristic of the technological society. There needs to be an administrative organization of modern propaganda to ensure that the above three characteristics of propaganda are correctly coordinated. There is no need for any Ministry of Propaganda to achieve this when the political economy, through media consolidation, allows the vast majority of mass media sources to be controlled by a few corporations. This allows us to identify four social conditions for modern propaganda:

(1) pre-propaganda (education)

(2) organized propaganda (encirclement)

(3) action (policy)

(4) re-action (effectiveness)

Through administrative organization of the application of psychological and sociological knowledge, the propagandist is a conduit for technical calculation and a cog in a machine. This helps the propagandist to become invisible, concealed behind public relations and press releases, behind advertising campaigns, blogs, editorials, infomercials, news-reports, media punditry, public hearings, committees, conventions, town hall meetings, and all the means by which propaganda is disseminated due to the demands of technical necessity and opportunism.

"The aim of propaganda is no longer to modify ideas, but to provoke actions [or non-actions]. It is no longer to change adherence to a doctrine, but to make the individual cling irrationally to a process of action [or non-action]. It is no longer to lead to a choice, but to loosen the reflexes [or increase resistance]. It is no longer to transform an opinion, but to arouse an active and mystical belief." (Ellul, p. 25)

Providing that individuals continue to reproduce the rubber-stamps appropriate to their group membership, it does not matter what they think or how they feel. The opinion of individuals is irrelevant. What matters is group mobilization or demobilization. The task of the modern propaganda is to manipulate group behavior. The opinion of the individual is something that the individual will tag on in retrospect to justify intellectually their participation or opposition, which itself is irrational and the effect of propaganda, as if it were their own decision and choice. It is for this reason that rubber-stamping remains an apt term for public opinion, which gives the stamp of approval to courses of actions (or non-action) that the group is already committed to, as the result of propaganda techniques that short-circuit individual thought and decision. In this respect, public opinion is akin to the chorus of chants that people call out to declare their allegiance to a sporting team. The analogy with a sporting event, such as a football game, is instructive. The game will be played autonomously under a set of rules and plays by both sides alike, regardless of any rhetorical or symbolic justifications that members of either team or their supporters may make about why they *deserve* to win, and, regardless of who wins, the outcome will be the same. Like any team sport, membership of a party is a matter of rubber-stamping group identity and the need to belong to a group. This, whatever their team does to win is justified by winning. The content of the chants is irrelevant; what matters to the propagandist is that the crowd turns up, pays their money, and supports the team, or if individuals stay at home, they watch the game on pay-for-view TV, and shout out the same chants (even though there is no-one to hear them).

It is for this reason that the application of motivational research studies to advertising is directed to provide techniques to motivate the public to buy the product—whatever it may be—and to want it; perhaps later, to justify their purchase, individuals will give reasons and opinions for their purchase, as if wanting it was *their* choice. Their identity becomes bound-up with making such choices. Work and shopping become the dominant actions within a mass society.

"If the classic but outmoded view of propaganda consists in defining it as an adherence of man to an *orthodoxy*, the modern propaganda seeks, on the contrary, to obtain the *orthopraxy*—an action that in itself, and not because of the value judgements of the person who is acting leads directly to a goal, which for the individual is not a conscious and intentional objective to be attained, but which is considered such by the propagandist." (Ellul, p. 27)

This separation of thought from action is perhaps the most pernicious aspect of modern propaganda. By reinforcing and manipulating the irrationality of group behavior, it is intensifying the irrationality of the society as a whole. This is not to say that individuals become thoughtless or mindless. The thoughts of the individual, especially their doubts and questions, become increasingly private and divorced from their actions. The motivations of the individual to adapt to the needs of the group, to fit in, to work, to gain approval and rewards, do not require anything else from the individual's participation in the actions of the group. Where the individual's thoughts diverge from the group's actions, and the individual continues to participate in the group, the individual's thoughts will become increasingly private and although the individual may well feel alienated from the group, providing that they continue to participate in the group's actions, their actions will alienate them from their thoughts too. This drives the individual deeper into irrationality.

The individual is forced to escape into dreams and fantasies, or distractions, as their private life and public behavior become increasingly partitioned, and the relation between the two is irrational or non-existent. Alcoholism, drug addiction, television addiction, domestic violence, child and animal abuse, and sexual perversions, are all consequences of this partition, as the individual seeks private outlets for their frustrations, their alienation, and the irrationality of their existence. These become their only sense of power or freedom. Without the intellectual recourses to cohere thought and action (largely as a result of pre-propaganda conditioning during their education), the individual is left in a state of existential angst and nihilism, or compelled to conform their thought to group rubber-stamping, which includes the consolations of religion. Propaganda

"...does not censor out personality; it leaves man complete freedom of thought, except in his political or social action where we find him channeled and engaged in actions that do not necessarily conform to his private beliefs." (Ellul, p. 28)

However, it is essential that this freedom of thought is between conformity and nothing. The propagandist appeals to and manipulates group identity, motivations, emotions, and myths that individuals share with each other; to use the individual's desire to belong to the group, and the other group's members put pressure on the individual to conform to the group, against the individual. There is nowhere else to go but into to silence. Like Bernays, Ellul considered the phenomenon of mass mentality or group mind to be basic to understanding how propaganda works. The target of the propagandist is the organization of the group, through which the individual can be manipulated, even if the actual delivery of the propaganda is given as if it were personal and directed towards "independent" individuals. Ellul noted that propaganda satisfies important psychological needs by allowing suggestible individuals to feel forceful, "strong" individuals; to transform the fears and insecurities into strong convictions that give them a sense of personal identity. It allows anonymous and conforming individuals to feel as if they are persons. Hence the group mind or mass identity does not require that the individuals are all assembled together because they can be reached by mass media, such as newspapers, radio, television, and movies. They can be alone and part of the group mind at the same time.

"Readers of evening paper, radio listeners, movie, or TV viewers certainly constitute a mass that has an organic existence, although it is diffused and not assembled at one point. These individuals are moved by the same movies, receive the same impulses and impressions, find themselves focused on the same centers of interest, experience the same feelings, have generally the same order of reactions and ideas, participate in the same myths—and all this at the same time: what we have here is really a psychological, if not a biological mass. And the individuals in it are modified by this existence, even if they do not know it. Yet each one is alone—the newspaper reader, the radio listener. He therefore feels himself individually concerned as a person, as a participant. The movie spectator also is alone; though elbow to elbow with his neighbors, he still is, because of the darkness and the hypnotic attraction of the screen, perfectly alone." (Ellul, p. 8)

Propaganda is most effective when a person is alone in a mass, and as a result cannot exist without mass media.

Propaganda must be all-pervasive to effectively isolate the individual. Propaganda must reach and encircle the individual through all-pervasive mass media, playing on emotions and ideals, will and needs, through the individual's conscious and unconscious mind, and connecting both his public and private life. It mediates all human relations and gives the individual a complete worldview—a means of explaining life and immediate incentives for action (or inaction) and an organized system of myths and personal identities; a system of given interpretations and intuitive knowledge expressed through rubber-stamps. The result of propaganda is that the individual is subjected to a totalitarian outlook that does not tolerate any divergence or dissent; it leads to an absolutist attitude, with its one-sided interpretations and prejudices that controls the whole individual and opposes any other influence or worldview. The alienating and dissociative effect of propaganda explains in part why fundamentalist Christians in America are often (unconsciously) at odds with the words and teachings of the gospels (and opposing in many cases), while simultaneously expound them. This should not be misunderstood. It is not simply a matter of hypocrisy. It is a product of the way propaganda dominates and polarizes public discourse and behavior via groups, which includes churches as well as political parties. It is for this reason why fundamentalist Christians in America are leveraged by the wedge-issue of abortion into also opposing public healthcare and education for the poor, any kind of public welfare provision, including food stamps, and any kind of restrictions on the access to firearms, while supporting tax cuts for the wealthiest members of society, including arms manufacturers and the pharmaceutical industries (even when they perform research on embryos). They see no contradiction between the words and teachings of Jesus and their support of the Republican Party. One exists in the private realm and the other in the political realm. This forms a partition in the psyche of the individual. By securing a natural alliance between the Republican Party and Christian evangelicals, through the wedge-issue of abortion, irrespective of the many points of ideological opposition between political power and religious doctrine, this opposition is concealed by propaganda. As long as the political opponents of abortion pay some lip-service to Christian terminology and principles, the support from fundamentalist Christians is secured regardless of the politician's own voting record and their immorality (including fornication, adultery, and homosexuality). Churches become transformed into instruments of propaganda, without their congregation even knowing it. We find no better example than the rhetoric of televangelists like Pat Robertson. Instead of being concerned with devotion to God, spirituality and worship, these instruments are concerned with wealth, power, and influence over the State.

Let's not make the mistake of believing that propaganda only connects with negative aspects such as prejudices and false beliefs. It also connects with our highest values, aspirations, hopes and dreams. Via our visions and ideals, propaganda connects with our imagination via mythology and ideology. It is this positive operation of propaganda that is the most dangerous of all, and can be seen in operation among people of all political persuasions and loyalties. Whether conservative or progressive, libertarian or communist, socialist or fascist, all people succumb to propaganda when they connect their notions of the good and just with an ideological or mythical image of human nature and how society should be. Propaganda crosses the divide between facts and values, allowing truth to be replaced with ideals and abstractions; allowing reason to be replaced with images, formulae, and slogans. Criticality is eclipsed by wishful thinking; denial and self-justification negate evidence and experience. No better example of this can be found that the media coverage and political discourse about climate change and global warming. Threats of unemployment or higher costs of living are taken as inevitable consequences of any changes in the status quo, all the while an imagined future (no matter how utopian) is placed on a pedestal as a justification for all sacrifices. Yet, if new virtues and attitudes are being promoted, they must be secured and established within the already existing practices and discourse of groups, as it they always were the virtues and attitudes of that group. They must be presented as eternal truths—as self-evident and natural; as something the target population should have known all along, as something they did know all along. Ideally, they should be connected with some past "golden age" and they are now under threat and need to be preserved or defended. Another method of doing this is by introducing these new virtues and attitudes as being something that "the enemy," "those other people," "they," don't understand, and thereby anyone who is "a true patriot," "an intelligent person," "one of us" must get it. In this way, people will keep their doubts to themselves, unwilling to appear "on the wrong side" or "stupid," and even if they do not grasp the new orthodoxy, they will fake it in both word and deed. They must preserve their identity with the group at all times.

It is thereby essential that the propagandist makes use of overt and covert propaganda. Overt propaganda is developed without any attempt to conceal that it is attempting to influence people. Of course, due to the pejorative connotations of the word "propaganda," this word is not used to describe overt propaganda. Instead, words like "advertising," "public information," and "issue advocacy," are used. Covert propaganda is designed to be used without its target audience knowing that it is being used. One of the methods of convert propaganda (as well as pedagogical methods, subliminal images, news reporting, opinion editorials, fiction, movies, cartoons, jokes, art, etc.) is to expose anything that challenges or opposes the propaganda message as being overt propaganda (by implication, false and a lie), while the covert propaganda "raises questions" and "puts the record straight." The combination of overt and covert propaganda has become so sophisticated that overt propaganda is used as a mask to conceal covert propaganda, to create public awareness of "a problem" and to demand "the solution" that the propagandist has already inserted into the frame by which the problem was introduced. For example, instead of overtly running a campaign for the privatization of water, allowing corporations to buy up land for the purpose of building their own reservoirs and selling the water to communities, farms, and cities, in municipalities counties, or states wherein that practice is currently illegal, the propagandist will purchase a series of news stories and documentaries—seemingly independent—"exposing" a few cases wherein overly-zealous officials have fined ordinary people for collecting barrels of rainwater. Such stories will play on a public distrust of "government"—a disgust of "control" and "over-reach"—and emphasize that rainwater is a natural recourse that should be freely owned by everybody. In the name of "public ownership" of rainwater, the reader or viewer will be left with a feeling of opposition towards regulations that prevent people from doing something as natural as collecting rainwater. They will complain about this to other peers as yet another example of "Big Government" bureaucracy. They might join a campaign against it, signing and distributing petitions, writing letters to their political representatives, and giving donations to lobbyists or political parties to do something about this outrage. Without realizing it, they will work against the public ownership of rainwater, by working against the laws that prevent multinational corporations from collecting huge reservoirs of water, damming up rivers, and holding farmers, citizens, and industries to ransom.

Again, we need to be aware than all effective propaganda is based on truth. We should be wary of the most enduring falsehood about propaganda that it is based only in lies and fiction. As both Bernays and Ellul observed, such a fabricated form of propaganda is soon discovered, exposed, and more than likely backfire. The problem with this enduring falsehood about propaganda is that it leads to the error that people often make: if an interpretation of carefully selected facts is based on verifiable facts, it cannot be propaganda. This leads people to believe that if you can do a Google search and find some corroboration, it cannot be propaganda. People who make this error are particularly susceptible to propaganda because they believe that the ability to verify the facts of the matter makes them invulnerable to propaganda. This error is intensified among an already propagandized population because they tend to only accept facts from their favored "trusted" sources and dismiss all statements of fact from other sources as being lies. These people tend to consider themselves to be invulnerable to propaganda because "we know the truth" and they are aware of "the lies." The old Nazi term *Lügenpresse* (which literally means "lying press") has become vogue among the so-called Alt-Right on chat forums and social media. One of Goebbels' tactics was to disseminate secretly false information about Germany to foreign journalists and enemy intelligence agents without them knowing it to be false. When the enemy press reported this information, Goebbels was able to use this to show to the German people how the enemy press lied and used propaganda. This denial of critical or opposing sources of media as having absolutely no truth to them—itself a form of absolutism typical of the heavily propagandized individual—leaves them unconsciously vulnerable to propaganda in the form of interpretations of carefully selected facts into the minds of the target audience, and connect it to the group identity through appropriately witty and succinct rubber-stamps and opinions, via which the group members can express and share their collective truths and worldview. The propagandist can tell lies, invent stories, falsify facts, fabricate evidence, purchase false testimony, etc., all of which can be used to elaborate their interpretations of current events. Yet these must be based on some verifiable facts, from which the propagandee can draw the conclusions given to them.

Propaganda is particularly effective when it takes a set of facts and overly speculates on their meaning and consequences in a way that reinforces the fears and prejudices of the target demographic. It is for this reason that the propagandist can use *carefully selected* statistics and research findings—all of which can be checked and verified for their accuracy—as the basis for their interpretation of the meaning of these facts and tendencies. It is this interpretation (or "spin") that presented a biased and prejudiced half-truth as if it were the whole of the truth; while its basis in fact can be verified and confirmed by anyone who shares its biases and prejudices, as being another confirmation and corroboration of their own truths and worldview. Of course a couple of subtleties need to be noted at this juncture. The propagandist can start by denouncing some widely publicized facts as being a lie (the fact may be true or false, as long as it is hard to prove) and then build his interpretation of the reasons for the lie on top. Conspiracy theories or counterpropaganda often take this form. Another approach is to take a fact out of context, without explaining it, and use it as the foundation for the construction of propaganda. In this way, the propagandist can control the framing of debate in such a way that her interpretation forms the center position—by implication, moderate—for subsequent debates and interpretations to be measured against. For example, she may take the fact that illegal immigration is a crime out of the historical, geographical, and political contexts that explain why illegal immigration occurs, in order to form the framework for debates on whether any immigration reform based on amnesty is "soft on crime" or "rewards criminal behavior." This form of propaganda respects some detail (some fact or definition) to the point of making it an irrefutable absolute that can form the basis of criticism and caricatures of any other position or interpretation. In the example given above, by taking the fact out of context, the absolutism on this issue can be isolated from others. In this way, the focus on the criminality of illegal immigration as the central issue can ignore that its proponents often willfully ignore the law when it suits them, say by drinking and driving, speeding, parking illegally, not paying all their taxes, littering, taking illegal drugs, etc., and their focus on this particular crime is completely arbitrary, even though based in fact.

It is also important to mention that all facts are carefully selected in relation to some thesis, but what distinguishes the propagandist is that he will select the facts in the light of whatever conclusion he wishes to promote. Silence regarding inconvenient, anomalous, or even contradictory facts is one of the hallmarks of the propagandist. If this come to light, she is able to either dismiss them as irrelevant or as lies. Again, a heavily controlled and factionalized multimedia environment is advantageous for this purpose, as well as reducing the chances that these awkward facts will come to light. Furthermore, by presenting carefully selected facts out of context, the propagandist can use suggestion, innuendo, hypotheticals and questions to guide the target demographic "to come to their own conclusions," which just so happened to be the same conclusions that he wants them to reach. In this way, the propagandist can clearly create a space for the members of the target demographic to discover for themselves that they are "in the know" and can "see the truth" for themselves. The propagandist can even play act that they are "just thinking out loud" or "just asking questions," while she is bringing the target demographic into the fold of "truth-seers." This places the onus on anyone opposing this conclusion *to prove* counter-claims or a negative, which, of course, is difficult or impossible.

It is even more difficult to prove the intentions of the propagandist to be false than it is to refute their interpretation of the facts. For this is the realm of opinion and inference, within which we all have the right of free speech and thought. Even when the consequences or actions of the propagandist seem to run contrary to his intentions, he always can blame circumstances or others. The skillful propagandist can always explain how her best intentions were thwarted by forces out of her control, and call upon others to ally with her to overcome these forces and help her realize her good intentions, whatever she may claim them to be. If people feel those intentions to be good and they are persuaded by her propaganda, they can be rallied against any force, or enemy, even ones that were previously unknown to people. When we are dealing with interpretations and intentions, we can only guess at the latter and consider the former to be a matter of opinion, and, hence, it is impossible to expose lies and falsehoods. In this way, the skillful propagandist is able to intermix interpretations of the facts and value judgements by which one side of a conflict can be condemned and the other justified for committing the same actions. The most outrageous speculations or innuendos can be simply asserted as questions. While a fact always (and unavoidably) has a different significance depending upon one's perspective, the propagandist takes full advantage of this to proffer her interpretation as if it were the only reasonable or logical conclusion, even when she is exaggerating or diminishing the significance of events, or disguising or insinuating intentions.

However, one of the hallmarks of propaganda is that the propagandist always declares the goodness of necessity of their own (or client's) intentions, while casting suspicion and innuendo on the intentions of whomever they oppose. The propagandist nearly always interprets facts in moral terms, using pathos and emotions to force their argument to its conclusion, and present that conclusion in the tones of moral indignation and purity. For the propagandist subtleties and complexities are to be dismissed as indicators of

94

moral weakness or deceptiveness, especially when the propagandist (or her clients) are doing or have done the same. Thus the propagandist will accuse others of war mongering or aggression, when it is a propagandist (or his clients) who wishes to start a war, and anyone who attempts negotiation or diplomacy will be accused of "appeasement" or "cowardice" in the face of aggression and provocation. Almost without exception, all wars are started in the name of self-defense and peace. It is for this reason that propaganda is a form of deception that uses truth. Its hidden task is to distract the propagandee from the propagandist's intentions by presenting interpretations of the facts as revealing the hidden interpretations of others, while declaring their own intentions to be the opposite. Censorship hinders the propagandist, who operates most effectively under the same conditions as free speech, which provides cover for the propagandist, who can retreat under the guise of opinion, commentary, speculation, and "just asking questions." Both free speech and propaganda flourish in the same culture, even though they counteract each other. In an authoritarian regime, the effectiveness of government propaganda is reduced *because* of its measures to silence free speech and counterpropaganda. These measures expose government propaganda as being propaganda. Whereas in a regime that allows free speech and open criticism, propaganda can be easily concealed as free speech to the extent that it becomes almost impossible to tell one from the other. In a totalitarian regime, people feel themselves to be engaged in free speech and able to say whatever they like, while at the same time disseminating propaganda without knowing it to be anything apart from free speech. They feel themselves to be free. Under such conditions, genuine free speech and critical discourse are simply unthinkable. Here we can see how an authoritarian and totalitarian regime are very different. The former controls people through fear and its show of strength, whereas the latter controls people by being the only thinkable possibility.

If we find merit in the above analysis of propaganda, we can see how propaganda can be based in truth and simultaneously promote a lie and distortion, which the propagandee either wishes to believe or uses as a veil to conceal some undesirable truth about reality. Thus propaganda is part of the realm of masks: of theater; of spectacle. This insight brings us to Ellul's sociological definition of propaganda:

"Propaganda is a set of methods employed by an organized group that wants to bring about the active or passive participation in its actions by a mass of individuals, psychologically unified through psychological manipulations and incorporated in an organization." (Ellul, p.61)

Propaganda can either be tactical or strategic. The former seeks some particular outcome, say purchasing a product or voting for a candidate, whereas the latter seek to change behavior or establish long-term commitment to a particular leader, party, or ideology, or change culture. Strategic propaganda need to be sociological, whereas tactical propaganda is primarily psychological (and the form that most people associate with propaganda), but tactical propaganda is only possible because of sociological pre-propaganda preconditioning through education. The old model of propaganda tended to look only at tactical propaganda—but in isolation— and therefore was unable to explain how propaganda works at all. Sociological (strategic) propaganda operates by integrating individuals within a group who identify themselves with specific (tactical) propaganda as the expression of their identity and individuality.

Through advertising, public relations, public information, government sources, mass media, and social programs, sociological, strategic propaganda produces a cultural interpretation of society, a "way of life," and relates cultural practices and customs to specific institutions and a worldview (within which the role of the individual human being is defined.) The individual, by adapting and conforming to these cultural interpretations, practices, and customs, thereby integrating their understanding of how to live with the institutions provided to them, makes them his or her own. It is relatively easy at this point for the propagandist to convince the propagandee that their worldview and way of life is natural and good, normal and real, and they live in the best society, freely; by confirming and affirming their correctness and success in adapting to this worldview and way of life, the propagandee confirms and affirms themselves and their freedom, becoming a propagandist in the process; integrating themselves within the group identity, thereby confirming and affirming their individuality.

While advertising and public relations use both forms of propaganda, as do economics, religion, and politics, this does not mean that people cannot have genuine economic, political, or religious thoughts and experiences. What it means is that the population in general do not, but have these fed to them as "off-the-peg" opinions and doctrine. Through generating social and cultural changes, propaganda inserts ideology, theory, and religion into life styles, attitudes, behavior, and discourse, as well as satisfying psychological needs through group identity; it establishes the social order as natural and necessary. The acts of the ruling elite—whether explained in economic, political, or theological discourse— are not only made acceptable to the ruled majority, but are supported (and even demanded) by the ruled majority due to the effectiveness of propaganda. In this way, propaganda can be seen to be the opposite of force and oppression. It generates complicity and conformity; individuals adapt themselves to the norms of the group through unconsciously sharing propaganda and disseminating it between them.

"Such propaganda is [essentially] defense. It is rarely conveyed by catchwords or expressed intentions. Instead it is based on a general climate, an atmosphere that influences people imperceptibly without having the appearance of propaganda; it gets to man through his customs, through his unconscious habits. It creates new habits in him; it is a sort of persuasion from within. As a result, man adopts new criteria of judgement and choice, adopts them spontaneously, as if he had chosen them himself. But all these criteria are in conformity with the environment and are essentially of a collective nature." (Ellul, p. 64)

It is through the conformity and adaption of the individual to society, through all-pervasive and strategic propaganda, that generates the level of social cohesion and integration required by a totalitarian society, and this is achieved without needing to resort to authoritarian and oppressive methods. It is this aspect of all-pervasive and strategic propaganda that presents the illusion of an open and free society. This illusion is reinforced across all media to the extent that the individual's conformity to it is expressed as spontaneous affirmation and celebration of their own freedom. Whether the totalitarian society is capitalist, communist, or theocratic, the more the individual adapts and conforms to it, the freer they feel themselves to be. In this respect, a totalitarian society need to be understood as very different from a fascist regime or dictatorship. It does not need to use the methods of state terrorism, oppression, fear, and violence. A totalitarian society depends on the repression and compliance of the individual to it; it relies on his mobility to imagine any alternative or even wish to. While we still think of propaganda in relation to the crude tactical propaganda of Nazi Germany or the Soviet Union under Stalin's dictatorship, we cannot hope to understand its power. These crude propaganda techniques only show us prototypes of modern propaganda. Through education, cultural media (movies, art, literature, etc.), social media, and group identity, using all the technologies of the public relations and mass communication, modern propaganda indirectly influences the individual to identify themselves in terms of shared prejudices and a worldview that provides the means for individuals to understand the world and their place within it, and to find solidarity and commonality with their fellow citizens and neighbors.

Narrowcasting:

Understanding the psychological need for allegiance (group identity) is the key to understanding how modern propaganda works in a liberal democracy. People seek out others who share the same convictions, fears, beliefs, and talking-points. A sense of solidarity with others and the vindication of one's own identity becomes satisfied by the choice between television and radio shows, newspapers, websites, or even baseball caps. When sharing the same opinion on wedge-issues is the litmus test of whether convictions are shared, political speech becomes a process of group-membership identification through Shibboleths and rubber-stamps. This is where strategic propaganda finds its power. People can find media personalities, pundits, comedians, talk show hosts, actors, musicians, pastors, or even politicians who voice the same convictions and rubber-stamp their allegiance by sharing the same opinions on a range of wedge-issues. Even questions betray group-identity. Ask the wrong question and you are out. Modern media provides specialized media channels and sources through which people can hear or read their own opinions echoed or reflected back at them by someone famous or important, thereby allowing that personality to act as someone who brings people together as members of the same group. Whether or not one says that Rush Limbaugh or Glenn Beck makes a valid point or not, on any issue at all, is a declaration of group-identity rather than a response to a single comment or statement taken in isolation. Liking or disliking a media personality becomes a Shibboleth or a rubber-stamp that someone else is in the same group and a possessor of the correct opinions, even when people do not know what opinions the person has or whether they are good opinions to have. A liberal person cannot like Ann Coulter, just as a conservative person cannot like Rachel Maddow. An otherwise liberal-minded person would be ostracized by the fellows if they were to agree on even a single point of criticism of Barack

Obama made by Rush Limbaugh, regardless of the merits of that criticism, or whether that person disagreed with everything else he said. Even the suggestion, made in the abstract, that Limbaugh's comments might have some merit, as a hypothetical possibility, would be enough to get one ostracized. Just as a conservative person will be ostracized if they like a Michael Moore film. In this way criticisms of political figures can be suppressed by their supporters simply by getting their opponents to voice them—Leftist criticisms of Obama could be silenced by having Rightist pundits say them, and vice versa. Conversely, the same policies supported by Republicans under a Republican administration can be opposed by Republicans if leftwing media personalities support the same policies implemented under a Democratic administration. In this way, the assassination of Osama Bin Laden became a cause of concern for Republicans when ordered by the Obama administration, even though the Republicans demanded it under the Bush administration. Similarly such extra-judicial assassinations were celebrated by Democrats when ordered by Obama, along with the use of drones and missiles against civilians, and the suspension of habeas corpus, yet these same actions were decried by Democrats as unconstitutional and tyrannical when ordered by Bush. Often people simply don't know what the policies of government are or have been, or where they stand on them, until they discover whether their group is in favor of them or against them. As a result, the audience is readily propagandized to believe almost anything is true or false, regardless of whether it has any evidence or corroboration, and whether an action is right or wrong depends on whether their group affirms or opposes them.

It is also important to keep public focus constantly shifting. One of the important propaganda methods used by mainstream corporate media, across the board, and increasingly across the Internet-based news, blogosphere, radio, and television, is to focus intensely on a few events, issues, and personalities, and move on rapidly to the next, without any connection or commonality drawn between them, almost a random, as if they reflected the spontaneity of life itself. Of course, the choice of events, issues, and personalities are carefully framed to match the needs and interests of corporations, political parties, and anyone with sufficient money to send news stories, infomercials, op eds, blogs, videos, and advertisements throughout the multimedia environment within which the majority of the developed and developing world has become immersed. Large sections of humanity commute to work in a portable virtual world, beamed at them via their phones, and many have migrated in part to live in it, and others live there almost entirely. Within this virtual world people can be *distracted* by the editing and selected highlights of the unfolding story of the world, as they are led by the shifting focus of interest and concern, from issue to issue, event to event, personality to personality, and led away from the possibility of democratic communication, organization, and political action. Instead, the population is led into maze of information and entertainments from crisis to crisis, reducing the time for reflection, rewriting history, and maintaining short memories and attention spans.

Even the questions of control over the Internet, surveillance, and misinformation lurch from crisis to crisis, with the mass mind, after a suitable period of hysteria and breast beating, soon forgets yesterday's crisis as if it had never happened. Concerns are soon forgotten about government mass surveillance technologies (remember PRISM or even TIA?), corporate ISPs and the control over content (GOOGLE "PURGE"?), near 'comic book' shadowy organizations that are widely covered by media and always, somehow, manage to evade capture (ANONYMOUS? Who are they? How do we know?), whistle-blowing organizations that provide "classified information," reported by media but it is never questioned whether the information is true or false, or misinformation (WIKIPEDIA? Why wasn't their website taken down? Could they be a CIA misinformation operation? How could we know?). Questions about social media and data mining, cookie tracking, and other methods of governmental and corporate surveillance, if these questions are asked at all, are never followed up. Politicians are never pressed. Answers are never sought. Even after terrorist attacks, the mainstream media debate is limited to raising awareness of some issue or need for new powers of government surveillance, such as encryption of iPhones or messaging phone apps, without any follow up about how these new powers are implemented. It is simply a matter of informing the population that they are being watched and recorded, and like Jeremy Bentham's famous prison, *the Panopticon*, the idea is that if people believe they can be watched at any time, they will regulate their own behavior. The function of these "crises" is to increase paranoia and self-suppress free speech, as well as justify massive new governmental powers and the erosion of rights.

100

Yet, this has become hardly necessary any more. The fast pace of propaganda in mass society has effectively eroded any possibility of deep analysis or questions. By generating a virtual flux of ever changing propaganda, fed through newsfeeds on social media or on corporate-owned websites on mobile phones, the manipulation and direction of the fundamental currents of society, through the framing of media news and opinion, creates public passivity and resignation; while presenting the illusion of participation and communication, by representing reality as a disconnected series of events, issues, and personalities, over which the vast majority of people have no control whatsoever, except to express their opinion, approval or disapproval via clicks and sharing links. This presents the illusion of community through the Internet, but in reality leaves the individual further isolated and alienated from democratic participation and action. Even before the Internet, in the 1960s, this trend was apparent.

"Between *news* that can be utilized by propaganda and *fundamental currents* of society the same relationship exists as between waves and the sea. The waves exist only because the underlying mass supports them; without it there would be nothing. But man sees only the waves; they are what attracts, entices, and fascinates him. Through them he grasps the grandeur and majesty of the sea, through this grandeur exists only in the immense mass of water. Similarly, propaganda can have solid *reality* and *power* over man only because of its rapport with fundamental currents, but it has seductive excitement and a capacity to move him only by its ties to the most volatile immediacy." (Ellul, p. 44)

Not only is the attention of the individual dragged along, following the framed waves of events, but a wave has hardly passed by before she considers it outdated and her attention is directed to the next. Even if events, issues, or personalities are still of significance the individual consigns them to history, and therefore he forgets them. They will only be apparent to him again if they are used again, although interpreted and selected specifically, to present some spin on a new wave of events, issues, or personalities, to frame his possible responses to them.

With intense seriousness and concern for her times, the attention of the individual is kept fleeting and superficial, changeable and malleable, and without consequence or weight. Even deep-seated convictions and passions are directed through the channels and contours of a partitioned and fictionalized multimedia environment; his words only preach to the converted—as it speaking them into an echo chamber—gaining him the reinforcement and catharsis he needs. Or, she receives hostility and finds her words distorted or ignored by those members of some entrenched and oppositional faction, and she is repelled by them, feeling nothing but frustration and dissatisfaction, in need of the reinforcement and solace given by her own group identity, to hear her own opinions echoed and refined by those of like mind. He might make an angry post on Facebook or Twitter. She might leave comment that someone is an idiot.

Through the waves of timely patterns of events, issues, and personalities, the individual is reduced to a series of conditional responses, and thereby he becomes one with the waves, as a channel and vehicle for propaganda and mass distraction. The individual forgets specific facts and retains only a general impression (provided to him by propaganda) which he uses to interpret the current patterns of society, as presented to him via the multimedia environment.

"Hardly has an event taken place before it is outdated; even if its significance is still considerable, it's no longer of interest, and if man experiences the feeling of having escaped it, he is no longer concerned. In addition, he obviously has a very limited capacity for attention and awareness; one event pushes the preceding one into oblivion. And as man's memory is short, the event that is supplanted by another is forgotten; it no longer exists; nobody is interested in it anymore." (Ellul, p. 44)

In this way, the public's attention has been focused on specifics, and the overall problems facing the world and their causes go unnoticed or ignored, or at most vague and aloof. Dots remain unconnected and no general analysis of the overall human condition is undertaken, except in a greatly reduced and superficial form to interpret current events, issues, and personalities, according to the needs of propagandists and propagandees. The act of dissemination, not objective reality, gives news its significance, and hence the public can be brought to a state of shock and grief over the tragic death of a single child, while, at the same time unnoticed, and unreported, tens of thousands of children die of starvation, neglect, and war. And, in this way, propaganda works most effectively with those people who engage with multimedia interpretations and representations of social currents and political events, issues, and personalities. Hence we see that individual prejudices and fears, and psychological needs are necessary for propaganda to work, but they are insufficient. What is also needed is a sense of participating in a collective center of interest, shared by those who feel themselves to be informed about current events and the most important issues of their day. The propagandee becomes propagandist, without knowing that they are either, as by sharing their opinions with other, they refine, reinforce, and proselytize the worldview.

It was for this reason that Ellul considered the *politically undecided* (distinct from indifferent) to be the most susceptible to propaganda. This is only partly true. Without question, within limits, they are manipulable and easily swayed, for a time, but they brush off propaganda as easily as they are swayed by it. They move this way and that; they are mentally promiscuous. But, it is not the undecided who are the most susceptible to propaganda. It is the person with certainties that they have acquired through propaganda, who has an irrational commitment to a worldview that feels "self-evident" and "indisputable," a matter of "faith" or "intuition," who becomes the most zealous and fanatical consumer and disseminator of propaganda. They actively seek out any information (text, image, video, or audio) that confirms their worldview; they seek out like-minded others who reinforce their worldview by sharing it with each other, and more often than not, sharing common enemies and scapegoats; they seek out people to challenge and oppose, to position themselves in opposition to and thereby test their own infallibility; and, most importantly, receive their greatest confirmation by convincing others of their truth and bringing them into the fold of true believers.

It is this desire to bring others into the group of "truth seers," convinced of their collective worldview and invulnerability to propaganda that reveals them to be concealing, if they are aware of them at all, their own irrationality, prejudices, and fears. Hence anyone who challenges them is the enemy or dismissed a stupid, a fool, or a sinner. Anyone who disagrees with them is deluded or a liar. They act with sympathy or hostility to educate or silence the opposing voice, depending on their own confidence in their ability impose their discourse on the wayward mind and induce their complicity and consent in repeating the required prejudices and worldview; repeating the required rubber-stamps to demonstrate their belonging to the "inner circle" of those "who know-what is going on."

Here we see that "truth" belongs to the collective identity—a mark of belonging that is shared by all who do belong and share this identity as their own—made by the individual into their own. Unable to explain how they can be so certain of their knowledge and insights, they gain the certainty they seek by seeing their knowledge and insights reflected back to themselves from the mirror of the agreement and compliance of others. The echo is the measure of the truth of whatever they utter. Without the echo, they have only the sound their own voice, and, beyond that, nothing at all. These are the people who are most susceptible to propaganda: the people who use propaganda unconsciously to conceal their own nihilism under a mask of certainty and zeal.

By indoctrinating truths and ethics into the individual, strategic propaganda creates a personality structure—a template—for the individual to flesh out for themselves. Individuals subjected to strategic propaganda are susceptible to tactical propaganda and respond appropriately to crisis or dramatized events.

"What starts out as a simple situation gradually turns into a definite ideology, because the way of life in which man thinks he is so indisputably well of becomes a criterion of value for him. This does not mean that objectively he is well off, but that, regardless of the merits of his actual condition, he *thinks* he is. He is perfectly adapted to his environment, like a "fish in water." From that moment on, everything that expresses this particular way of life, that reinforces and improves it, is *good*; everything that tends to disturb, criticize, or destroy it is *bad*. (Ellul, p. 67)

This definite ideology becomes a form of cultural normalization and psychological standardization, which tend toward totalitarianism. Whether Right or Left, their intellectual life and personality are given over to the collective identity of the group; while this is not so much of the problem for the Leftist propagandist, for whom all categories of history and social being, or for the Right Wing propagandist for whom all things find the origin in the genius of the Party, the Leader, or God, it is an insurmountable problem—catachresis ('missing the mark')—for either the Leftist or Rightist propagandee who still seeks to find the foundation of their thoughts and action illuminated by the clarity of an intellectually free and rational mind. Only those who feel no need to question their own certainties are free from the doubts and tensions of the genuinely open mind.

The collective identity leads the propagandized mind towards the collective foci of interests, concerns, and problems. The self-identity of the propagandee is measured by how they understand and deal with these

104

interests, concerns, and problems, as a propagandist of the word and deed. When their individual and collective foci become identical, that person is simultaneously a propagandee and propagandist, both a leader and led, and lost to propaganda until their own experiences and life events tear them away from the group. Only disassociation from the group through alienation and rupture, through internal conflicts and betrayals, can save them from the grip of propaganda. They cannot be talked out of it by an outsider. They must escape from its ruins. Clearly the more intensely a group shares the collective foci of interests, the susceptible individual members are to propaganda. However, through mass media, even as isolated individual can share the collective foci, perhaps even more intensely given their isolation. This isolated individual can feel that they are attuned to deep insights into current events and their causes, rubber-stumping every insight that they have as its own confirmation, and can develop intense fanaticism and extremism, as a result; whereas the group member can be as equally lost to propaganda and the group identity, but, unless the group demands extreme or fanatical action as proof of loyalty and commitment to the group, the member will find catharsis and satisfaction in simply belonging.

As Joe Bageant put it, in the opening sentence of his book *Deer Hunting with Jesus: Dispatches from America's Class War*.[44]

"On the morning of November 2, 2004, millions of Democrats arose to a new order. Smoke from neoconservative campfires hung over all points southward and westward. The hairy fundamentalist hordes, the redneck blue collar legions, and other cultural Visigoths stirred behind distant battlements. In university towns across the country, in San Francisco, Seattle, and Boulder, in that bluest of strongholds, New York City, and in every self-contained, oblivious corner of liberal America where a man or woman can buy a copy of *The Nation* without special-ordering it, Democrats sank into a Prozac-proof depression. What, they wondered, happened out there in the heartland, the iconic one they'd seen on television and in magazines, the one bright with church spires, grange halls, stock-car races, and community heritage festivals. And why had the working class so plainly voted against their own interests?"

Bageant terms the vision of America sold to Americans by corporate media as *the hologram*. Corporate media dominates the dissemination of information

---

[44] Joe Bageant, *Deer Hunting With Jesus: Dispatches from America's Class War* (Three Rivers Press, 2007)

and opinion in America to present a manufactured worldview of what it means to be a good American—this is the hologram. It is the totalitarian worldview produced by the propaganda machine that channels and frames public discourse within America by controlling the questions and remaining silent about anything that does not fit in with the corporate agenda, while demonizing or marginalizing anyone who raises criticisms or presents facts in contradiction to the propaganda machine. Intensified media consolidation, TV, radio, and newspapers, as well as books and Internet sites, give voice to the interests of fewer people—the owners of media corporations—and threatens to turn media into a total propaganda machine in service to these interests. Media pundits represent themselves as reflecting the concerns and views of their target audience, but they express and represent the message and interests of their employers. Cable TV, radio, newspapers, and the Internet have become factionalized, with people only interested in channels and sites that reinforce their own opinions and views. What has happened to the promise of the Great Conversation? Where are public debates and the frank exchange of views? It seems to me that they have all but disappeared; replaced by the propaganda machine and the hologram. Under such circumstances, the breeding ground for extremism is fertile, distrust and contempt abound, and public debate is almost impossible. Without public debate, democracy is stifled and the public merely become pawns of the propaganda machine.

With the consolidation of mass media and the Internet, media in America has become quite partitioned and factionalized. I term this as *narrowcasting*.[45] This is the mainstream media tendency to tailor the content of TV and radio talk shows and website content to appeal to targeted and politicized audiences, to reinforce their already held beliefs, assumptions, fears, prejudices, and worldview. It is the opposite of *broadcasting*. It does not challenge deep-seated views and assumptions. It does not inform. It draws its target audience together into a clique of kindred spirits, akin to a cult, by appealing to their values, myths, and aspirations. Pundits tell their target audience whatever they want to hear, who the good and bad guys are, and why the world is in the shape it is in—all of which reassures people about their own understanding of the world, and reaffirms the sacrifices and

---

[45] I first introduced this term in *Debunking Glenn Beck: How to Save America from Media Pundits and Propagandists* (Praeger, ABC-CLIO: Santa Barbara, CA: 2011)

choices they had made. Their existence is affirmed. Narrowcasting, often in the guise of entertainment and information, exploits the psychological need for meaning, being in the know, and belonging. People seek out and trust the sources of media that satisfy their needs, and they begin to identify with their choices of media, to exclude other sources of media—especially ones that promote opinions critical of or even different from their own, to the extent of feeling hostile towards or repelled by any media source that challenges or contradicts their trusted media sources. Such an audience is now prepared for—ready to receive—propaganda and misinformation.

Narrowcasting remains an important idea if we want to understand how mass media works to precondition its target population demographic for propaganda and misinformation. Propaganda is largely constructed through using combinations of selective coverage, censorship, framing debates and questions, spin, repetition, juxtaposing images, subliminal messages, falsehoods, and deception—but it is always plays on people's emotions, such as their pride or fear, or preys on their ignorance and vanity to bypass their skepticism and personal experiences. This can help us understand how propagandists are able to drive wedges between people—to divide people against each other—in order to distract and alienate a target demographic against its own best interests. This is especially important when the economic elite—the owners of multinational conglomerates, including media corporations, public relations firms, and marketing agencies—are using that propaganda machine to distract the public from the corporate takeover of the political institutions of America in order to maintain for themselves a monopoly over government access to ensure a favorable regulatory environment for maximizing profits and their control over markets, labor, and resources.

How does narrowcasting work? A successfully narrowcasted audience is inoculated against all alternative or contradictory media sources. They are "in the know" and anyone who disagrees with them cannot be trusted. This is akin to being in a cult. Viewers, listeners, and readers seek out the media sources that confirm their prejudices and worldview. They are inoculated against all other media sources. Such an audience is now ready for the next stage: propaganda and misinformation. Narrowcasting develops into a form of self-censorship in the sense that the successfully narrowcasted audience will neither tolerate nor seek out alternative media sources—as they are all liars and propaganda, "the liberal media." Cable TV channels like Fox News—owned by Rupert Murdoch's News Corporation—target a specific demographic, the nationalistic and conservative white working and middle classes, and take any other demographic as a bonus. The style and content of the channel is tailored to appeal to their sense of patriotism, personal responsibility, and hard-nosed realism, as well as the near universal dislike of taxes. Hard work and individual achievement are celebrated, but what is ignored is that hard work still results in poverty for many people. Yet we are to believe that failure is simply due to laziness or government interference. Slogans, symbols, graphics, and music are important parts of Fox News's presentation. Kitsch abounds. Interwoven into this are the messages of the day—correct opinions to be had if you are a conservative and patriotic—and the ongoing narrative against "the government," "socialism," "progressives," "radicals," and "the liberal media." The aim is to bypass critical thinking and reasoning by appealing directly to emotions and fundamental values. The focus is always on perceived threats characterized in terms of a slogan such as "the War on Drugs," "the War on Terror," or the "War on Christmas," and blaming the Democrats or "the Left" for obstructing the necessary means to deal with these threats or even for having caused the threat. TV viewers are provided with ready-made refutations of people they should disagree with—refutations that support the policies of the Republican Party—as any patriotic American should, which, oddly enough, are repeated and reinforced by their friends, neighbors, other people they know at work, and in the newspaper and on the radio too.

Fox News presents itself as "fair and balanced", as if in virtue of being on the air as the sole herald of fair and balanced reporting and commentary, as opposed to "the out of touch" and "biased" reporting in "the liberal media" (which often includes competing corporate media such as MSNBC, CNN, CBS, and ABC, as well as the obvious candidates like *The New York Times*). Narrowcasting exploits the irrationality, fear, and ignorance of its target audience—reinforcing and intensifying these psychological reactions—to discredit alternative sources of information and education in favor of a value-based narrative that appeals to a mythical idealization of America juxtaposed with exposés of threats to that idyllic, narrow view of white, property-owning, and suburban America. This leaves the target audience open to misinformation. It is of little surprise that polls conducted by Farleigh Dickinson University and the University of Maryland suggest that people who only watched only Fox News are not only more misinformed about contemporary political issues than people who got their news from watching other cable TV channels, but were more misinformed than people who did not follow any news at all.[46] It should also be of little surprise that, as the Pew Research Institute has shown, Republicans in general are far more likely to reject science, especially global warming, given the endless assault on science and global warming disseminated by Fox News and the propaganda machine in general.[47] Critics have given example after example of how Fox News, selects topics that favor Republican Party talking points—misrepresenting these as news—to distort the facts to fit the message of the day, blur the distinction between reporting and commentating, discredit and smear the political opposition to the Republican Party, and suppresses any information that can problematize or contradict its reporting.[48] However, let's not make the mistake of thinking that this is a something that only occurs among viewers of Fox News. It is also not new. In a poll performed by *Tide* in 1947, Americans were asked their opinion of "the Metallic Metals Act."[49] Of the 70% who responded with an opinion, 21.4% considered the act to be beneficial to the United States, 58.6% felt the matter should be left to the

---

[46] *The Huffington Post* reported (Nov, 21, 2011) a poll from Farleigh Dickinson University that showed that Fox News viewers are less informed than people who do not watch any news http://www.huffingtonpost.com/2011/11/21/fox-news-viewers-less-informed-people-fairleigh-dickinson_n_1106305.html ; and (Dec, 17, 2010) a poll from the University of Maryland that showed that Fox New viewers not were much more likely to believe false information than viewers of any other cable news channel http://www.huffingtonpost.com/2010/12/17/fox-news-viewers-are-the-_n_798146.html . Almost on a daily basis, media watchdog Media Matters of America exposes errors or misrepresentation of facts on Fox News: http://mediamatters.org/ .

[47] See a summary of the 2008 Pew Research Study "A Deeper Partisan Divide over Global Warming" http://www.people-press.org/2008/05/08/a-deeper-partisan-divide-over-global-warming/ or the full report http://www.people-press.org/files/legacy-pdf/417.pdf . This tendency has also been addressed in detail in Chris Mooney, *The Republican War on Science* (Basic Books, 2005).

[48] Fairness and Accuracy in Reporting (FAIR), "Fox: The Most Biased Name in News," July 2001, http://www.fair.org/index.php?page=1067 ; Jeff Cohen, *Cable News Confidential: My Misadventures in Corporate Media* (Sausalito, CA: PoliPoint Press, 2006). See also Robert Greenwald's 2004 documentary *Outfoxed: Rupert Murdoch's War on Journalism* http://www.outfoxed.org/ and Media Matters for America http://mediamatters.org/ for daily updates on misinformation on Fox News.

[49] See Fredrick C. Irion, *Public Opinion and Propaganda*, p. 698

market, 15.7% believed that the act benefited foreigners but not Americans, and 4.3% flat out opposed it. Of course, there was no such act as "the Metallic Metals Act." In a mass media culture, the public is conditioned to have opinions, and it simply does not matter whether those opinions are based on experience, facts, or any knowledge whatsoever. Let's not make the mistake of thinking that MSNBC, CNN, CBS, and ABC are actually "liberal media" that are struggling to inform the public and counter the lies of Fox News. They also distort and manipulate the facts and disseminate propaganda. This game of 'good cop, bad cop' played by corporate media is designed to frame public debate, present the illusion of a wide spectrum of views, and continue the myth that there is actually a free press, media diversity, and choice between media outlets in America.

Alongside Fox News are all the thousands of AM and FM conservative talk radio shows across America, most of which are provided by the corporation Clear Channel Communications, with over 110 million listeners.[50] Every day, workers across America listen to these channels, in the background, largely to keep them company while they work, before they go home to collapse in front of the TV. Cable television channels such as Fox News, along with conservative talk radio present themselves to their audience as the voice of "mainstream America": white conservative working and middle class America. They do not pretend to present a wide spectrum of political views. Instead, they present a coordinated assortment of right wing positions, chiefly those that satisfy corporate interests, promote consumerism, and increase ratings through controversial, sensationalist, and politically incorrect speech. Vilifying "the liberal media" is an essential component of narrowcasting. Of course the accusation of "liberal bias" in "the liberal media" was a worn out cliché by the end of the 1970s. Today, it is laughable. Whether on MSNBC, CNN, CBS, ABC, or Fox News, corporate media promote the interests of their owners and sponsors. The difference between these media corporations is largely one of competition over market share for specific demographics and commercial revenues. Their pundits spar off each over—all part of the show. Cable TV reporting and

---

[50] See Clear Channel Communication's website: http://clearchannel.com/ See also *Broadcast Blues* (2009) by Radio and TV producer Sue Wilson (http://www.SueWilsonReports.com) about the perils of media consolidation.

commentary have blurred the distinction between news, entertainment, and propaganda.

On the Internet, we have seen the growth of right wing "news" sites, such as Glenn Beck TV, Inforwars.com, and Breitbart.com. Their target audience tends to be self-identified "conservatives" who feel alienated and dissatisfied with a modern society and government, and Glenn Beck, Steve Bannon, or Alex Jones's anti-government and anti-progressive rhetoric and oratory feeds this "conservative" sense of loss about the erosion of the cultural importance of family, church, and nation, hence responding to the experiences and truths of their target audience, and reinforcing their prejudices and worldview; but, misdirecting and deceiving this audience about the causes of their dissatisfaction and alienation, either blaming socialists, in the case of Beck, blaming "the Left" and "multi-culturalism" in the case of Bannon, or blaming some globalist conspiracy for One World Government, in the case of Jones, turning attention away from the takeover of society and its political institutions by multinational corporations and international investment banks, and leaving their audience to further recede into their paranoid private realm, in a state of quietism and inaction, except perhaps doing their bit as obedient workers, disseminators of propaganda, and good consumers, especially when it comes to purchasing provisions, guns, and ammunition in preparation for the apocalyptic scenarios fed to them by the likes of Beck and Jones.

As I said in *Debunking Glenn Beck*, Beck waves the red flag of his warning about a socialist takeover of America to the bull (the target demographic of white, nationalistic, and conservative working class Americans) to distract them from the corporate sword that is carving up America and the rest of the world. Anything outside of their cult following of "truth seers" and "patriotic Americans"—especially anything from outside of America—is taken as suspicious and not to be trusted. Any contradictory facts or interpretations can be explained away as part of some conspiracy. Alienated from any concept of good government, distrustful of democratic participation as being manipulated by socialists or globalists, the target audience is turned against organized labor and progressive movements—the very same forces that defend the interests of the working and middle classes against the corporate takeover of America—and, cunningly, disguises their integrative propaganda as agitative propaganda, leaving their target audience with a cathartic illusion of rebellion and resistance while being relegated to a politically impotent private realm and worldview based on a mythical and idealistic view of America and the world.

On FM and AM talk radio the situation is even more extreme, with some hosts using racism and sexism to attract attention and ratings, and some even calling for armed rebellion against Washington DC or the reformation of the Confederacy, with their narratives rife with anti-government, anti-liberal, anti-feminist, anti-immigrant, and anti-democratic rhetoric. Their positive message is that they stand for American freedom and values—but this message remains abstract. Even if the level of bigotry and hate-speech that now dominates political discourse in talk radio remains background or unheard by most people, it reflects the growing polarization of American politics and the erosion of public debate into a "them v. us" struggle to the death. Even though it appeals to only a small minority, extreme right wing discourse and narrowcasting have consequences for how public debate is framed by the media for generations of people. It moves the "mainstream" view further towards the right, presenting the status quo as being the moderate position and the view of "the average American", and anything to the left of that being "radical" or "liberal". The so-called conservative pundits explore positions to the right, seeking to promote corporate interests, regardless of whether behind military ventures or in need of whipping up opposition to regulations, people's own rights, unions, or anything that gets in the way of big business, or even just to serve as a distraction. These pundits pronounce themselves to be "hard talkers" or "realists" taking on the "political correctness" of "the liberal media" and exposing "the enemies of America." Narrowcasting of this kind is designed to drive wedges between people and divide the working and middle classes—pitting public sector workers against private sector workers, educated against uneducated, urban against rural, and progressive against conservative-minded people.

These methods constrain, divide, and direct public opinion to promote the interests of the elite through mass media by channeling thoughts and attitudes to keep them within acceptable bounds, and thereby prevent the possibility of any effective challenge to established privilege and authority. This results in self-censorship and the framing of permissible public opinion. These techniques can also be used to create crises and whip up public reaction to distract the public while presenting the illusions of critical

112

journalism and transparent government. In this way, "national problems" and "crises" are created by the government through the use of propaganda to create public demand for an already planned policy and to present "a solution" to this problem, as if the government was responding to the public demand. This allows a government to represent itself in the media as accountable and representative, when in fact it is creating that demand in the same way as the advertising industry creates demand for products. Media is increasingly synonymous with the propaganda machine, which operates to control what is known and censor anything that threatens to inconvenience privilege and power, while serving the interests of privilege and power, and to keep the attention of the population both distracted by and focused upon divisive issues and sensationalist stories.

Under such conditions, democratic participation has become quite unfeasible, except in a few small communities, and incapable of providing an administrative basis for the organization of modern society. If democracy were to be possible, it not only requires a means by which the public could understand how mass media works and presents information to them, but it also requires a means by which the public could understand the relationships between politicians and mass media propaganda. These possibilities are undermined by deliberate and selective use of facts, rhetoric, symbols, or art as propaganda to achieve social influence directed towards or against any opinion or idea for or against any public policy or law, without any reasoned or critical reflection on the necessity and implications of that public policy or law. This is largely affected through narrowcasting and oppositional politics. This appeal to emotion rather than reason appeals to the irrational and visceral within us to connect disparate discourse about events with associated meanings, symbols, images, and implications. It taps into our psychology— our self-identity—in a way that reinforces or even intensities our fears, paranoia, or prejudices, giving a sense of meaning and belonging. Combined with "them v. us" rhetoric and misinformation, reasoned and thoughtful public debate and deliberation between people with different opinions, experiences, and worldviews becomes impossible. Other people are seen as "the enemy" or "brainwashed" simply because they have different opinions or ideas about policy and the future. One's opinions become bound up with one's sense of self-identity, defined more in terms of affirming a worldview and community rather than in terms of any ideology, and often in the negative sense of self-identify—*as not being a member of some vilified group*. In this way, "conservatives" and "liberals" are defined as opposite groups; without giving these terms any substantial meaning.

The hostility that narrowcasting generates towards "them" undermines pluralism. It also destroys the possibility of open and rational communication because it makes listening and mutual understanding (and respect) completely impossible. Instead, it generates and intensifies contempt between people. A heavily narrowcasted population can always be fed lies, as they will never read, listen to, or watch any source that could expose those lies, and even if they do, they will always interpret the exposure as being a lie (and therefore confirm their suspicions about the source). In this way, the political opposition can always be demonized using the most fantastic fabrications without a shred of evidence, or wild conspiracy theories, alongside assortments of lies, half-truths, interpretations, carefully selected facts, chosen studies, and edited news. Not only does this intensify hostility between groups of people, especially those of opposing political views, or religious or ethnic divisions, but it also undermines and erodes the possibility of communication, which is the foundation of democracy. The heavily narrowcasted population not only increasingly lives in a fabricated universe— the hologram—but they live in such a heavily partitioned and factionalized society that it becomes impossible to develop the lines of communication and deliberation that make modern society function and work as a democratic society. Elections become a matter of media control and bombarding the population with propaganda, lies, and distractions. There is no possibility of making a rational choice between candidates in such an environment. When propaganda is systemic and used to intensify divisions within society over a long period of time, rather than only just before elections, this leads to such an entrenchment of hostilities and alienation between people to such an extent that violence is inevitable. The systemic use of propaganda on the domestic population is a precursor to civil war.

However, often propaganda uses evidence and corroboration to its advantage, even showing the opposite conclusion suggested by evidence or corroboration. Narrowcasting works by feeding the audience interpretations of the evidence that supports the audience's shared convictions, or confirms their suspicions about "their opponents." Connections between interpretations and events can be carefully selected and fed to the target demographic, using any number or kind of media source, across coordinated

114

(yet seemingly independent) media channels and outlets. Through these interpretations, individuals have their need for information and allegiance (belonging) satisfied, while having the required opinions and talking-points fed to them, the belief of which becomes a condition of group-identity. Thus allegiance to a political party, religion, ideology, or community is reinforced through narrowcasting, especially in terms of stances on wedge-issues and their justification, alongside the propagation of opinions, interpretations, lies, falsehoods, innuendo, and ideas, and the framework of a whole vocabulary to use as rubber-stamps and a set of "off-the-peg" refutations and counterpoints. This inoculates people against criticism and opposing viewpoints, allowing them to be dismissed without listening to them, and suppress any challenges or questions that might introduce doubts, contradictions, or alternative ideas. This entrenches people into their narrowcasted group, thereby suppressing their critical faculty and intellect in general, and ultimately results in a narrowcasted audience believing anything at all with conviction, as long as it is shared and reinforced by members of the same group and the same media sources. Even when lies are exposed as lies, the target audience will simply deny it and carry on regardless.

We need to look beyond the truth-status of opinion and statements of fact when analyzing propaganda in a heavily narrowcasted media. We need to look at its psychological function and consequences within society. Most importantly, we need to look at how it erodes criticality and rationality, and leads to intellectual inauthenticity and political alienation. We need to see how the all-pervasive echo-chamber and hologram of mass media propaganda distracts the population from the realities of government and the political process, and erodes the possibility of democratic participation and deliberation. We need to look at how mass media narrowcasting operates to divide people against each other, while reinforcing prejudices and false beliefs—how propaganda operates through group-identity and the real targets of propaganda are the attitudes of people towards each other. This results in polarization and ignorance; encirclement of attitudes around fears and scapegoating—creating and reinforcing the "them v us" attitude. Narrowcasting operates by intensifying and reinforcing attitudes of conformity, belonging, and hostility through rubber-stamping and sloganeering; to present a simulacrum of political involvement and thinking under the guise of free speech, all the while suppressing and circumventing the conditions through which free speech is possible and occurs.

Opinionating is not free-speech; it is parroting—and propaganda undermines free speech.

Propaganda and Democracy:

As I have argued above, we need to look at how the public relations and advertising industries in America have become enmeshed in mass media, manufacturing social trends, motivations, allegiances, facts, and personality—using the lessons of behavioral psychology to reduce the framework of public debate (especially in social media) to stimulus-response mechanisms. We need to look at how mass psychology and sociology reveal how pre-propaganda works from childhood through education and mass media to manipulate psychological needs to suppress the possibility of critical thinking, enlightenment, self-reflection, communication, and democracy. Propaganda is a form of psychological warfare that reduces public opinion to a series of knee-jerk responses to stimuli, leaving the population paralyzed through terror, hatred, fear, false flags, smokescreens, and scapegoats. Mass media is a mechanism for mass distraction, organized through media consolidation, 'astroturf' movements and other faux forms of "political mobilization," social media, bloggers, think tanks, movies, music, and mainstream media news—in sort, totalitarian control over the minds of the population through the culture industry to lead to the illusion that the individual's attitudes and opinions are forms of free-speech or "spontaneous participation."

The creation and manipulation of "spontaneous participation" through propaganda is not new. It is as old as the proverbial hills. Yet through the technologies and administrative methods of the twentieth century it reached hitherto unknown levels of refinement and sophistication. It was evident during the Chinese revolution and "the Hundred Flowers Campaign," which, through systematic and all-pervasive *propaganda of agitation* campaigns, political mobilization seemingly arose at a grassroots level, even though those campaigns are orchestrated by the Communist Party apparatus. The idea proposed by Chairman Mao was that if the masses were to take on slogans and talking-points for themselves, the people would organize themselves into propagandists and agitators working for the Party, working towards the goal proposed in the original propaganda campaign, but consider themselves to have orchestrated it spontaneously.[51] Propaganda of agitation consists in taking real misery and suffering, poverty, and oppression, as points of departure for the manufacture of coherent explanations, the designation of enemies and scapegoats, and the propagation of myths, stereotypes, and an ideology. This leads to popular mobilizations operating along social divisions, intensifying polarization, and conforming to ideological promises and policies as proposed by the Party, through the control over education and mass media. Today, in America, the propaganda of agitation is directed towards immigrants, especially Mexicans, and Muslims.

In this media environment, it is quite impossible to ask questions about the direction and vision of society. Whatever the ideology, democracy depends on the communication and deliberation of idealized visions of the future to be reached by the policies or strategies advocated by the population, for themselves, and for future generations. Narrowcasted and heavily propagandized populations are incapable of doing this—they only exist in the 'now' of whatever they are currently fed to be outraged about. It is essential that the idealization remain generalized and aloof, expressed in vague value statements and grand visualizations. America needs to be great again—but what does greatness mean? That question will not be asked. We might be told it will involve jobs, money, and winning, but there will be no details or any strategy discussed beyond building a wall between the U.S. and Mexico, or banning Muslims from America. Propaganda can only make vague promises and talk in empty concepts and value statements. Over-specified predictions work against the propagandist if they don't come true. (It was for this reason that, during WWII, Joseph Goebbels protested against the predictions of victories that streamed from the Führer's office.) Or if predictions are made, it is important that they are sufficiently far into the future that they will be forgotten if they don't come true. Hence, in 1961, Khrushchev had little to fear when predicting that communism would be achieved in the USSR by 1980. It also remains possible to use scapegoating or esoteric constructions (designed to appear to be expert explanations but so abstract as to explain anything and nothing) to explain away failed predictions if anyone should so happen to remember them.

---

[51] Roderick MacFarquhar (ed.), *The Hundred Flowers Campaign and Chinese Intellectuals* (New York: Praeger, 1960)

Yet, if we can remember as far back as 2008, the original Tea Party started as a grassroots movement of working and middle class Americans who were disenfranchised by Bush's and Congress's bailing out of banks and insurance companies to the tune of 800 billion dollars, and they called for government accountability and the audit of the Federal Reserve. They opposed the bailouts. These were the same bailouts that were supported by MSNBC, CNN, CBS, ABC, and Fox News (predictably, Fox News switched to opposing the bailouts, once Obama had been elected). Corporate media across channels, as well as newspapers and stand-up comedians on HBO, and *The Daily Show* and *The Colbert Report* on Comedy Central, were all quick to focus on racists and extremists in the Tea Party, as well as examples of ignorant slogans on placards, humorous spelling mistakes, and misspoken errors of historical fact. Similarly the corporate-owned media mocked the Occupy Wall Street protests—portraying them as anarchists or people protesting without reason (as if their objection to the bank bailouts and lack of any accountability wasn't evident.) This alienated moderate and middle class people from the Tea Party and Occupy movement—and without any other avenue to protest the bailouts they were pulled back into the arms of the Democratic Party, with the promise of new financial regulation, oversight, and protections, along with the promise of campaign finance reform. Hope and change. Those people skeptical about this promise and Barack Obama in general—a sentiment heightened through narrowcasting by right wing media—were drawn back into the arms of the Republican Party, despite its policy opposing any financial regulations at all, steadfast in its refusal to support any audit of the Federal Reserve—instead calling for further deregulation, lower corporate taxes, and cuts in government spending on social programs to reduce the deficit and national debt. Dissenters could find catharsis and solace in the libertarian and states' rights platitudes and slogans offered by Ron Paul, while the Tea Party candidates for election to Congress in 2010 all came from the extreme right of the Republican Party, promoting a radical agenda that ranged from removing all social programs and regulations to imposing theocracy on America. This assault continues to date, including intensified attacks on women's rights, gay marriage, and public sector workers, social security, Medicaid and Medicare, and even public lands and the National Parks.

Regardless whether it is integration or agitation, capitalist or communist, all modern propaganda must direct itself to material progress and consumerism to associate any policy or proposal with increased or decreased material prosperity, and to secure the status quo of the economic order as either being the best or least worst of all possible worlds. Even agitation propaganda in America today talks of protest and demands on the government, or returning to some "golden age" of the Constitution. In this respect, within limits, environmentalism or conservation campaigns utilizing propaganda are more likely to succeed among affluent classes by talking of environmental destruction leading to the collapse of systems vital to human health, or how the damage to the overall planetary ecology with term human survival prospects, providing such campaigns do not require measures that will reduce the affluence of those classes. Among poorer classes, environmentalism or conservation campaigns are easily opposed by propaganda campaigns based on the fear that they will cause job losses or raise taxes. Combined with almost complete media blackouts of protests, like the 2016-17 Sioux protests in North Dakota about the DAPL pipeline, allowing the police and government to act with impunity, until the foreign press picked up the story, the public either remains oblivious to such events, or simply gets to see a sanitized or carefully crafted version of them.

Today, the propaganda of agitation is part of a broader propaganda of integration, which is designed and organized to integrate individuals into the system and body politic as deeply as possible; to channel agitation; to establish a totalitarian worldview as natural and spontaneous; to ridicule all alternatives and make them irrational or unthinkable; to isolate critics; to disintegrate connections within traditional cultures; and, to marginalize opposing political groups and organizations. This results in the individual's whole existence being mediated by propaganda—lost in the hologram of narrowcasted mass media—and this results in mass conformity and control being represented as freedom of speech and political action. The collective self-discipline of a highly propagandized population results in the mutual reinforcement of the myths of freedom and truth becoming transformed into ideological unity—all without any real content or meaning apart from some vague sense of belonging to "us" and not being "them."

The aim of the propaganda of integration is for oppositional voices not to be heard or seem insane; thereby exhausting the opposition by forcing them to make increasingly huge efforts to even make their basic premises heard. In this way, the opposition becomes marginalized, misrepresented, and ridiculed until their voices fall silent. It is a psychological war of attrition and victory goes to the last one standing. The myths and truths of the victor become posited within a totalitarian worldview as the norms and beliefs of reasonable people—they become common sense! Such a worldview is naturalized through repetition in everyday speech; consequently the status quo becomes objectified as reality. Political realism—or moderation—becomes the mask of the propaganda of integration, whereas populism become the mask of the propaganda of agitation. By controlling the framework of public debate, the individual molds himself to fit that framework; consequently the manufacture of public opinion and consent becomes "spontaneous." Such an individual considers herself to be informed and free, when she is completely brainwashed.[52]

However, through narrowcasting, the prejudices and worldview—rubber-stamps and myths—of the target group are reinforced as norms and natural. As long as the individual feels the need to fit into the group, as long as resistance to the group results in feelings of alienation and nihilism, the individual will eventually conform to the group, in thought as well as action. Once that happens, the individual will feel a sense of greater feelings of empowerment and freedom of thought, as they conform to the group and his or her private beliefs and doubts grow increasingly silent and forgotten, and ultimately his or her own sense of personality will cohere entirely with their identity within the group. At that point, the individual is effectively lost to brainwashing and group-think and they are no longer an individual at all. They have become an automaton. Once a person has become lost to group action, completely identifying themselves with the group, it becomes easy for propagandists to insert demand for further actions, even those actions, that would seem at odds with the group's own myths and prejudices, and these actions will be rubber-stamped as confirmations of the truth of those myths and prejudices. It is thereby possible for someone to declare themselves to be a good Christian, while at the same time expanding hatred and committing violence, even though such acts are completely at odds with the teachings of Jesus Christ, but through their conformity to the rubber-stamps of group-think they can confirm that these acts show their faith and commitment to

---

[52] A.M. Meerlo, *The Rape of the Mind: The Psychology of Thought Control, Menticide, and Brainwashing* (New York: World Publishing Company, 1956); see also Milton Meyer, *They Thought They Were Free: The Germans 1933-45* (University of Chicago Press, 1954)

Christianity, which is understood through the interpretations and myths of their Church. Criticisms of the propaganda becomes interpreted and received as a criticism of their faith.

Here we can see how propaganda functions as the justification and authority for any course of action, and as a result the past actions of the group members themselves act as reinforcements for the propaganda, further intensifying the feelings of justification and authority. When this intensification reaches pathological levels of zealotry and fanaticism, the group is under such a shared degree of psychosis, that it becomes possible to indoctrinate them further no matter how extremist the course of action, extravagant the myths, or one-sided the prejudices. The proselyte becomes a militant, due to the effects of propaganda with the group's organization; thereafter it becomes easier to turn the militant into an assassin or terrorist; self-righteous and self-justified, while being completely lost to the group-think of whatever movement they identify with.

In the light of the above analysis, we can revisit an important question: What do we mean by myths? We tend to think of myths as fables or the tales of ancient gods and heroes, but, as Ellul claimed, in modern society, we too have our myths, but we are unable to see them as such. For us, they are self-evident truths and dominant explanatory tropes that underwrite our worldview. As Ellul put it,

"By 'myths' we mean an all-encompassing, activating image: a sort of vision of desirable objectives that has lost their material, practical character and have become strongly colored, over-whelming, all-encompassing, and which displace from the consciousness all that is related to it. Such an image pushes man to action precisely because all that he feels is good, just, and true." (Ellul, p. 31)

Wise leaders, the master race, the revolutionary proletariat, the Founding Fathers, the religious icons, the free market, all examples of myths upon which stories, histories, ideologies, and a world-view can be built. The task for both the educator and the propagandist is to juxtapose and connect particular myths with particular conditional reflexes. In this way, individuals in groups act in the name of the myth, without there being any logical or necessary connection between the myth and the action.

By using myths, propaganda explains and justifies the conditions of the individual—allowing the individual to feel free and in charge of their own destiny, while conforming to the dictates of their circumstances—and gives the individual reasons, pathos, and convictions in the face of ignorance, uncertainty, and the intense social pressures of money, work, and success. Propaganda bridges the psychological needs of the individual and the sociological trends and currents that exist within the culture already. This bridge allows the individual to identify the satisfaction of their psychological needs with their membership of a particular group. It does this by connecting the myths learned during individual's childhood (through pre-propaganda conditioning and education) with the rubber-stamps of the group, either reinforcing those myths as truths or denouncing them as lies, depending on the psychological disposition of the individual towards their own childhood educational experiences and the needs of the propagandist. Myths become a statement of personal identity and lifestyle choice—expressed and shared collectively through declaration of patriotism, flag waving, celebration of national heroes, and praise of their party and its leaders. Once strategic propaganda is well developed and culturally entrenched, these statements become rubber-stamps—literally slogans on bumper stickers, baseball caps, or social media memes—that can be shared through specific groups via narrowcasted media.

In this way, the individual adopts the sociological identity, rubber-stumps, and broad ideology of the group as their own, thereby further reinforcing and disseminating them. The individual's personal identity becomes synonymous with the group identity, as they adopt the archetypes and stereotypes of the group into their own idealizations of self and normal behavior, and any dissent, doubts, or deviations from the group identity is relegated to the private realm to be either maintained in secret or repressed into silence. The individual will readily adopt the political message and rubber-stamps of the moment, presenting them as their own opinion, if the propagandist can insert them into the group's repertoire via narrowcasted media sources. These can be dropped and forgotten, or even replaced and reversed, depending on the needs of the propagandist, without too much resistance or inertia providing that the propagandist takes care to respect the language and prejudices of the group, and manipulates them carefully. In this way, the same policy supported by the group when their political party is in power can be opposed by the group when "the opposition" is in power and continues that policy. While this is partly explicable in terms of the double-standards and hypocrisy of political expediency, it is also a deeper manifestation of the irrational psychology that is generated by propaganda when it is the means of establishing sociological cohesion and satisfying individual psychological needs. Once rubber-stamps and myths become the means to establish personal identity through group identity, the content or consistency of those rubber-stamps and myths becomes irrelevant. Supporting the team takes priority over all other concerns, and anyone who deviates from this priority is likely to receive hostility and be excluded from the group.

As well as the myths of the free market and American exceptionalism, there are other myths that are indoctrinated into American children through educational pre-propaganda conditioning and media propaganda. These includes:

- the myth of technological progress (as the basis of a better society);

- the American Dream (that wealth and prosperity are achieved through individual enterprise and hard work*);

  * This is an extension and combination of the pre-capitalist myths of the Protestant Work Ethic and Providence.

- the Pursuit of the Happiness (that individual happiness is the ultimate good);

- Nationalism (that human interests are subordinate to the national interest, as interpreted by leaders);

- the Founding Fathers**(that a semi-mythical group of historical figures, infallible heroes who defined the whole nation for all time);

  ** This is an extension of the myth of The Hero, a form of myth shared by most human cultures.

- Social Naturalism (that the current social order is the best of all possible worlds and is the inevitable result of natural forces and laws, understood and represented in either scientific or theological forms);

- Elitism (that the current ruling elite achieved their position due to their abilities);

- Equality (that America is a classless society);

- Democracy exists in America.

The contradictions and inconsistencies between these myths, as well as the cultural tensions and ideological conflicts they cause in society, and their contradictions with experience and history, can all be concealed through the skillful application of propaganda based on these myths, especially within the cultural context of highly narrowcasted mass media disguised as a competitive market of ideas.

By building upon and reinforcing these myths, propaganda becomes a cohesive force within America, to the extent that any challenge to this propaganda (even by calling it "propaganda") can be represented as anti-American propaganda disseminated by "haters" or "the blame America first crowd," while the dissemination of propaganda can be represented as patriotism and free speech, as "self-evident truths." Within the cultural context of highly narrowcasted mass media, wherein people's personal identity is so invested in believing these myths to be "self-evident truths," the act of even calling them myths or questioning them will result in the conditioned-reflex of hostility, along with whatever appropriate rubber-stamp responses are available to that particular group, and will fall on deaf ears. Even the words on this page would result in such hostility for even mentioning these myths *as myths* that are bound-up with pre-propaganda conditioning, propaganda, and group identity, that they would be considered by some to be treasonous, or dismissed as "liberal lies" or "leftist propaganda."

This helps us understand how a worldview can be riddled with contractions and inconsistencies, and yet still function as a worldview. For example, one of the contradictions that has arisen as a result of the power of multinational corporations and international finance over the U.S. government is the contradiction between nationalistic rhetoric and rhetoric in favor of globalization (with its consequences e.g. unemployment, loss of industry, tax havens, outsourcing, reduced trade tariffs, lower capital gains tax, higher income and sales taxes). Not only is this contradiction concealed by the propaganda of scapegoating (e.g. blaming unions and migrant workers), but there is a considerable effort made by propagandists (on behalf of their employers) to equate the national interest with the interests of the

124

economic elite. Hence any policy that advocates any form of "protectionism" can be lambasted as against the national interest (and costing jobs, etc.) if it increases the share of profits that go to the American workforce rather than to shareholders and the owners of international finance houses, banks, and multinational corporations. This has resulted in a disjoint between the nationalism of political propaganda and the corporatism of political policies. So-called "free trade agreements" like NAFTA and CAFTA, and TTIP and TPP, result in the loss of sovereignty and democratic oversight in favor of the profits of multinational corporations, often preventing elected bodies in nation states from passing laws that prevent corporate operations (e.g. laws that ban GMOs). Investors can even be compensated for the loss—"regulatory takings"—of national or local laws that cost corporations money when they comply with them.

Another example is the way that the oil and coal industries in America have spent billions of dollars lobbying politicians and creating propaganda to denounce and discredit climate scientists and prevent climate change from being discussed seriously as an impending problem that requires careful decision making within Congress and in mainstream media. Climate change denial has become the new political norm in opposition to the reactionary measure of introducing new taxes as a means of social engineering. The root problems of excessive consumption and waste are simply ignored. The short-term quarterly profits report and news cycle perpetuate short-term thinking, and the problems we face as a species are perpetually deferred to the future, regardless of their future costs and consequences, if they cost money now. Long term thinking and strategy are eclipsed by the politics of immediate gains.

Changes in political leadership (the election of a new president) have little effect on economic policy, military strategy, or energy policy beyond minor shifts in emphasis on regulatory mechanisms. The demands of technology and the profits of shareholders leaves political leaders powerless, with no more control over events than a newsreader has over the news. Means have become ends—the means not only limit the possible ends open to us, but they also define them. As Ellul put it, "If politics is still defined as the art of the possible, nowadays it is the technician who determines with growing authority what is possible."[53] In many respects, the real work of politics is conducted behind the scenes by bureaucrats and corporate advisors, and the political struggles of party politics, committees, and protests are illusions and distractions—theater or like professional wrestling—to maintain the charade of democratic inclusion and accountability, whereas, in objective fact, the parameters of choice and action have been heavily conditioned by the technological framework wherein problems and their solution emerge as public policy. Our thinking and perception have become constrained by this framework.[54] Objectively, the purpose of the political realm is to distract us from the extent that technology dominates human thought and modern society has become a juggernaut running out of control, full steam ahead, to its inevitable collapse and destruction. Our only choice is either to cling on, be left behind, or be crushed under its wheels. This juggernaut is none other than the globalized corporate state, otherwise known as the industrial-military complex in the service of international capital and finance, combined with the corporate media and telecom industries to become the invisible world government.

Ideology has become totally subordinated to the needs of propaganda in the service of the juggernaut. Its role is primarily one of distracting the population from the operations of the juggernaut and their disastrous consequences for life on Earth. Whether concealing or disguising it, this presents the illusion of political competition, struggles, and choices, when in fact there is none at all. Ideology is in fact a thin veneer over the cultural nihilism that lies at the heart of modern politics. This does not mean that beliefs, presuppositions, and assumptions have disappeared, but it does mean that these things have political use or function only within propaganda campaigns, and they shift and change in accordance with the dictates of political expediency. What has disappeared is any authentic revolutionary force and a passion for the radical transformation of society in accordance with a vision of a good society. Instead the situation is one of the mindless conformity to ongoing economic activity, generated by technological activity and mass consumption, moving in accordance with the profit motive and

---

[53] Jacque Ellul, *The Political Illusion* (trans. Konrad Kellen, New York: Alfred Knopf, 1967), p.38

[54] Ellul, *The Political Illusion*; see also, Karl Rogers, *Participatory Democracy, Science and Technology* (New York: Palgrave Macmillan, 2008)

technological innovation, without any space for ideological or philosophical reflection on what constitutes a good society. The goodness of money and technology—both of which are in essence manifestations of the desire for power—is taken for granted as a self-evident truth.

Mass media assails the individual with what is "now," with opinion, with controversy, crisis, and urgency, to the extent that only that which is present is important; the individual can only be excited by "current events" as fed to her through the Internet and mainstream media channels. Whatever happened yesterday is of no concern whatsoever except in how it relates to the moment. Otherwise it is forgotten, as if it had never existed. "The news" is nothing more than a framework of consumer items from which he can choose to digest, to talk about, to have opinions on, and use to declare his allegiance to his party, his social group, and his nation. The individual will be fed opinions and positions on which she will demand that action must be taken by politicians, by the "they," on her behalf. He will adopt those positions as his own, as evidence of how well-informed he is, as a statement of his identity. Such a media generates shallowness of reaction as to erode the possibility of thoughtful reflection and criticality. The individual leaps from opinion to opinion, without any regard for consistency or coherence; without regard for anything apart from the drama of the politically expedient facts of the day, and how they relate to her own self-righteousness and his own intensity of feeling. Politics has become completely ephemeral—nothing other than entertainment and distraction—which serves as a form of mass mind-control, legitimation, and catharsis. Democracy has become yet another mode of consumerism—a team sport—within which the average citizen is only a spectator. Party politics within the two-party system is little more than a decoy—bait—to distract the masses from real problems and their causes. Vision is replaced by promises and slogans—like "Make America Great Again"—which means anything and nothing, and are discarded the moment the election is over, when "the demands" of "political expediency" take over. Any and all promises are forgotten by the collective amnesia of the masses as they are lost within the never ending and always changing news cycles and feeds of mainstream mass media, whatever the talking points, crisis, or national tragedy of the day; to be replaced with another tomorrow, or within a few days, as the mass hysteria of the nation is generated and channeled with almost seamless ease. A nation brought to the edge of the sofa in terror, with great gnashing of teeth, at the prospect of an imminent nuclear strike from North Korea, can be redirected within a few days towards a national controversy over the causes of a school shooting, or outrage at the lewd behavior of a scantily-clad pop singer, as if the threat from North Korea had never existed. The situation is reminiscent of the activities of the Ministry of Truth in Orwell's *1984*, but there is no need to falsify records and change the news, as the mass focus moves on and forgets they had ever seen them.

This state of affairs is further compounded with propaganda is used to reinforce a worldview that stands in contradiction to the facts. This leads to denial and a faux skepticism regarding the facts. The notion of "a conspiracy" or "hoax" is the standard go-to reaction to deal with pesky facts that simply cannot be denied. The new vogue of denouncing "fake news" is a case in point—as if fake news never existed before—and anything that does not fit into the hologram or contradicts it can be dismissed as "fake news." This vogue is itself a product of propaganda and narrowcasting. No matter how absurd or tentative a conspiracy theory, it will be believed rather than face the consequences of the facts and having to question, reevaluate, and change one's behavior. One of the ironies of the modern era is that the greater access to information and up to the minute news, available across a wide variety of media, has resulted in the entrenchment of ignorance. By this, I do not mean that people lack knowledge; instead what we see is the growth of a steadfast refusal to know the facts, even a hostility towards them, all justified by the vacuous repetition of slogans and clichés, without any concern whatsoever with the possibility of error or objectivity, and understood only in relation to the individual's identity. Statements of group-identity—shibboleths or rubber-stamps—have replaced reason to the point that the mere fact that a person is a member of another group instantly discredits anything he could possibly say. It does not even need to be heard to know that it is wrong. It is wrong by association, by definition. It is wrong *a priori*.

In a media environment wherein counterpropaganda and contradictory information exists, narrowcasting is essential to provide the mechanism and outlets to inoculate the target demographic against counterpropaganda and contradictory information, by creating a resistance and sense of suspicion against its sources (utilizing rubber-stumps such as "the liberal media" or *Lügenpresse* for example, or even full blown conspiracy theories of New World Order control over mainstream media to promote communist and atheist lies), and also to reinforce the sense of belonging, truth, and catharsis, thereby satisfying psychological needs, by reinforcing the myths and beliefs of the old world view. In this way, for the target demographic, the translation between the old and new worldviews is not only established without contradiction or challenges, but it is actively defended by the target demographic. Critics can be represented as liars and "haters," and alternative news sources and outlets can be represented as propagandists. All other media and opinions can be represented as part of a global conspiracy to persecute the target demographic, who can represent themselves as under siege, as the last remaining holdouts of truth and civilization against the barbarian hordes. Anyone who exposes or cites these alternative media sources can be represented as a propagandist or a "useful idiot" manipulated by propagandists in the sense of "the liberal elite," "international communists," "globalists," or however the nemesis of "conservative" America is represented. Of course, this is something of a recycling of the old "Jewish banking conspiracy" myth, but it is also new in the sense of an inoculation of the group mind against any source of information or even a question that challenges the worldview of a heavily propagandized and narrowcasted population.

Of course, by concealing the takeover and asset stripping of America by multinational corporations, banks, and investors, and the outsourcing of American industries and capital to Asia, along with its natural recourses and wealth, under the guise of the mystical free market and American exceptionalism through corporate and military power, the real nemesis of conservative America is—ironically—the very same "conservative" corporate media that they depend upon for information, analysis, catharsis, criticism, and commentary. Narrowcasting is a mechanism that undermines the ability of its target demographic to learn how to adopt and develop an effective strategy of survival and success in a complex and changing world. No better example of this can be seen in how "conservative" corporate media undermines and distorts science and environmentalism when their conclusions contradict the bottom-line profitability of multinational corporations. By playing on the ignorance of their target demographic, propagandists reinforce, entrench, and intensify the power of propaganda to distract and redirect.

Even the most minute and careful analysis of news in mainstream media will not allow us to draw accurate conclusions about world events from it. The appeal to statistical methods, presented out of historical context as objective fact, leads to an erosion of memory, presents false continuities, and prevents the news from being anything other than a series of images and sound-bites presented one after the other. This suppresses political thought, despite any passion for participation in political discourse that the viewer might have, and prevents the development of critical thinking and the making of predictions. Taken as a whole, this presents the illusionary view that the media will supply the viewer with up to date information, today, tomorrow, and every day, and that citizens can rest assured that all the information they need will be supplied to them, and political affairs will take care of themselves. This is further compounded by narrowcasting when statistics and facts are carefully selected and interpreted to reinforce the prejudices and worldview of the target audience; to present them with opinions and "evidence" to counter and shout down the voices of others. Through framing and the selection of news and opinion, the focus of the audience can be directed. Through media consolidation, this focus, along with a collection of facts and talking points, can be carefully corroborated, coordinated, and repeated via seemingly independent sources to give them some sense of truth and objectivity, which may be television or radio channels, newspapers, blogs, or comedians. The "diligent" online surfer will be able to "fact check" to their satisfaction simply by finding sources that reinforce whatever it is that they want to believe. Yet, if we look more carefully at these seemingly independent sources, we often find commonality of terminology, slogans, headlines, phraseology, prioritization, references (if any), and reinforcement of the message of the day. It should be apparent to close discourse analysis that there sources are not independent at all.

Of course the "urgency" of the need for political action in the face of the never-ending succession of unrelated "crises" and "scandals" not only plays into the hands of those for whom it is advantageous to suppress the memory and criticality of the citizenry, which prevents foresight and understanding, but it creates a public demand for the immediate implementation of whatever "solutions" and "necessary steps" are presented in mainstream media. Narrowcasted media not only fills the partitions of party politics, but also frames the entire "public debate" in terms of party politics, and, hence, there is no debate at all. Any other ideas, concerns, issues, or events are suppressed or marginalized, and dismissed as unthinkable, impractical, extreme, naïve, biased, or irrelevant, and, by doing so, bolster and reinforce the media framing of politics along party lines. Propaganda also is developed to utilize people's fears about and vision of the future, say by promoting an apocalyptic vision or utopic myth, depending on the already existing beliefs of the target demographic and the needs of the propagandist (and his or her clients). By associating an apocalyptic myth of the destruction of America or the rise of tyranny with the political opposition, both the Democratic Party and Republican Party propaganda machines can play off the fears of their target demographics, thereby positioning themselves as the only means to stop the opposition gaining power (and destroying America or establishing a dictatorship); both parties can focus on the other party, thereby concealing that they lack any real solutions to real problems through focusing on divisive social issues (or scapegoats), or that the differences between the two parties are largely cosmetic. Obviously there are differences between the parties— on the environment, women's rights, and ethnic minorities, as well as on public services and domestic policy—but what is common to both parties is the use of the same divisive methods to turn the target population against each other and maintain the "them v. us" structure of the two-party system and maintain the status quo of the corporate state and industrial military complex. Hence the illusion of competition can be maintained to satisfy the public need for these to be a real competition, without running the risks to the status quo associated with the unpredictability of real competition. In this way, the illusions of democracy and representation are maintained to avoid all the problems that would arise for the ruling elite of democracy and representation do not exist. Propaganda is a form of mass hypnotism and crowd control, providing that it satisfies real psychological needs and maintains the illusions of freedom of speech and political competition, and generally distracting the population from the real causes of their alienation, dissatisfactions, and problems.

Propaganda not only distracts individuals from the causes of their problems, but it provides them with the means to justify their own exploitation to themselves as something they have chosen. Of course many of the tricks of the propagandist are well known and have been used successfully, time and time again, throughout history. Through scapegoating specific ethnic or religious groups, or specific groups of immigrants, resentments about unemployment and low pay, or a lack of public services, can be projected against the scapegoats and translated into racism and bigotry. In this way, the ruling elite have divided the ruled majority against each other, time and time again. Likewise, through misrepresentation and fear mongering, the target demographic can be turned against itself to prevent it from organizing itself and better negotiate its own position in society in relation to the ruling elite. One of the greatest coup d'états of propaganda in C20th American history was how the American working class was turned against organized labor and unions through "Red Scare" anti-communist propaganda, the fear of capital flight and unemployment, alongside the use of violent union-busting tactics, and a series of laws that forced unions into hierarchical and bureaucratic forms that facilitated anti-democratic structures and corruption.

"...propaganda must not concern itself with what is best in man—the highest goals humanity sets for itself, its highest and most precious feelings. Propaganda does not aim to elevate man, but to make him *serve*. It must therefore utilize the most common feelings, the most widespread ideas, the cloudiest patterns, and in so doing place itself on a very low level with regard to what it wants man to do and to what end. Hate, hunger, and pride make better levers of propaganda than do love or impartiality." (Ellul, p. 38)

Propaganda must stay at the human level. It must not propose aims so lofty or ideal that they will seem unachievable; this creates the risk of a boomerang effect. There must always be the prospect of "winning." Propaganda must concern itself to simple, elementary messages that ultimately are vacuous and can never be falsified (confidence in our leader, our party... hate our enemies, etc.), without fear of being ridiculous or discredited. It must speak the most simple, everyday language, familiar, individualized—the language of the group that is being addressed, and the language with which a person is familiar. What has often been termed "the dumbing down" of America is in reality symptomatic of the power and all-pervasive character of modern propaganda. Political theater and spectacle have become the form of political expression, especially during election campaigns or when passing controversial legislation. Public discourse has become simply the propaganda of integration and agitation, resulting in shallowness, short-term memory, docility, and gullibility: Thus the cycle of erosion of rationality and democracy continues unchecked.

Yet this is nothing new. It has been known for a long time. As Schumpeter put it in 1942,

"Knowledge of facts and logic no longer play the part attributed to them by the classic doctrine [of democracy]. I am particularly struck by the almost complete disappearance of the sense of reality. For the average citizen, the great political problems are grouped among the distractions reserved for leisure hours. They are not even on the level of fads, and exist only as the subject of idle conversation. To him, these problems seem far distant… basically, the citizen has the impression of living in an imaginary world."[55]

Democratic deliberation, according to the classic doctrine, requires that citizens have a grasp of the past—their history—memory and continuity to analyze present events and their consequences. When mass media falsifies the past or rapidly presents news and information as 'snap shots' of events taken out of context, without any reference to their history, it prevents and erodes memory, disrupts continuity, and obscures politics. Via sensationalism, moralism, punditry, and propaganda, mainstream media prevents democratic deliberation as it leaps between scandals and crises. Almost stroboscopically, mass media presents reality in flashes and glimpses, disconnected and isolated; this leads to passivity, apathy, consumerism, and indifference towards the larger picture. To put it in stark terms, modern propaganda results in cultural retardation and undermines the conditions on which democracy depends.

The State is able to place itself outside all ethical constrains and even above the law, while using propaganda and misinformation to keep the population distracted and present the illusion of critical media, political opposition, and competition, when in fact there is a close collaboration between government and media corporations to preserve the status quo. Even apparently radically opposed political parties, say the Republicans and Democrats, share a common interest in preserving the status quo, they are dependent on the same media corporations for being elected and re-elected, and they receive donations from the same economic elite and serve their interests. This is deeply troubling when the State's monopoly over the use of police forces and the military, which act outside of ethical and legal constrains when deemed necessary to do so, are placed at the service of preserving the

---

[55] Schumpeter, 1942, *Capitalism, Socialism, and Democracy* chap. xxi

status quo that benefits the economic elite, which itself has an oligopoly control over media and telecommunications corporations in an increasingly deregulated and consolidated market. This is the *route* to fascism in response to any popular resistance to the corporate state.

In order to prevent popular resistance, the collaboration between state and corporate power—the corporate state—results in the combined use of propaganda and state violence (suppressing protests, breaking up unions, arbitrary arrests, indefinite detention, police surveillance, etc.) to keep the citizenry disorganized, fearful, fragmented, and incapable of mass action. In addition, propaganda is used (especially in the guise of critics of the government) to keep the population turned against each other, distrustful, alienated, and isolated from even the possibility of democratic participation. Through the use of the mechanisms of oppression and repression, the vast majority of the population can be reduced to a mass of apathetic consumers, incapable of resisting the operations of the corporate state. The use of propaganda in this way is a form of coercive violence—using fear and terrorism to oppress a population—but it is also, for the reason I have given above, extremely damaging to society in general because it intensifies irrationality, repression, alienation, and factionalization, all of which destroy possibility of democracy. Turned against itself, incapable of rational debate, communication, and critical thinking, such a population is taken to the point of civil war, retrained only by the military and police power of the state. Such a population turns inward into criminality, consumerism, fetishism, while the state becomes increasingly necessary to preserve the peace and *simultaneously* protect the economic elite from social change, civil unrest, and public scrutiny. Once it has been achieved, the economic elite can invisibly act as rulers, with impunity.

Once the majority of the population has been subdued and politically isolated, even if guaranteed a specific level of income and consumption, along with entertainments and distractions, the system tends towards totalitarianism within which the social order is continually reproduced for the benefit of the ruling elite. The state simply becomes an instrument—an autonomous administrative machine—to reproduce the totality of the system by whatever means its agents deem expedient. The ordinary citizen is driven further into the private realm of work, consumption, and family, and anything that threatens to change the social order either seems unthinkable or is treated as a personal threat. The individual will demand the security of the state and find their identity in terms of their place within the totality of the system. Regardless of an ideology they may expose—which in itself will be little more than rubber-stamping their party allegiance and group identity—they will support the system as if their life depended on it. To oppose the system is not only done at great risk, but in a totalitarian system it is unthinkable, madness, or simply criminal.

Hence we can see that one of the common misconceptions of propaganda is that there is a clear distinction between the propagandist and the propagandee. On this view, some behind the scene elite and their agents conspire to trick and deceive the mass into believing all sorts of lies and falsehoods that benefit the elite and keep the masses distracted from their subordinate and passive position in society. While this scenario may well be true, it does not help us understand the nature of propaganda. Without doubt, the general population are subjected to mass media distractions and deceptions that benefit the industrial-military complex and the ruling elite, but it is the notion that propaganda is a voluntary and rationally manipulated instrument that is the greatest obstacle to understanding and counting it. The *technological* definition of propaganda, as a device or instrument, is only partially true, so if we *reduce* our understanding of propaganda to this definition, we cannot hope to gasp it fully. What we need to also include is the psychological and sociological relationships to information and mythology that underwrites both the dissemination and reception of propaganda. By understanding of propaganda in this way, we can see that its deepest and most fundamental characteristic is that of an *irrational mode of communication and reflection on the meaning and truth of the world.* Combined with its technological aspect, which is essential for modern propaganda to exist at all, with all its entailments of specialization and professionalization, we can see that as proponents of an irrational mode of communication, propagandists are also propagandees, effectively acting as channels for propaganda and enrolling others into the dissemination (propagation) of propaganda, thereby transforming propagandees into propagandists, without their conscious realization of their own irrationality. In this way, apart from all the usual obvious forms of propaganda, in most part propaganda remains invisible and tacit, with propagandees/propagandists unaware of their own irrationality and complicity in disseminating propaganda. In this respect, we can see that modern mass society is held together by the irrational reinforcement of its norms and shared worldviews by propaganda, and therefore is an irrational society.

If we can accept and grasp the truth of the above argument, we can see that propaganda is not simply a device used by the ruling class (be it political, economic, military, or technological), just as religion is not simply a device used by the ruling class, but is an all-pervasive property of mass society as a totality that also has sway over the ruling class, even though they clearly enjoy the privileges and power of their position, and leads the ruled class to be complicit in their own subjugation and the social compliance of each other to the status quo.

"... nowadays propaganda pervades all aspects of public life. We know that psychological factor, which includes encirclement, integration into a group, and participation in action, in oblivion to personal conviction, is decisive. To draw up plans for an organization, a system of work, political methods, and institutions is not enough; the individual must participate in all this from the bottom of his heart, with pleasure and satisfaction." (Ellul, p. 119)

And, furthermore, react with hostility towards anyone who exposes propaganda and the irrationality of its propagation. Hence, we can see that Bernays was both propagandist and propagandee when, under the sway of a conception of propaganda in terms of a technological definition, he reduced his analyses of propaganda to being an instrument to change public opinion, habits, and culture, to be used by intelligent men, while irrationally as zealous about smoking tobacco as about not smoking tobacco, depending on the contingent needs of the moment. It is for this reason that Bernays could use propaganda to justify a coup d'état in Guatemala and the establishment of a military junta to suppress democratic movements without questioning the morality or consequences of this. Bernays was unconsciously and irrationally under the sway of propaganda, hence such questions were unthinkable and his own complicity in mass murder, torture, and oppression was concealed by the irrational justification of his own actions in terms of providing a value-neutral, objective, and scientific method.

Due to the participation of the masses in political affairs, alongside the threat of the revolution, the ruling elite need propaganda to distract and direct the masses in accordance with an agenda that serves the interests of the ruling elite. In this way, the illusion of democracy and representative government can be maintained, while the masses can be placated and kept in a passive and subordinate condition. Through mass media propaganda, the public can be informed and presented with the spectacle of a critical media, and through mass communication technology (such as the Internet) individuals can express their opinions in response to the news and views that are fed to them on a daily basis. This brings both a sense of participation and catharsis. If legitimate government governs with the consent of the governed, and democracy requires that government is responsive to public opinion, then propaganda functions (and is needed by the state) by obtaining consent and presenting the illusion of accountability and representation. Public opinion is kept in flux, diverting its focus from one issue to the next and forgetting the past, and the individual is kept in an irrational relation with information and opinion. Even when individuals become cynical or critical about politics and media, the function of propaganda is to keep their attachments to the group-identity and "necessity" of party-politics and supporting "their" party (like team-sports) as being "the lesser of two evils" or in response to wedge issues that media-led politics uses to divide the masses into opposing camps. The government does not consult public opinion in order to decide policy; instead, it consults public opinion in order to learn how to refine or modify its propaganda.

Once the state has become autonomous and the system has become totalitarian, virtues such as truth, justice, and freedom become eclipsed by power and political expediency. They become whatever the agents of the state deem them to be, and the good becomes whatever the state does, as an *a priori*. Hypocrisy and reality blur together as the self-justification, made in moral terms, of the use of force and the abuse of power is all-pervasive. This leads to a disjoint (a divide) between speech and action. Rights can be removed in the name of preserving rights. Acts of terrorism and murder committed in the name of security and peace. Aggression committed in the name of defense. Oppression and brutality committed in the name of freedom and democracy. Moral terms (including ethics and ideology) are used to glorify and affirm a policy, regardless of its reality and inconsistency with the expounded moral principles. As Ellul argued,

"The 'moral hemiplegia' afflicting the Left and the Right are anterior. And the values, the humanism, and so on are invoked only to ward off free choices, justify our determination, and glorify our positions. This is a complete throwback to Christian hypocrisy. It is not because of the value of man that they are, say, Leftists, but being Leftists, they invoke the dignity of the human personality—of course from the Leftist point of view. For those opposing them are *only* people who negate this so-called human personality! It is not for reasons of honor that others are Rightists, but, being Rightists, they invoke honor against a Left that knows only how to dishonor, vulgarize, and debase all it touches." (Ellul, p. 84)

In other words, the policies of both the Left and Right are not based on a moral or political philosophy, but, instead, use morals and ideology to justify their policies, which are themselves justifications for the autonomous use of force and power. Moral sloganeering or rubber-stamping is a form of *doublespeak*, as William Lutz defined it, that conceals or prevents thought by divorcing language from the world and limiting the capacity of thought to grasp the world.[56] The extent that this kind of doublespeak is required to sustain *necessary illusions* (as Chomsky termed them, that underwrite any faith we may have the democratic character of the current political economy) shows us the extent that we buy into a psychologically comforting world view that legitimates the status quo, even when we seek to inform its inequalities and injustices and improve society.

The juggernaut cannot be stopped, but it can be apologized for—given justification and explanation—in terms of pious abstracts, which maintain the illusions of choice and control. It is due to the autonomy of the political machine, hypocritically justified by both the Left and the Right in their own terms, irrespective of its reality, or by invoking abstracts such as "the general will" or "the will of the people," that results in "democracy" and "dictatorship" becoming indistinguishable, except in the style of rhetoric and symbolism. "Opposing" political parties converge to the point of conforming to the operations and structures of the political machine, which now mediates values and ideals as its justification rather than being adjusted or directed by them, regardless of what it does. Hence, all the atrocities of the twentieth century were committed by people who were under the spell of the illusion that they were acting in the name of justice and for the improvement of mankind, whom *in reality* they were in denial of the autonomy of the political machine, in denial of how they were under the sway of propaganda justifying this autonomy, and its negation of justice, goodness, and truth. This

---

[56] William Lutz, *Doublespeak* (New York: Harper Collins, 1989), p.1

delusion—this sense of denial—is itself the product of propaganda. It can be found among Leftists in America who believe that *somehow* they can drag the Democratic Party to the Left *as long as* they continue to support it and vote for its candidates, regardless of the Democratic Party's consistent and undeniable move to the Right. Likewise, Christian fundamentalists continue to support the Republic Party, believing that *somehow* it will champion their values and truths, regardless of how many times those values and truths have been brushed aside in the name of political expediency by a political party that champions only the aspiration of unchecked corporate power and the accumulation of wealth. For proponents of both parties, the autonomy of the political machine has become synonymous with "democracy" and "the republic" respectively, and, despite the propaganda value of a narrow set of wedge issues (such as immigration, same-sex marriage, gun laws, and abortion) to maintain the illusion of opposition and competition, both parties are largely indistinguishable, except in terms of rhetoric and symbolism.

Human dignity, freedom and happiness are not guaranteed outcomes of the autonomous political machine. Ellul notes that one of the errors made by democrats and republicans, liberals and conservatives, is the naïve belief that the rule of law and moral restraint are sufficient to moderate and constrain government. It is as if the ink and parchment of the Constitution were themselves impermeable barriers to the excuses of government, the autonomy of the political machine, and propaganda. They have ignored the century long history of psychological warfare conducted on the people to preserve the status quo and privileges of the economic elite. History shows us, time and time again, case after case, where this naïve belief preceded the rise of terrible dictatorships. Just as the German democrats, republicans, and liberals thought that they could moderate Hitler and did not have to take his words seriously, so democrats, republicans, and liberals in Poland thought that they could deal with the communists under the direction of Moscow and Stalin. As *Reichspogramnacht* (Reich Massacre Night) or *Kristallnacht* (Night of Broken Glass) in Berlin, Nov. 9, 1938, showed, the veneer of civilization can be easily cracked and moral restrained ignored, as Nazi Stormtroopers destroyed Jewish businesses, burned down synagogues, arrested tens of thousands of people, and murdered many, while ordinary German people watched passively or even joined in the brutality. The lesson of this terrible event and the holocaust that followed for the next six and a half years is that human rights and moral constraints do not mean anything at all, unless people are willing to defend them, to defend their neighbors, and place morality, values, and law over and above the autonomous operations of the political machine. People cannot passively expect good outcomes; instead they must actively participate in the organic process of community life in order to ensure that it is shaped and governed by moral restraint, ideals, values, and aspirations to live a good life, in the spirit of solidarity with all.

2.

...and the Free Press

"Information is an instrument of power." —Arthur Sylvester,

(Assistant Secretary of Defense, October 1962)

Too many of us have taken the existence of a free press for granted. The history of struggle for ownership and control over the dissemination of knowledge and information demonstrates example after example of propaganda, censorship, distortion, distraction, suppression, and deception. The democratic role of corporate media—as if it is a "free press"—is an example of something that is, at best, only formally true (by equating a "free press" with mass media), and, at worst, a form of self-deception. The very notion that there exists an independent media in Western "democracies"— acting as the free press—is open to question. Yet the idea that it is an important democratic institution to counterbalance governmental abuses of power is a commonplace notion that is propagated by journalists and some academics, with little regard to the actual practices of mainstream corporate-owned media in supporting the government and acting as its mouthpiece, framing criticisms, disseminating opinions and slogans, or limiting damage by disseminating propaganda and spin. Since at least the early twentieth century, the commercial interests of privately owned newspapers had created an intrinsic editorial selection bias in favor of news stories that either benefited advertisers or avoided offending them.[1] This created an editorial bias against covering stories that might offend advertisers and the interests of the owners. It also extended this editorial bias against any story that might result in withdrawn access to government sources, which have become the

---

[1] Will Irwin, *The American Newspaper* (Iowa State University Press, 1969, first published in 1911); see also *Propaganda and the News* (New York: Whittlesey House, 1936)

141

main information source for corporate media. Journalists have been constantly pressured to act as propagandists when governments snubbed critics and only cooperated with complicit reporters.[2] Editors also avoid any story that might result in lawsuits or legal consequences. Reporters are pressured to support the opinions and prejudices of media owners, investors, and advertisers to favor the ideals and norms of the economic and political elite. If access to political leaders is cut off to media sources that do not play ball, this leads to a culture of "self-censorship" within corporate media, wherein criticisms of the government's policies are either silenced or marginalized, or channeled into the two-party political game. This has created an intrinsic pressure on journalists to maintain friendly relations with government officials, alongside the internal editorial pressures for reporters to support the opinions and prejudices of newspaper owners. When the media supports and repeats governmental statements persistently and uncritically, irrespective of the facts or their inconsistency with previous statements, there is strong evidence for the case that media is engaged systematically in the dissemination of propaganda in support of governmental policies and agendas. Once the government is the major source of information and provides the framework of analysis, the media become the means of disseminating governmental information and the official line, masked as impartial investigative journalism based on relevant facts. Once the primary role of media is one of making sure that the governmental agenda remains unchallenged then we see the propaganda machine at work. The operations of this machine should be evident when journalists and editors apply a double standard of criticism and rigor depending upon whether the news or facts are favorable or unfavorable to government claims or statements, so it is important to maintain the illusion of "the free press" by pretending that there is some conflict between the media and the government, when at best there is little and at worst none at all. Divisions and dissent within the media (including criticisms of the government) only tend to occur when the economic elite disagree with each other about policies or see an opportunity to further their own agenda by changing government personnel or public policy.

---

[2] George Seldes, *You Can't Print That!* (Garden City, 1929); see also *Freedom of the Press* (Bobbs-Merrill, 1935)

All media are instruments of power. Whether or not any news item is covered, or how much it is covered, can change the public perception of events. The truth or falsehood of any statement or report is irrelevant; all that matters is its effectiveness in achieving public support for a policy or politician. Media can serve as a distraction from events in the world, thereby hiding events or problems, as well as direct the public attention to specific events or problems, creating problems where there are none, and generally acting as gatekeepers for any political activity or debate. Yet, the free press is largely considered to be fundamental to a democratic society, supposedly acting as a vigilant safeguard and watchdog against governmental malpractice. Why? Without a free press, government can operate in the dark or use propaganda with impunity to deceive the citizenry. Transparency and accountability—both of which are essential for democracy—require the vigilance and truthfulness of the free press, itself acting as a vital fourth estate, alongside the executive and legislative branches of government, and an independent judiciary. The existence of a free press is essential for maintaining the accountability and representative nature of government, thereby providing the foundation for an informed citizenry to participate in the democratic process. In order for democracy to work at all, there must be a free press alongside a public commitment on the part of the citizenry to discover the truth and act on it. Through rational deliberation and communication, a free press provides the possibility of persuasion and political debate to change minds or achieve compromise to find solutions to shared problems, as well as keeping people informed about the operations of government, new policies and laws, and proposed projects. It is for this reason that "freedom of speech, or of the press" is specified in the First Amendment of the U.S. Constitution:

"Congress shall make no law respecting an establishment of religion, or prohibiting the free exercise thereof; or abridging the freedom of speech, or of the press; or the right of the people peaceably to assemble, and to petition the government for a redress of grievances."

This amendment has been taken as a fundamental condition for democracy by the Supreme Court of the United States. In New York Times v United States, 1971, SCOTUS ruled, "In the First Amendment, the Founding Fathers gave the free press the protection it must have to fulfill its essential role in our democracy. The press was to serve the governed, not the governors."

Taking this at face value, it would seem that "the free press" is simply a press that is free from governmental oppression or censorship, just as "free speech" is speech that is also free from governmental threats or coercion. Free speech is anyone being able to say whatever they please, and the free press can print or publish free speech. Seems straightforward, right? What is free speech? To answer this question, we need to make a distinction between free speech and other forms of speech. Free speech does not always need to be based on literal truths about one's experiences, reflections, or facts about the world. Poetical and metaphorical forms of language, including songs, film, and music, are also forms of free speech. Fiction and satire can also be forms of free speech. So can comedy. These forms also expose double-standards. Free speech is speech that is free from constraints (such as fear of punishment, censorship, reprisals, etc.) and it is free from inconsistences, double-standards, and distortions (lies, suppression, repression, etc.). Free speech is the utterance of truth in all its fullness and authenticity. On this definition, propaganda is not free speech. A lie is not free speech. Of course a person is free to speak a lie, but the lie itself is not free speech. Why not? Because the purpose of a lie is to trick and deceive another person that something is true when it is not. This presents a fraud as real. By manipulating a person in this way, one has coerced them through using their own trust against them. This not only disrespects them, but also places them in an unfree relation with the speech. It is harmful to freedom because it is based on concealment and distortion of truth. A lie is no more free speech than is the blurry mess that one sees after being poked in the eye is free sight. A lie is no more free speech that identity-theft or fraud is freedom of association. Whether the individual is free to believe or disbelieve a lie is neither here or there. Only an irrational or insane person would knowingly choose to believe something that is false. By giving a person a counterfeit truth—by lying to them—one abuses the relation of trust to trick a person into believing something that they would freely disbelieve if given the truth. We can no more claim that a lie is free speech than we can claim that knowingly passing counterfeit money is the free exchange of currency. By deceiving another person, we have not only prevented them from developing a free relation with truth, but we have also prevented ourselves from doing so.

144

It is essential to remember that speech does not occur when there is only one person. It is a social activity between people already situated in a culture, with a history, using a language learned from other people (parents, teachers, friends, etc.). Speech is an exchange founded on relationships. Free speech is not simply the unrestrained utterance of opinions, gibberish, or lies. It is not some abstract right to say whatever pops into our heads. Free speech involves a free exchange founded on free relationships, which involve trust and mutual respect between individuals, and occurs in the context of sharing ideas, values, experiences, and truths with other people. Both propaganda and lies involve the disrespect and suppression of other people's freedom, even when they are free to reject (or ignore) propaganda and disbelieve lies. They are forms of coercive speech. The problem is that both propaganda and lies conceal their nature to present themselves as truth, and it is this act of concealment that makes them coercive and abusive of other people's trust. Taking this into account shows us that propaganda is based on an unfree relation with truth and is the opposite of free speech. Following the implications of this can help us understand that not only does "the free press" need to be independent from constraints imposed on it by vested interests, be they commercial or political, but it also *must* be based on free speech. Newspapers, television channels, radio stations, internet sites that disseminate propaganda and lies are not a free press. They are a fraudulent and counterfeit "free press" masquerading as something they are not, in exactly the same way that the freedom to vote is undermined by election fraud or the freedom of religion is undermined by persecution. Propaganda disrupts and abuses the public trust and political discourse in exactly the same way that infomercials and fake news disrupts and abuses the free market by undermining the ability of people to do their own research and make informed decisions about which products are the best. By masquerading as a free press, while disseminating propaganda and lies, media sources undermine freedom of choice by misrepresenting commentary or news reports as free speech, abusing the trust of viewers, listeners, or readers, and placing them in an unfree relation with content and sources.

The deliberate dissemination of propaganda and lies are harmful to the public; it is an act of psychological violence made in an attempt to place the recipient in an unfree relation to truth that erodes the possibility of free speech, disrupting the sharing of knowledge, undermining moral consistency and judgment, and open and informed consent upon which democracy and

145

legitimate government depend. The fact that people can always turn off the radio or television set, or look at other newspapers or internet sites, is neither here nor there. To claim that propaganda and lies are part of free speech simply because anyone can choose not to listen to them is like saying that bigamy commits no offence because marriage involves choice. A person cannot enter freely into marriage with a bigamist if one does not know that they are already married. That person was deceived and entered into the marriage under false pretenses. It is akin to saying that election fraud is not an abuse of the political system because one can always move to another country or jurisdiction. The truth is that it was a sham and people were cheated out of a choice. The deliberate deception of people undermines their freedom in so far as freedom is based on choice and knowingly entering into relationships and associations with others. The concern here is the distortion of reality and the circumvention of freedom that occurs when people are deceived into entering into false relationships and thereby trust and believe others who are lying to them, or using propaganda to manipulate them, are intensifying the irrationality of prejudice, bigotry, and hatred towards other economic classes, groups of peoples, races, political parties, genders, etc., and thereby preventing or distorting the possibility of making rational and informed decisions.

The promotion of "hate speech" through the dissemination of propaganda and lies is not an example of free speech. Telling children that the Nazi holocaust never happened is not free speech. It is violence. Hate speech is no more free speech than rape or sexual assault are examples of sexual liberation. It is akin to abusing and manipulating the trust of children in order to groom them for pederasty; it is the opposite of free sexual development and relationships. Hate speech opposes free speech because it is only possible to achieve it by manipulating the irrationality, fear, and ignorance of its target audience, closing their minds and undermining their capacity for free thinking, and thereby undermining the possibility of intellectual freedom. It is abusive and dangerous. It is for this reason that prohibitions of hate speech are not violations of free speech, but are in fact means of protecting free speech by protecting the conditions that are necessary for free speech to occur at all. Similarly, prohibitions of propaganda and lies in media would not be violations of free speech. Such prohibitions would protect people from violence and abuse by protecting the conditions under which free speech occurs, just as outlawing counterfeit currency protects the conditions under which monetary exchange has value and meaning. Media outlets that knowingly disseminate propaganda and lies should lose any protections due to them under the category of "the free press"—such as the First Amendment protections of the US Constitution— simply because they do not apply to them, just as the deliberate selling of dud or dangerous ammunition is not protected by the Second Amendment and the right to bear arms, or the selling of forged art works as genuine artifacts is not protected as freedom of expression. There should not be any constitutional right to abuse, manipulate, and deceive the public under the guise of "the freedom of the press."

In a mass society and media-driven culture of rapid news-cycle turnover, based less on substance and content and more on personality, celebrity, scandal, innuendo and gossip, the shallowness of the experience of media leads to conditions within which the dissemination of propaganda can flourish. The individual lives vicariously through the personalities of others, which further erodes his individuality, rationality, and authenticity by circumventing the deep-seated and painful existential and intellectual struggles a person must go through to develop these aspects of character. Once again, wearing a dramatic and symbolic mask becomes a substitute for the development of identity and personality. Media functions to provide artificial short cuts to real psychological and social needs. This allows the individual to adapt to her conditions without engaging with and changing them, and to live within a simulated environment without being conscious of it. The satisfactions offered by propaganda are ersatz and provide emotional decompression and intellectual stimulation at a superficial level, thereby allowing the individual to remain under the impression of being deeply informed and engaging with the world without having to think or even question reality. Through the media personality, the individual can feel a sense of intimacy, empathy, and solidarity—as if someone else feels what the individual feels and knows what she is going through—with both the personality and the audience. A kinship or even community of fans grows around the media personality, giving an artificial sense of belonging and the satisfaction of real psychological and social needs. The technological medium becomes a substitute for human relations and conceals the alienation and anonymity the individual would otherwise feel. This can be particularly intense and effective when political commentary and opinion are presented in the form of comedy.

So, while we may well agree with the 1971 ruling of the Supreme Court, that a free press is necessary to preserve political freedom and democracy, we can still ask: are the press living up to this responsibility? Are the daily functions and operations of governance well reported? Are we learning what is really being done by our representatives in our name? With its dependency on commercial advertising and ratings—as if paid for speech is free speech—as well as political access and obligations to shareholders and its owners, does the media censor coverage of the operations of government and the record of our representatives? Clearly, it does. Yet it also distracts. It is commonplace to say that news reporting focuses on scandals, sensationalism, gossip, and bad news. The average newspaper reader, radio listener, television watcher, internet browser does not learn about the thousands of trains or aircraft that arrived at their destination that day. Instead, she learns about the crashes, accidents, strikes, and delays. The same is true about political and economic news. The individual is informed about crises, corruption, depressions, recessions, problems, and conflicts, not about progress, the everyday activities of political institutions, economics, solutions, and peaceful resolutions. If positive news stories are covered at all, they are buried deep within the cycle, and only mentioned once. The news-cycle has a short attention span and the individual is confronted on a daily basis with an intense, albeit shallow, barrage of disturbing and upsetting news and opinion, one after the other, ranging from increased taxes, wars, deaths, disease, crime, terrorism, and impending environmental collapse, all interweaved with gossip, sensationalism, scandal, and trivia, and advertisements selling products and services. All of this forms a cultural background to her everyday life of work and family, all while coping with the stresses of an increasingly abstract and all-pervasive modern society, and yet being utterly powerless to do anything about world events.

Of course this should be unsurprising. Much of everyday and ordinary life is considered too "boring" to be newsworthy, but the individual is given the impression that she lives in an apocalyptic era over which she has no power whatsoever. Human life is portrayed as impotent, fragile, expendable, destructive, corrupt, and depraved, while the individual is left with the feeling that catastrophe looms over her head. Everything threatens his safety. He feels himself to live in a brutal, unjust, and violent world. He feels alienated and forced to retreat into the private realm. Yet, the individual cannot accept this. She cannot live in a state of constant dread in an incoherent, absurd, and terrifying world. She cannot live in chaos. The individual is forced to respond and restore order; to make sense of things. Of course she can choose to be heroic and do something about it—to make a stand—and make the world a better and meaningful place through her own efforts and sacrifices, either individually or cooperatively with others. Political action remains an option. He may well forge ahead with his own intellectual struggle to make sense of this world, challenge the status quo, and help others to question and reflect on their own reality and truth. She may choose to change the world by changing the self; by seeking out paths to her enlightenment and the enlightenment of others. But these choices are difficult and risk confronting their own futility and failure. Most people do not make these choices.

An alternate choice remains that of hedonism and seeking out pleasures and distractions to conceal and forget the deep sense of existential dread and alienation in the face of a world over which the individual has little control, if any. People will seek solace in sex, drugs, and rock 'n' roll. Or conform to the more socially acceptable path of consumerism (shopping) and entertainments. Political activism becomes clicktivism on social media like Facebook and Twitter. Of course this choice is a form of self-denial, ultimately self-destructive, and leads the individual nowhere at all. He will donate to charity, sign and share online petitions, read self-help books, go to the gym, try the latest diet, and concentrate on "self-improvement," all the while continuing and maintaining everyday life of family and work, and paying the bills. Of course the individual may choose to embrace nihilism in the face of chaos and confusion, and find some consolation in that. Alternatively, she may choose to be stoical and develop a *philosophical* attitude. Yet most people will not choose this path. Instead, he will become desensitized to media, while being immersed in it, ignore his own sense of dread and mortality, and become callous and indifferent to life itself. Or she turns to the consolations of religion. This is not to say that choosing a religious or spiritual path is itself a form of escape from reality, but it is escapism when that choice is shallow and simply paying lip-service of doctrine and ritual in order to feel better and avoid confronting reality and deeper truths.

News stories lose their shock-value or frightening character when they offer cues or information for which the listener already has ready explanations in his mind, or can easily find one. The great power of propaganda is that it gives modern man comprehensive and intelligible explanations for events, allowing the individual to both understand those events and position themselves in relation to them, without which he could not live with the news. Individuals are reassured by propaganda when it provides explanations for events, and promises solutions for what otherwise seem as chaotic and insurmountable problems. Propaganda allows the individual to blame someone for the problems presented by media—scapegoating—and also believe that someone, somewhere is solving them or knows how to solve them. Propaganda helps the individual cope with work, taxes, and war. Most commonly of all, the individual will demand that something must be done to solve the endless stream of problems he sees and reads in the news, every day, every moment of every day. And this *something* must be *done by somebody else*: by politicians, government, corporations, bureaucrats, scientists, administrators, judges, activists… by a nebulous and abstract "them." She will post her demands, her outrage, her anger on social media to the "them," before sitting back—her work is done—and moving on to the next social problem or issue that needs solving by somebody else. He insists that he is kept "informed" by "the media," by newspapers, television, radio, and the internet. Sometimes she reads books too. He likes to have opinions about world events, policies, and issues. She likes to have certainties, beliefs, and a sound sense of her own values. He needs general answers and explanations. She needs an affirmation of the meaning of her own life. He needs to feel important, competent, and knowledgeable. She needs to know the facts about the influences over her life. Of course we can point out how the irrational relation to information is a consequence of ignorance, laziness, and a lack of reflection on the part of individuals—who feel the need to have opinions and be 'in the know' about any and all questions of their day without actually researching and studying—but the problem of propaganda is deeper than this. We cannot hope to counter propaganda without dealing with *the problem of alienation*. This is a fundamental problem in modern society. This problem brings us back to the basic problem of authentic human relations within a technological and capitalistic mass society. This is the problem which we must address if we are to understand what is meant by free speech.

When media satisfies our need for meaning and truth, or at least presents the illusion of so doing, the individual develops a strong psychological and existential need for media. When this happens, the individual is susceptible

150

to propaganda. The individual becomes addicted to it. Propaganda gives the individual explanations, justifications, and the reinforcement of values. It gives the individual a worldview and identity. It gives the individual the resources to reinforce and affirm their beliefs in their own values and the meaning of their existence. It tells him who are the main players and what the important issues of the day are. It tells her what she needs to think in order to feel secure in her knowledge of the world. It allows the seeming maelstrom of news and opinion to be placed under categories and associated with meanings, values, and groups. It tells him what to affirm and what to reject. It allows the looming sense of catastrophe to be abated as something that will be solved by "them," or something made meaningful in terms of some greater purpose, history, progress, or divine plan. It is on the foundation of prejudices and worldview received and reinforced through propaganda that the individual exercises judgment, selects or rejects facts, and forms their perspective and opinions. The perspective and opinions of the individual allow him or her to associate and identify with groups, and, consequently, propaganda has become the foundation for group membership and identity politics. Shared propaganda (albeit unconsciously shared) has become the Shibboleth of modern society and has become fundamental for individual identity and political participation. Of course the propagandized individual does not consider themselves to be propagandized. For such individuals, they are "informed" and "in the circle of truth." Only others are effected by propaganda. For the propagandized individual, propaganda is "free speech," "information," "truth," "reading between the lines," "joining the dots," "reasoned interpretation," "commonsense logic," or whatever euphemism they use to rubber-stamp their own speech and thought. While rubber-stamping is clothed as individual self-expression or free speech, it is actually quite different. It is a mode of conformity, wherein through emotional and impulsive reactions, one identifies with a social group by imitating them. It is a manifestation of "the herd instinct," as Nietzsche termed it. Of course it is pernicious when the individual is unaware of propaganda, as for them propaganda only effects other people, but, the most pernicious aspect of propaganda is that it essential for the individual in modern society to make sense of their own existence and identify with others. It is this aspect of propaganda that makes it psychologically addictive.

This has been known for almost a century. Walter Lippmann—a political journalist who wrote propaganda pamphlets during World War I—argued that the manipulation of public opinion, via mass media, was antithetical to the development of an enlightened, informed, and democratic public capable of exercising freedom of choice and rational decision-making.[3] However, he considered the public to be incapable of critically analyzing public policy and distinguishing fact from propaganda.[4] He was concerned with the extent that urbanization and mass society had resulted in heavily-mediated communications between people and political leaders, which had created the conditions for the majority to be highly susceptible to propaganda, and the public tended to resort to stereotypes in order to understand the world in terms of a pseudo-reality.[5] Mass media had provided politicians with the means to manufacture consent, while legislation was becoming so complex that elected lawmakers could not understand the laws they agreed upon and were increasingly dependent upon bureaucrats and technical experts for précis and explanations. Under such conditions, democratic participation (in Thomas Jefferson's sense) had become quite unfeasible, except in a few isolated rural communities, and was incapable of providing the administrative basis for the organization of modern society.[6] If democracy was to be possible it not only required a means by which the public could come to understand how mass media worked and presented information to them, but it also required a means by which the public could understand the media relations between politicians and the public. Rather than demand the better standards of education and greater levels of public participation required for the emergence of a critical, engaged, and informed *demos*, Lippmann hoped that political experts and social scientists could independently provide the public with information and help insulate the public from propaganda and other kinds of opinion manipulation.[7]

It was this kind of appeal to professionalization and professional ethics that underscored the defense of the nascent public relations industry by practitioners such as Ivy L. Lee and Edward Bernays. Lee argued that truths are not self-evident, but, rather, they are claims based on interpretations of

---

[3] Lippmann, W., *Liberty and the News* (New York Harcourt & Brace, 1920)
[4] See also Lippmann, W., *The Phantom Public* (New York: Harcourt & Brace, 1925) and *A Preface to Politics* (New York: Mitchell Kennerly, 1913).
[5] Lippmann, W., *Public Opinion* (New York: Macmillan, 1922)
[6] See also Lippmann, W., *Drift and Mastery* (Madison, WI: University of Wisconsin Press, 1985), first published in 1914.
[7] See also Lippmann, W., *The Good Society* (Boston: Little & Brown, 1933)

the facts, and, therefore, the "evil" of propaganda is the failure to disclose its sources.[8] For Lee, the establishment of professional journalistic codes of practice to expose deliberate lies and concealed sources formed the basis for an ethics of mass media. For Bernays, the uses of propaganda and public manipulation techniques by professional public relations representatives were essential for modern democracy in a mass society if they resulted in the dissemination of diverse and competing interpretations and symbols, educating an otherwise ill-informed and obstinate public about pluralistic and conflicting truths and desires.[9] These uses of propaganda allowed dissenting minority views to be heard within the public sphere and, thereby, would provide genuine opportunities for challenging widely established interpretations and assumptions. Given the absence of Platonic guardians, acting as a committee of wise elders, the use of propaganda in a competitive market countered the public tendency towards parochialism and ignorance. Hence, according to Bernays, the public relations professional had ethical obligations towards wider society, as well as their client, and, therefore, should not promote deceitful or antisocial clients. Bernays provided a pragmatic argument for this ethical obligation on the grounds that professional public relations were more likely to be successful in commercial terms if they genuinely catered to the public interest and promoted socially beneficial causes. Providing that this ethical obligation was met, the use of propaganda in professional public relations in a competitive market constituted a legitimate form of public education and would have a positive contribution to democracy in a mass society. It was based on the perceived need for a feedback relation between public relations and the public interest, as the democratic basis for mass media, which led George Gallup to develop the random-sample poll as a means by which politicians and public relations professionals could learn what the public opinions and interests were and how best to cater to them.[10] The professionalization of journalism went hand in hand with the manufacture of consent through the use of propaganda.

---

[8] Lee, I.L., *Publicity* (New York: Industries Publishing, 1925)
[9] See also Bernays, E.L., *Propaganda* (New York: Liveright, 1928); see also *Public Relations* (Norman, OK: University of Oklahoma Press, 1952)
[10] Gallup, G., and Rae, S.F., *The Pulse of Democracy* (New York: Simon and Schuster, 1940)

Another consequence of the increasing cost of propaganda is that corporations and corporate-owned media become the gate-keepers of the political process, such that it is, and the two-party system becomes completely locked in. Not only is it impossible for any third party to amass sufficient money to gain the mass media access required to compete with the other two parties, but the most third party candidates can hope to achieve is to be a spoiler and benefit their opposition. Left wing third party candidates benefit the Republicans. Right wing third party candidates benefit the Democrats. This not only has the overall effect of making elections closer and more partisan, but also of reducing "debates" to the trotting out of the same wedge-issues, thereby allowing the two parties to both satisfy the same corporate interests while seeming to oppose each other, and thereby ensure that the status quo is maintained. New ideas, innovative solutions to real problems, and democratic participation are all suppressed, eroded, and eventually destroyed, all the while the political process is reduced to sound-bites (or Tweets) and a personality contest. The increased costs of mass media, due to the costs of advertising and technologies, have resulted in increased levels of corporate control over mass media. Mass media consolidation has resulted in more media outlets becoming owned by fewer media corporations, despite increasing numbers of media outlets, which has transformed the 'media barons' into a new cartel "constituting a Private Ministry of Information and Culture" capable of setting the agenda and framework of public debate, controlling the dissemination of information, and dictating the conditions under which a political candidate is likely to be elected to public office.[11] By serving the economic elite, while sustaining the illusion of being an independent watchdog, mainstream mass media has distorted and suppressed the public ability to learn about and understand public policy. For over a century, systematic media consolidation has resulted in corporate-owned mass media becoming a business that sells mass audiences or readers to advertisers, and promotes news as entertainment and a commercial product (nowadays often inserting infomercials into news, promoting products, and acting as a conduit for official government statements). Reporters are pressured to support the opinions and prejudices of media owners and advertisers, which tend to support the political status quo. The demands of access to politicians and the commercial interests of

---

[11] Bagdikian, B., *Media Monopoly* (Boston: Beacon Press, 1997), first published 1987

privately owned newspapers has created an intrinsic editorial selection bias in favour of news stories that either benefited advertisers or avoided offending them, and aid the government in justifying or selling a policy or need for reform.[12] As a result, newspapers, radio stations, and television channels tend to favour the needs and norms of the economic and political elite, and cannot be said to be a free press in any real sense. As Benjamin Ginsberg put it,

"In the United States, in particular, the ability of the upper and upper-middle classes to dominate the marketplace of ideas has generally allowed these strata to shape the entire society's perception of political reality and the range of realistic political and social possibilities. While westerners usually equate the marketplace with freedom of opinion, the hidden hand of the market can be almost a potent an instrument of control as the iron first of the state."[13]

This idea of media "self-censorship" in response to "market forces" was central to Noam Chomsky and Edward Herman's propaganda-model of mainstream media performance, wherein bias and censorship tend to be the consequence of commercial and political pressures and constraints, rather than any conscious media conspiracy.[14] Even though Chomsky and Herman provide many examples of deliberate deceit and distortions of the facts by journalists, they primarily analyzed mass media, in terms of a model of corporate oligopoly, as a system for transmitting messages to the general population that utilizes the systematic use of propaganda "to amuse, entertain, and inform, and to inculcate individuals with the values, beliefs, and codes of behaviour that will integrate them into the institutional structures of mass society."[15]

This conformity to the status quo serves the owners of mass media (the economic elite) and conceals conflicts between class-interests by building "filters" into the structures of information gathering, selection, and

---

[12] Irwin, W., *The American Newspaper* (Ames, IA: Iowa State University Press, 1969, first published in 1911); see also *Propaganda and the News* (New York: Whittlesey House, 1936)

[13] Ginsberg, B., *The Captive Public* (New York: Basic Books, 1986), p. 89

[14] Herman, E.S., and Chomsky, N., *Manufacturing Consent: The Political Economy of Mass Media* (New York: Pantheon Books, 2002), first published 1988.

[15] *Manufacture of Consent*, p.1

dissemination. Chomsky and Herman's model explained media choices regarding 'newsworthiness' as the product of five dominant "filters":

(1) The interests of the owners of increasingly consolidated media;

(2) The interests of advertisers—the main source of income for mass media;

(3) Reliance of media on governmental and corporate sources for information;

(4) Avoiding "flak" and the increased costs it brings (where "flak" refers to criticism in the form of letters of complaint (emails, phone calls, or petitions) from the public or powerful media watchdogs; law suits; political speeches or proposed regulation; public hearings or investigations, etc.);

(5) "Anti-communism" as a national creed and control mechanism (In the United States and the United Kingdom, after the dissolution of the Soviet Union, this has been replaced by "anti-terrorism.")[16]

Due to these "filters", the premises and interpretive framework of the debate are set. Reporters and editors—the gatekeepers—even when acting with journalistic integrity and professionalism, unconsciously become agents of propaganda and censorship in favour of the status quo because "the constraints are so powerful, and are built into the system in such a fundamental way, that alternative bases of news choices are hardly imaginable."[17] Dissenting views or alternative sources of information are filtered out. The increasing pressure for successful financial performance, within an increasingly deregulated advertising-based media system, will prioritise the appeal of programming to advertisers, as well as increase the time available for advertising, and this will inevitably marginalise or eliminate any programming that could offend advertisers. This greatly effects the placement, tone, context, and treatment of news, as well as the volume of coverage.

---

[16] See Chomsky, N., *Hegemony or Survival: America's Quest for Global Dominance* (New York: Henry Holt, 2003); and, Chomsky, N., *Failed States: The Abuse of Power and the Assault on Democracy* (New York: Henry Holt, 2006).
[17] Chomsky and Herman, *Manufacturing Consent*, p. 2

"Messages from and about dissidents and weak, unorganised individuals and groups, domestic and foreign, are at an initial disadvantage in sourcing costs and credibility, and they do not often comport with the interests of the gatekeepers and other powerful parties that influence the filtering process."[18]

Furthermore, due to their uncritical reliance of governmental statements, especially during conflicts or wars, reporters often present these statements as objective and factual, while non-governmental sources are considered suspect, biased, and often ignored. Consequently, "enemies" of the current government are vilified for the same kinds of actions that "allies" are allowed to commit without any media criticism or concern. As Chomsky and Herman showed, mainstream media have consistently portrayed people abused by enemy states as *worthy* victims, receiving a sustained and high level of attention and indignation, while those abused by the US government, friendly states, or client states are portrayed as *unworthy* victims, as collateral damage or somehow deserving of their abuse, when they are portrayed at all. When the mainstream media supports and repeats governmental statements persistently and uncritically, irrespective of the facts or their inconsistency with previous statements, there is strong evidence for the case that media is engaged systematically in the dissemination of propaganda in support of governmental policies and agendas. Once the government is the major source of information and provides the framework of analysis, the media become the means of disseminating governmental information and the official line, masked as impartial investigative journalism based on relevant facts. Once the primary role of mainstream media is one of making sure that the governmental agenda remains unchallenged then the propaganda-model should be applied. Also, this model should be applied when journalists and editors apply a double-standard of criticism and rigor depending upon whether the news or facts are favourable or unfavourable to government claims or statements. As Chomsky and Herman showed, citing examples of mainstream media reporting of events in Eastern Europe, Latin America, and Indochina, reporters and editors have consistently applied double-standards of criticism and rigor in favour of serving the propaganda needs of the US government.

If these claims are true then it is evident that censorship and propaganda are the dual aspects of the media collusion with government and this

---

[18] *Manufacturing Consent*, p. 31

collusion has caused a crisis in democracy by manipulating or preventing public participation in decision-making processes. Far from being a free press, mainstream media has become coercive and manipulative of news reporting and the dissemination of information to the public. In this way, so-called democratic governments can rely on market mechanisms to establish media conformity, silence critics, and marginalise opposition.[19]

"To confront power is costly and difficult; high standards of evidence and argument are imposed, and critical analysis is naturally not welcomed by those who are in a position to react vigorously and to determine the array of rewards and punishments. Conformity to a "patriotic agenda," in contrast, imposes no such costs. Charges against official enemies barely require substantiation; they are, furthermore, protected from correction, which can be dismissed as apologetics for the criminals or as missing the forest for the trees. The system protects itself with indignation against a challenge to the right of deceit in the service of power, and the very idea of subjecting the ideological system to rational inquiry elicits incomprehension or outrage, though it is often masked in other terms."[20]

As well as suppressing or falsifying facts, along with leaving the official version and assumptions unchallenged, the standard tactic of media conformity to government policy and the state-corporate status quo is to generate an "historical amnesia" that conceals failures and reversals of policy.[21] This takes the form of media silence and revisionism.[22] This is the technocratic tendency to conceal its operations and create institutional barriers to public participation (otherwise known as "interference") in the

---

[19] See also Chomsky, *Necessary Illusions*, chap. 3; Lance Bennett, W., *News: The Politics of Illusion* (New York: Longman, 1988); Preston, Jr., W., Herman, J.S., and Schiller, J.S., *Hope and Folly: The United States and UNESCO,* 1945-1985 (Minneapolis: University of Minnesota Press, 1989); Chomsky, N., *Media Control: The Spectacular Achievements of Propaganda* (New York: Seven Stories Press, 2002); Rampton, S., and Stauber, J., *Weapons of Mass Deception: The Uses of Propaganda in Bush's War on Iraq* (New York: Penguin, 2003); Barsamian, D., and Chomsky, N., *Propaganda and the Public Mind: Conversations with Noam Chomsky* (Cambridge, MA: Southend Press, 2003); Snow, N., *Information War: American Propaganda, Free Speech and Opinion Control since 9-11* (New York: Seven Stories Press, 2003).
[20] Chomsky, *Necessary Illusions*, p. 9
[21] See also Huntington, S., *American Politics: The Promise of Disharmony* (Cambridge, MA: Harvard University Press, 1981)
[22] For examples of media serving as "adjuncts of government" see Chomsky's *Necessary Illusions*, chapter 4

development and implementation of public policy. Western media often rely on the use of doublespeak in developing interpretations (such as representing an act of military intervention and the establishment of a puppet regime as "democracy promotion") to misrepresent double-standards or blatant hypocrisy, which presents the illusion of freedom of the press while serving the propaganda needs of the government.[23]

Even though the commonplace understanding of propaganda tends to consider the uneducated sector of the population to be the most vulnerable to propaganda, we can see that the educated elite (the "opinion leaders") are the prime targets of propaganda and also its main purveyors. Academics, journalists, and intellectuals consider themselves to "the opinion leaders" and, hence, are targeted as being the means to stifle dissent and independent thought. The educated elite are used to keep debate within permissible bounds and establish a consensus that endorses the assertions underlying propaganda campaigns. In this way, assertions can be publicly established as unquestionable truths—doctrines—and maintain strict boundaries to debate within public media, academia, and other intellectual circles. Anything outside these boundaries is immediately marginalized as being the irrational views of extremists, cranks, and the ill-informed. In this way, the intellectual elite both conform to the established agenda and promote it. Thus, to use one of Chomsky's examples, the US media and intellectual elite vigorously debated how best to deal with the Nicaraguan Sandinista threat to US security and the US government's efforts to promote democracy in Central America, while there was hardly any debate or discussion about whether (or how) Nicaragua could be a threat to US security, whether the US government was really attempting to promote democracy, or why those "fledgling democracies" supported by the US (such as Guatemala and El Salvador) have the worst records for human right abuses in Latin America. Today, we can see similar doctrines regarding Iran's development of nuclear weapons, the privatization of public services and lands, the so-called "free trade agreements," the use of genetic modification for agriculture "to feed the world," the domination of global finance and trade by corporations and banks, the regulation and centralized control over food and alternative medicine, and the deregulation of media and communications technologies, to name a few. It is within this framework of permissible opinion that the

---

[23] Chomsky, *Necessary Illusions*, chapter 5

boundaries of information are disseminated to the individual citizen. Similarly, through media "self-censorship" and news blackouts, facts can be suppressed and particular problems can be obligated from public awareness. Some people will still chant "Free Tibet!" in the West, but the situation of the Tibetan people under Chinese occupation has simply been forgotten and goes unreported.

Propaganda threatens to subvert the possibility of an enlightened citizenry based on socially conscious, critically thinking, informed, and rational individuals. It threatens to drive societal development towards the creation of an irrational and totalitarian mass-society. Hence, our concern with propaganda should run deeper than increasing our awareness of techniques of mass persuasion and public manipulation, with all their pernicious distortions of democratic participation in deciding on this or that policy, but should be central to our critical understanding of the development of the whole of modern society. In the face of mass society, with its overcrowding (overpopulation), duality of work and leisure, totalitarian focus on money (which is experienced by most people as wage labor and bills), isolation and alienation, and its crisis of meaning, propaganda fills the inner void felt by the individual. Propaganda becomes both a source of and substitute for meaning and belonging in the face of solitude and its challenges. As such, propaganda satisfies deep-seated psychological needs and is more than a source of cultural narratives. Propaganda allows the individual to move beyond the ordinary and everyday knowledge (based on experience and reason) to feel that he grasps the whole world and knows his place within it. It provides the individual with a substitute for knowledge and allows her to have opinions about everything. It provides him with a sense of knowing the world through his intuition, emotion, and "gut instincts" rather than having to take the laborious route of knowing the world through rigorous study and research, as well as critical self-reflection of the methods of interpretation, experiment and analysis, experience and logical reasoning. It allows her to know the world beyond her experience and imagination; to connect with a wider sense of humanity and history beyond her immediate environment, her family and friends, and the reality of her life. It allows him to interpret and explain his life and its causes. While the individual remains "in the know" through propaganda, playing his part within groups and organizations, given to him through the rubber-stamps of group-identity, he will continue to reinforce his prejudices and worldview, *as his own*, even though it was given to him by others. Such an individual retains an inauthentic and irrational relation with ther life, consciousness, and being. While others can challenge and question the prejudices and worldview of such an individual, she can only really help herself by confronting and challenging her own irrationality. Who can do this? Is this not a case of lifting oneself up by one's bootstraps? Ultimately, the individual needs to experience a shock or catastrophe of such deeply personal proportions that it shatters or cracks his worldview by revealing to him, in his own terms, the rift between his worldview and prejudices and the reality he experiences. It is only when the individual experiences the contractions and flaws, inconsistencies and errors, and limitations of her own worldview that she has the opportunity to distance herself from it and rediscover her own innocence, and, as a result, learn what she does not know and what she falsely has believed to be knowledge. This can be a genuine moment of liberation and enlightenment that arises when reality shreds one's illusions, myths, and conceits. Of course there is always the danger that the individual will panic and run fearfully towards alternative sources of propaganda (counterpropaganda) and re-establish an irrational relation with knowledge and truth. It takes real courage to resist the temptation to become once more giddy and secure in "the circle of truth" offered by propaganda. The desire to be "in the know" once more risks a return to the ersatz truth of propaganda, acting as a mask to conceal ignorance and uncertainty from others and, most of all, from oneself.

In modern society, the individual cannot stand not knowing. Without great intellectual courage and the virtue of humility, he cannot accept his state of innocence. She needs to assert herself, to see herself as someone who knows the truth, who is important, who has something to say. He needs to feel that he is somebody and be considered as such by others. She needs to express her authority, her position, and have an opinion on everything. Propaganda allows the individual to feel that her opinion matters in mass society; she feels important in relation to the whole range of political issues and society as a whole. His opinion is of fundamental importance as an expression of self-identity and meaning, and provides him with authority, conviction, satisfaction, and a sense of his own cleverness. Propaganda not only allows the individual to engage in political discourse, but transforms a state of ignorance and impotence into a sense of political action, dramatic meaning, and democratic participation, through which the individual gains her place in history and culture, and escapes the humdrum of modern life.

Of course these feelings are a sham. The social instinct for "wisdom" in modern society is often completely frustrated and replaced with an instinctive need for self-expression and assertion. Though some routes of satisfaction of this narcissistic instinct exist through the culture industry—in novels and the movies—and thereby give the reader or watcher the feeling of self-esteem he so desperately craves (by identifying with the hero, for example, or being a maverick anti-hero), that is often not enough. The individual seeks out propaganda in response to this deep-seated need for truth and meaning. It is the Band-Aid over the chasm of alienation.

The individual's frustrations, resentments, and bitterness can be channeled and given meaning by projecting them onto an enemy who is to blame. Fear and anxiety are projected onto some other: Jews, Communists, Fascists, Capitalists, Liberals, Conservatives, Feminists, Fundamentalists, Illuminati, Aliens, the Devil, etc. Some "they" is to blame. Thus her own feelings of worthlessness in modern society can be transformed into self-righteous indignation, into hatred and anger towards someone else, some other group, some race or religion, some political party or politician. In this way, the causes of his conditions can be disguised as the fault of someone else entirely, who can become an object of hatred and disgust. Propaganda generates *the politics of contempt*. Through scapegoating, propaganda has a therapeutic and compensatory psychological function that allows an individual to be part of something bigger, and to transfer his own inadequacies and frustrations into something heroic and noble, part of some great struggle, and part of history. Myths, symbols, and abstracts inform reality and make it meaningful in terms of the group-identity of "us" and the hatred of "them." Heightened anxiety and fear, often little more than the consequence of change and uncertainty, can always be effectively used by the propagandist to scapegoat and demonize a group of people (immigrants, for example) as being a threat or destroyers of the individual's "way of life." Liberals, atheists, feminists, socialists, and homosexuals have often been targeted in this way, as destroyers of morality, tradition, and culture. Ironically, the more an individual succumbs to the lure of propaganda, the more she substitutes the mask it provides in place of herself—to conceal herself from herself most of all—and the more of an individual she feels herself to be, the less of an individual she actually becomes. His personality becomes a caricature—a façade—as he performs the stereotypes of his group-identity like a puppet on a string, all the while feeling empowered, liberated, and connected to the "truth" of his own condition, via the explanations given to him by propaganda, and thereby defining himself in relation to society and history as a whole in terms of a pseudo-reality.

Most of all, propaganda deludes the individual into thinking that they are a free and self-determining person. In the sense that freedom of action (of deed, speech, or thought) is always based on the knowledge of the true, good, and just—the knowledge of a rational cosmic order—propaganda, by acting as a substitute for knowledge, acts as a substitute for freedom as well. In this regard, we can clearly see that nature of the relation between propaganda and the free press: They are not merely opposites, as propaganda acts as a substitute for free speech and masquerades as it, but they undermine each other. By acting as a substitute for free speech, propaganda appeals to irrationality and group-identity (belonging), reinforcing the prejudices and worldview of the individual, thereby reinforcing the individual's own sense of themselves as a knower and free speaker. In this way, even though he is doing little more than rubber-stamping and repeating the "truths" of their group, simply parroting the opinions and myths given to him, the individual believes that he is engaged in intellectual freedom and free speech. In actuality, the terms "intellectual freedom" and "free speech" have become rubber-stamps used to conceal propaganda and allow it to function in the guise of being its opposite, all the whole undermining freedom of thought and speech.

Narrowcasting and the Free Press:

Narrowcasting is not new. In many respects, we find the origins of narrowcasting in organized religion and the demarcation of writing into doctrine to distinguish it from heresy, whereby people would only trust specific sources of writing and consider all others as lies (or diabolical in origin). It was developed to great success by the Bolsheviks and Nazis during their early years as political parties before they seized power. Both were able to use agitation and identity propaganda to create a sense of the party as a radical opposition and the vanguard of the revolution to the extent that they viewed themselves as the only "truth-speakers" or people "in the know." The propagandized Nazi or Communist felt that they were part of history and all other sources of media were suspect or reactionary (the 'lying press' or

Lügenpresse, as the Nazis termed them). Narrowcasting feeds off *suggestibility* and *confirmation bias*—that people tend to believe the first story they identify with and measure all other stories against it.[24] This prepares the individual to accept further propaganda as truth, providing it comes from trusted sources, and to distrust information from other sources as being propaganda or lies.

Narrowcasting in the United States does not fight against the privatization of the individual. It does the opposite. While agitation and identity propaganda are both used to gain support for political movements, organizations, and parties, as well as invoke outrage and group-identity, it is important for the kind of spectator-based mass politics cultivated in America, as the vast majority of people retreat into the private realm and play no part in politics. Apart from voting every 2 or 4 years, sharing petitions and posts on social media, and answering the questions of pollsters, or shouting each other down on social media, most Americans do not participate in politics or take any interest in it. Narrowcasting in the American media is largely designed to reinforce the alienation and apathy of the population, and repress political action beyond feelings of outrage and contempt at "the opposition," a sense of belonging to the group-mind, and "self-righteousness." Its primary function is to keep people divided, inoculate them against opposing views, and reinforce their prejudices and worldview. It undermines the possibility of democratic participation by creating a sense of fatalism: the status quo is too powerful, no resistance is possible, and there is no alternative. Anyone who disagrees is one of "them," a liar, idiot, or traitor.

This is why there is often a near total media blackout of mass protests (such as early Tea Party rallies, the Occupy Wall Street movement, and the anti-DAPL protests) *until* the police use violence and oppressive tactics to break them up. The more aggressive and brutal the police action, the more likely it is to be covered, without any actual discussion of the history of the protest or the aims of the protesters. Why is this so? The basic idea is to maintain censorship of the causes of the protests, while promoting a fear of the police (especially when showing how the police can act illegally with impunity) to fix the message "protest and this could happen to you" in the public mind, which is why particular focus is directed on showing police

---

[24] Marbury B. Ogle, *Public opinion and Political Dynamics* (Boston: Houghton Mifflin, 1950)

violence against old people, young or pregnant women, disabled students, journalists, and people peacefully petitioning their government (which is supposedly a First Amendment right), while also showing that there are no consequences whatsoever for the police. Corporate media mystifies the protesters and intensifies contempt for them. This is often combined with showing violent reactions of protesters, such as throwing objects, burning vehicles, or rioting, as if these were causal in the police violence. This is also to intensify the public sense of fear of protesting. It ignores any revelation of agent provocateurs working to cause violence and justify police action, while also collectively blaming all protesters for the actions of a few. There is rarely any follow-up of any inquiry or prosecution of police (while arrested protesters, including journalists, are threatened with extreme prison sentences) and rarely are police-chiefs or local politicians questioned about these incidents. Only official statements are reported. The absence of accountability is important because it maintains the public perception that "resistance is useless" and dangerous to the individual, and this is a method to promote the idea that people should "stay off the streets." It also for this reason that there is a media blackout of peaceful protests until violence occurs, so that people do not seek to join the protests and increase their numbers while these events are peaceful.

This explains why the media will report that police officers do not face any disciplinary action, even if they kill unarmed citizens. This is always stated as a matter of fact. There is no follow-up to why they were not disciplined or how and why the officer was exonerated. It is merely sufficient to broadcast that there was no disciplinary action or the officer was acquitted of all wrongdoing. Narrowcasted media is then in place to pick up the outrage in some channels (thereby acting as catharsis and reducing tensions) and justifications in others (thereby reinforcing conformity and prejudice), without any real analysis or debate of the actual facts of the case. The aim here is to reinforce the public perception that the police can brutalize or murder citizens with impunity, even arbitrarily, so the citizenry learn to behave and obey the police without question. It does not even matter if such events are rare, as they are blown up out of all proportion by the media, all the while maintaining only shallow coverage. The same can be seen in the coverage of mass shootings (which are rare, but dominate the news cycle) or terrorist acts (which are also rare in the US), without any discussion of causes, and alongside the call for new laws to deal with "the problem." This is a fundamental mechanism for the erosion of any belief in rights and constitutional protections.

This is also the function of so-called fringe media (like infowars.com). Their narrative often takes the form of conspiracy theories and agitation propaganda. This kind of narrowcasted media targets an already paranoid and alienated section of the population, and intensifies their paranoia and alienation. Under the guise of a concern for constitutional rights, and outrage at their violation, the loss of civil rights, and governmental tyranny, transmitted to a heavily narrowcasted audience, interweaved with conspiracy theories about some aloof and shadowy organization (Illuminati, Bilderberg group, etc.) that somehow is always untouchable while simultaneously (and surprisingly) poor at remaining secret and covering its tracks (like some bad Bond villain), the target audience's feelings of paranoia and alienation are justified, reinforced, and intensified, while the object of their fear and outrage is even further abstracted and removed from their experience. The audience will believe the assertion that such shadowy organizations have grand and evil plans (such as killing 90% of the world's population, for example) while somehow not killing or even framing (using child pornography etc.) the media pundit (i.e. Alex Jones) who exposes this diabolical plot. The contradiction between their unrestrained malevolence on one side and their restraint on the other remains unexplained. The aim of this kind of propaganda is to encourage (through fear) the further retreat of the individual into the private realm (stocking up on canned food, guns, etc.), all the while calling for the further erosion of rights and political engagement.

The effect of narrowcasting on a heavily propagandized population is extremely damaging. Propaganda does not simply change the opinions and behavior of individuals. It changes the individual as well. It causes unconscious psychological changes, impulses, emotions, and trauma to the individual's capacity to reason and reflect. It erodes the ability of individuals to think critically and impartially, thereby intensifying the irrationality of the individual's thinking and unconscious habits. The longer the individual is subjected to propaganda, the deeper its effects are driven into the individual's subconscious presuppositions and preconceptions about the world. Masked by rationalizations, self-justifications, explanations, myths, and abstractions, propaganda is driven deeper into the human psyche until it forms the foundations for the individual's worldview and identity. No clearer example of this can be seen that with racism and identity-politics. The prejudices of the individual become reinforced through repetition, and the ease of doing so becomes its own affirmation of their truth, which justifies and explains these prejudices in ways that lead the individual to believe that he is right to have them. Her bigotry is transformed into ideology through the circularity of its own confirmation through repetition within her social groups and cultural milieu. Ignorance is transformed into commitment and loyalty—into strength and faithfulness. Any doubts or questions are discarded, as an emerging butterfly discards its cocoon—and anyone who questions or criticizes them from within the group are soon denounced as "sellouts" or "cucks." The individual is not only under the sway of propaganda, but his very identity depends on it. She is clear and resolute in her own certainty, oblivious to the nothingness upon which it is founded.

Through group identity, these prejudices can be declared openly as "truths," further reinforced and shared by members of the same group. The conflicts and contradictions within modern society and mass media become lines of demarcation drawn to divide the population into partisan factions and camps. The existential investment of the individual's identity within the group reinforces their membership, thereby intensifying their fundamental commitment to the group in direct proportion to the intensity of the fragmentation of society into partisan camps. Propaganda intensifies the vicious circle of partitioning to such an extent that the individual's own zealotry and fanaticism ultimately becomes their whole identity—a mask—that secures itself by dividing the world into "them" and "us," all the while concealing itself and the nothingness that lies behind it. Its truth is reinforced and confirmed through the utterance of shared slogans as the Shibboleth of group-identity. The individual becomes increasingly hostile to the members of opposing groups in direct proportion to the erosion of any identity they once had outside of group-identity. Maintaining propaganda and intensifying their own irrationality becomes a matter of life or death, as well as the primary method to rubber-stamp their own sense of self and its rightness. Narrowcasting secures this sense of group identity and the divisions in the population. Armed with a set of ready-made, off-the-peg, explanations and justifications which are at hand to counter and dismiss criticism and questions, the propagandized individual is incapable of the kind of doubts and critical reflection required for rational inquiry and self-examination. Open-minded questioning becomes not only impossible but an enemy to the individual's own sense of being. Their mind is resolute in its faithfulness to their prejudices and worldview. All contrary facts are falsehoods. All opposing evidence is a hoax or a lie. All critical methods and intellectual virtues are part of a conspiracy. The identity of the individual depends on exorcising the demonic forces of contrary worldviews and ideas. It is not merely the case that the individual has become a parrot—or a puppet on a string—but narrowcasted propaganda has eroded the individual's mind and filled it with itself. It has eroded the very possibility of self-doubt and critical thinking upon which open-minded and rational discourse depend. It has created a void within the individual that transforms them into a ventriloquist's dummy, robbed of any authentic and existential subjectivity, and turns them into a speaking and writing object: an instrument of the dissemination of propaganda.

The transformation of the propagandized individual into an instrument has reconstructed a propagandee into a propagandist. The propagandized individual becomes a propagandist, although completely oblivious to this transformation. The individual becomes an automaton, thereby confirming their truth through increasing the numbers of people who utter it. She is not only liberated from the troubling difficulties of questioning and testing the deeply philosophical and human problems of epistemology, morality, and politics, but is, much more importantly, liberated from her own awareness of her inability to navigate and address these problems. Compromise and criticality—or even seeking commonality with others outside of the group mind—become quite impossible. He is free from any such problems that arise from attempting to reconcile comprehensively all the intellectual and moral standards, values, norms, rules, and conventions of society and culture, as well as the profound existential problems of the human condition. She now is empowered by the certainty of easily graspable stereotypes, slogans, and formulae. Group-identity becomes the measure of correctness, thereby transforming thinking into behaving, reflection into posturing, truth into slogans, and free speech into utterances of propaganda. The individual is lost in the hologram of narrowcasted propaganda and has no way of knowing or escaping it. In this sense, it is like a cult and the individual is brainwashed.

Propaganda gives the intellect of the individual a zealous character and this also gives narrowcasted media a cult-like aspect. Their media is the only free press. Their speech is the only free speech. It makes the individual feel special and "in the circle of truth." In this way, when they shout down or silence people they do not agree with, they consider this to be the exercise of free speech, but when others do it to them, it is an example of how the others condemn free speech. The propagandized individual is indistinguishable from the religious cultist, and the propagandist becomes akin to a religious leader or guru. Thus plunges the propagandized individual into a state of psychosis (akin to psychopathy). His responses become formulaic and reactionary—rigid in their reproduction of the orthopraxis of propaganda— and results in the suspension of both the social and imaginative dimensions of learning and inquiry. The socio-political process becomes one of passivity in its reception, even (and especially) when the propagandized individual acts with anger and aggression to the questions and doubts of others, and the propagandized individual becomes unable to adjust to any learning context other than that of receiving propaganda from his trusted source. Truth and information become instruments of psychological warfare, as she demands strict opposites—them v us, black v white, liberal v conservative, good v evil—without any real idea of how these dualities are constructed, or even what they mean. She views herself as a participant in a historical conflict or struggle without any knowledge of its history of constructed meanings. This self-aggrandizement in terms of a fictional conflict is quite typical of the psychotic personality. The tendency of the propagandized individual is to view everything narrowly in terms of these constructed dualities, reducing all interpretations to them, and deprive meaning of any dynamic structure of interpretation. Truth is given an emotional (and romanticized) content that is itself perceived as the test of its correctness. The quest for truth is transformed into drama, wherein the propagandized individual feels victimized and persecuted by anyone who questions and challenges his prejudices and worldview. He projects his own hostility onto others, and finds solace and comradery in his group identity and its reinforcement of his own personality.

Symbols and slogans no longer relate to experiences and facts about the world, but instead relate to personalities (heroes, leaders, and villains, etc.); group demands and rubber-stamped myths (usually presented as history) generate hopes and expectations, and, of course, the narratives by which group-identity is recognized and reinforced. Propaganda becomes the medium for group-identity and its confirmation of the value of its symbols, necessary for group-identity, thereby eroding the possibility and capacity of exercising moral conscience and intellectual freedom. Everything is in flux and expedient—moral absolutes today become replaced with their opposite tomorrow. Two plus two equals five. The group's use of symbols becomes a set of Shibboleths that act as replacements for thinking and logic, alongside any objective standard, which become so eroded by propaganda that the individual's capacity for free speech and thought not only become destroyed, but are also irrelevant. Once the individual conforms to the mediation of group-identity as their standard of truth and morality—which become increasingly intensified and partitioned by a heavily narrowcasted media— then their own subjectivity and freedom are given to them as objects to be incorporated into their personality as symbols of their identity, which can literally be worn as a slogan on a t-shirt or a baseball cap. The reconstruction of the individual in terms of the symbols and slogans of the group, transform the processes of indoctrination into a sense of belonging and the self-expression of individuality. The emergence of uniqueness and freedom from conformity and repetition is one of the most astounding and damaging coups of propaganda over the human mind and nature. The thoroughly inauthentic propagandized individual believes themselves to be liberated and that the opinions given to him by others are his own. These self-appropriated collective beliefs, values, and norms, which the individual identifies as her own, develop a degree of importance that would otherwise not exist in a person unaffected by propaganda. Through narrowcasting, the propagandist inserts stereotypes and images in the consciousness of the individual and provides him with a ready-to-hand vocabulary and phraseology through which he communicates in ways readily understood and accepted by fellow group members, and these stereotypes and images replace or suppress alternatives. The personal (or subjective) dimension of language acquisition is suspended (or at least greatly diminished) within the propagandized individual, as she develops the collective speech and thought practices of the group. After a while, the conscious subjectivity of the propagandized individual is completely eroded, leaving only the group-identity and its shared prejudices and worldview, around which all thought and language is tested and practiced. It is at this stage that the individual can be said to be indoctrinated or brainwashed. Authenticity and freedom of consciousness are completely eroded. The propagandized individual is effectively a cog in the propaganda machine.

One of the hallmarks of the propagandized individual is their readiness to call "propaganda" any idea or fact that they do not share. All of the thoughts and speech of the propagandized individual have become those of the group, and, consequently, she will assert her distrust of "propaganda" and will readily consider anything that threatens or undermines her capacity for self-justification to be propaganda. The current vogue in declaring anything that contradicts the hologram as "fake news" is an example of this. All other media sources are "fake news." It is not simply the case that the propagandized individual cannot consider any idea or question that contradicts or does not fit in with their prejudices and worldview, although that is indeed the case, but the inoculation against contradictory testimony or criticisms results in a sense of suspicion and hostility towards the source of such ideas and questions, and to those who speak or write them. Their capacity for critical thinking or even learning has been completely eroded. The propagandized individual has a need for self-justification within the group. Propaganda satisfies this need by providing ready-made responses, symbols, and images, and removes doubts and moral scruples. As it reinforces the prejudices and worldview of the individual, it prevents the individual's awareness of the double-standards and contradictions that he operates under. It now becomes possible for the individual to feel completely justified in supporting "a just and noble war," without any idea about the realities and causes of that war, nor being able to explain why that war is just and noble (or even what these terms mean), and to condemn "the enemy" and "their atrocities," even when "their" soldiers are committing exactly the same actions as "our" soldiers commit on a daily basis. Anyone who points out that atrocities are atrocities regardless of which side commits them is considered to be "a traitor" and "aiding the enemy." Anything that threatens or challenges her certainties and sense of self-justification must be opposed and silenced. Not-listening or shouting down others becomes the mode of political speech. Anyone who exposes the hypocrisy of the propagandized individual must be hated and reviled. Narrowcasted propaganda has created an adverse reaction to doubts, ambiguities, or criticism. Through narrowcasted media, the propagandized individual is not only inoculated against any opinion or criticism that challenges his prejudices and worldview, but is threatened by others and is driven to hate anyone who belongs to any other group. "They" are the problem. "They" are what is wrong with the country. By definition, any criticism or opposing statements of fact must be "propaganda," against which the propagandized individual considers themselves to be immune.

The inauthenticity created through narrowcasted propaganda is the result of the individual surrendering themselves to *a substitute identity*, created by someone else; this artificial identity replaces the individual's own personality and conceals that the replacement has taken place. The propagandized individual speaks the words of others, obeys the impulses of others, and becomes someone else; the substitute personality brings with it a sense of greater truth and connection with reality, as given by someone else, fulfilling the need for belonging and meaning, and allows the individual to explain the world and her place within it. The individual feels himself to be part of something bigger, all the while becoming further alienated from his organic and subjective personality without even knowing it. The more eroded the self, the more important the propagandized individual feels, and she becomes completely lost to an artificial world—the hologram—as given to her by others, and reinforced through group identity and the collective reception of propaganda. Essentially, this is how indoctrination and brainwashing work: substitution and erosion of the self and the framework of thought through which the self is understood. In a very real sense, propaganda alienates the individual from his thoughts, his critical and personal judgment, his reason and imagination, and his doubt and curiosity. The thoughts of the individual become suppressed and distanced from her—as something without meaning or significance—while, through propaganda, the symbols and images of propaganda replace thought, thereby channeling speech and its reception into the framework of the vocabulary and semantic structures of the group. The propagandized individual has surrendered to that framework when he makes it his own. It owns her by providing a strong sense of identity and certainty, and allowing the articulation of self-justification, and, by doing so, transfers the conscious focus of the individual to the group as the reinforcement and confirmation of the individual's identity. Of course the individual does not simply disappear or feel robotic. He is still someone who feels that he thinks and has an inner life. She is still the person who speaks, experiences the world, and to whom things happen, but she no longer has any mental and conscious connection with her organic and subjective self. If he feels any sense of alienation from that self, or its loss in any way, he simply lacks the intellectual and linguistic framework to express and understand it. It is ineffable and unspeakable. The organic and subjective self becomes repressed into the silence of the unconscious background and concealed under the dominance of group-identity and its given framework of self-expression and interpretation. Any vague feelings of dissatisfaction or alienation can always be projected onto "them" as contemptuous and evil.

Any contradictions or tensions that the propagandized individual feels between her sense of alienation and the group-identity become inarticulate and unthinkable. He represses and dissipates these contradictions and tensions simply because he lacks the cognitive means to identify and grasp them, all while propaganda continues to provide a satisfactory and easy means to grasp and interpret the world, and the individual's place in it. Any sense of ill-ease or loss can be projected onto others and reinterpreted as a consequence of the problems those others have caused. Doubts, contradictions, and tensions become a threat to the individual and therefore must be treated with hostility and blame. This is why the individual feels no sense of hypocrisy when she accepts and expresses moral double-standards as self-evident truths. The suppression of critical judgment and the rigors of consistency within the intellectual and linguistic framework of thought and speech is a response to the alienation of the individual from critical thinking and self-reflective integrity, but the propagandized individual is still capable of criticizing others. "They" are the hypocrites! "They" have no logic! "They" are liars! "They" are propagandists! Not "us"! Never "us"! Of course this act of projection of the double-standard can only occur with the limits of the framework of self-justification, as certain questions can never be asked even of "them." Some things must remain taboo and unsaid. When all the possibilities of thought and speech are made in relation to the group, the propagandized individual is no longer capable of judging for himself. In political contexts, the individual needs to always use ready-made value judgments and truth statements as rubber-stamps of self-justification; this is enhanced when these rubber-stamps are reinforced by self-declared experts and trusted media pundits (and especially comical and entertaining media figures). The propagandized individual feels that their own judgment is being confirmed in direct proportion to the extent that their own prejudices and worldview is being vindicated and confirmed. The justification of prejudice in the name of opposing political correctness is a good example of this. The effect of this is to atrophy the very critical faculties that are needed to counter it. We should not make the mistake of believing that this only effects stupid, ignorant, or poor educated people. Intellectuals, students, educated and informed people, and other members of the so-called "chattering class" are often the most zealous and dogmatic propagandized individuals, often manipulated without any awareness of it at all, with their access to newspapers, books, movies, and social media.

When the media personality is a propagandist (as most are), she can both agitate the audience by presenting to them explanations of their problems and also satisfy them by presenting a solution to their problems—this both provides catharsis (someone is doing something; someone thinks the same) and reinforces prejudices and the worldview of the target audience. However, this solution is illusionary. All it really offers is further dependency on that media source when the propagandized individual feels satisfied with the propagandist's artificial stimuli, as tension is first created (with the problems) and then reduced (with the solutions), thereby allowing the individual viewer or listener to engage in the political process vicariously and become further alienated from any form of political participation. Everything becomes abstract—a soundbite or symbol—and this functions as a substitute for thought and an intellectual tranquilizer, even when the pundit offers the most outrageous solution that will never be implemented (and therefore offers no solution at all) to what is more often than not a pseudo-problem or a conspiracy theory. Of course this tranquilization will act as a remedy, but only to "problems" deliberately manufactured or exaggerated for the purpose of offering "solutions." This has shown itself to be particularly effective when scapegoating immigrants (or foreigners in general) or heightening the fear of terrorism, thereby allowing the propagandist to wear the mask of patriotism (or nationalism) while simultaneous deceiving and distracting their target audience from the real causes of their problems by offering faux solutions to faux problems. For example, the role of so-called free trade agreements, multinational corporations, outsourcing, interventionism, and the global imposition of neoliberal ideology can all be ignored. The causality of mass immigration from Mexico to the United States, as the result of the destruction of the Mexican economy and its agricultural base, can be ignored all the while simultaneously blaming illegal immigrants and unions for unemployment and the lower wages.

The alienation caused and concealed by propaganda leads to a psychological dissociation between thought and action. The individual thinks without action, and acts without thinking. This results in paranoia and apathy, both of which further removes the propagandized individual into the private realm. Thoughts, doubts, scruples, uncertainties, and criticism all disappear into the private realm and are dissociated from public behavior and discourse. Hence a person can be lead to believe in the existence of an international conspiracy to kill 90% of the world's population and destroy nation states, for which the blame can vary (Jews, Communists, the Illuminati, the uber-rich, or even extraterrestrial lizard men), all the while the propagandized individual still goes to work, uses banks, shops, and acts as if everything is completely normal. The social conditioning generated by propaganda allows this duality between thought and action to continue, leaving the propagandized individual behaving out of habit, and act within the world without thinking, without having any need to reflect or analyze her ideas or thoughts about the world. Life becomes completely partitioned into the mundane (ordinary) on one side and the fantastic (paranoid) on the other. Thus people can become hysterical or deeply paranoid about the control over their government by "the one-percent" or by the oil companies, or how global warming is a hoax perpetuated by the Chinese (or climate scientists), all the while complaining on their iPhone about the price of gas while they fill up the tank of their car. Similarly, one can find numerous examples on social media of people complaining publically that Big Brother is watching their every move on the Internet and will send those who know about it to FEMA camps! They are both being watched and not watched at the same time. The propagandized individual becomes partitioned and fragmented—losing all criticality and self-awareness—and primarily aligned with his group identity and worldview, which does not need to be internally coherent or consistent, and can live entirely within a fact-free environment providing that it is shared by others and confirmed by their favorite media sources. He becomes a spectator of an artificial life, like a ghost haunting someone else. She becomes a mechanized part of the hologram. Self-doubts and questions become either suppressed or relegated to the private realm, cannot be articulated in public, and therefore silenced. The thrill of being "in the know" and in "the circle of truth" dominates over the need for rational thinking and action, and under these conditions it is possible for a person to believe anything at all, just as long as they feel special or insightful for believing it.

In a society wherein work, leisure, behavior, and discourse have become propagandized and mechanized, genuine democratic participation is impossible. The depths of authenticity and reflection required to deliberate, decide, organize, and act as a democratic community (*demos*) in cooperative and free association, simply are lacking. Political participation becomes mechanized, limited to quantifiable methods such as voting, donating, signing petitions, answering poll questions, clicktivism on social media, and declaring an allegiance to a political party (bumper sticker, lawn sign, etc.) become sufficient, and it simply is never asked or even considered whether they have any real or meaningful effects or consequences. That is irrelevant to the speaker. It does not matter whether they are heard. All that matters is their self-expression of allegiance. Reality becomes synonymous with and bounded by their act of self-expression—it becomes total. The subjective and objective become fused together as a unified expression of ego without any regard at all to its consequences. Even a committed campaign worker becomes dissociated from the meaning and purpose of the political process, apart from some vague goal of his side winning and the other side losing, without any concern with the effectiveness of the methods used. And today, few even participate even to that level. Most political participation has been reduced to Tweets and Facebook posts, judged only to the degree that they are shared or receive approval in the forms of "thumbs up." There is no longer any connection between public political participation and the shaping of policy and societal development. While it was always true that most people are mere spectators in the political process, the new methods of social media have concealed that from most people, leading to a mass delusion of political participation and objective meaning.

Of course this has been cultivated deliberately to protect the power and privilege of the ruling elite who own and control mass media, along with almost the total infrastructure (economics) and superstructure (politics) of society, who don't want the masses interfering with the process by which public policy and society are shaped. However, as I have argued elsewhere, this elitism is very damaging for society because it suppresses democracy and reduces the societal stock of available knowledge, skills, experiences, values, and imagination brought to bear to the task of envisioning the future of society.[25] This impedes the capacity of society to adapt to unforeseen consequences and changes in a complex and open-ended world that does not conform to human intentions. This retards the potential of society to adapt to changes in the natural world and our ability to respond to natural disasters

---

[25] Karl Rogers, *Participatory Democracy, Science and Technology* (Palgrave Macmillan, 2008)

and climate change.[26] By reducing the level of inclusion and dimensions of change in society, by reducing the degree of pluralism in the political decision-making process, to only satisfy the interests of the elite, society is not only less able to explore alternative solutions to the problems it faces, but it also is less able to even understand or identify those problems. For example, modern society becomes increasingly unable to explore and understand the need for changes to patterns of consumption and methods of production required to prepare for and deal with the problems of global warming and climate change, and understand those problems and their causes, when the only political and economic dimensions permitted are those that benefit the short-term interests (profits) of the elite. In a mass media culture wherein the media is increasingly owned and controlled by that elite, the level of misinformation and denial about there even being a problem at all becomes quite staggering, especially in a culture in which actually knowing what one is talking about is no longer a prerequisite for having an opinion on any subject. The hologram becomes divorced from reality.

This tends to become most apparent during elections—even though the mass hysteria and hyper-factionalization generated by mass media during elections heightens irrationality and further disables the capacity of people to be aware of media manipulation—due to the corporate dominance over the political system and mass media. The framework of available options of candidates and the content of political debate is strictly limited to those that satisfy the profit-motive of the elite to the extent that the national interest becomes synonymous with the interests of the elite. Anything outside this framework will receive no media coverage whatsoever, or ridiculed as extremist (idealistic, unworkable, impractical, etc.). A heavily propagandized audience will simply parrot those ridicules. When the profit-motive itself becomes the primary obstacle to change, especially among those who receive no share of the profits, the inertia of the system works against change, either concealing the need for change, misrepresenting the situation, or making any deviation from the status quo seem threatening. When the need for change is paramount for the long-term sustainability of the system itself, the short-term interests of the elite work against the long-term interests of everyone, while concealing or distorting those long-term interests; it is at that point that

---

[26] Karl Rogers, *Modern Science and the Capriciousness of Nature* (Palgrave Macmillan, 2006)

a threshold is crossed and the whole system is undermined and driven on a path towards self-destruction. Total collapse becomes inevitable (unless a revolutionary overthrow of the ruling elite permits new options to be considered) when the need for reform is suppressed. However, as I have argued above, one of the main functions of propaganda is to create a dissociation between the worldview of the population and reality itself. The usual outcomes of the dissociation are a divided population, denial, and paralysis, which not only leads to the continuance of the status quo but accelerates the further fragmentation of society towards its total collapse.

The removal of critics of the status quo from the public realm is the best way to preserve the status quo. A privatized population is politically impotent and is readily subjected to a "divide and conquer" strategy should there be any opposition to the policies the benefit the elite. This is also one of the primary effects of "the War on Terror" propaganda: to subjugate the domestic population into conformity to whatever the government declares necessary in the name of "security." The aim of the privatization of politics through narrowcasting is to create a passive population of consumers and workers, organized for the benefit of the elite, wherein the individual is only concerned with their selfish needs and can easily be turned against his neighbors or fellow workers, and by projecting his frustrations and resentments through scapegoating immigrants, unions, or specific minority groups. The response to the increasing divide between the so-called First and Third Worlds is to build a wall. This gives the elite a monopoly over government and a free hand in dividing up the wealth of the nation. The strategy of divide and conquer is particularly effective in an authoritarian society when privatization becomes the spontaneous reaction of the individual when there is disharmony and division within the population. Narrowcasting and propaganda are extremely effective in this situation. The individual retreats into the private realm or only identifies with a specific group. His skepticism towards other individuals or groups becomes justified in her own eyes by *a priori* interpretation of the actions of other groups as suspicious by definition. Whatever "they" do is suspicious, either part of some conspiracy or a lie. It is propaganda that sustains this attitude of suspicion, reinforcing privatization and skepticism, and leaving the government to act however it deems fit. Each citizen is left to care for their own personal happiness and is not given any route of public participation apart from paying taxes, obeying the law, and voting in elections. For most citizens, they have the same spectator relation with politics as they do with sports: they root for their team.

It is for this reason that there has always been a close connection between propaganda and ideology; in this way, ideology receives its intellectual justification among its adherents and becomes established as truth. Furthermore, this compels its adherents to propagandize and proselytize, and through propaganda, ideology is disseminated as a Shibboleth and symbol of "correct thinking." Due to the dominance of means over ends in modern society, narrowcasted propaganda has become an autonomous mechanism for the domination of a particular ideology over the framework of political discourse and debate. The individual is transformed into a partisan propagandee, and then into a propagandist, a conduit, and remains oblivious to the fact that they are a disseminator of propaganda. The professional propagandist becomes a specialist and understands themselves as being a propagandist only through professionalized industries of public relations and advertising, and even then only are dimly aware of the ideological dimensions of this. The end result is that the task of disseminating information becomes one of uniting people under an ideology. Narrowcasted media is self-represented as "the marketplace of ideas" and "the free press." Once the dominant aim becomes one of power, achieved through securing ideology into the framework of public discourse and debate, thereby transforming political speech into an instrument of propaganda, the content of ideology and its meaning are both empty and open to manipulation depending on the needs of the propagandist. Consistency and coherence are of secondary importance to the technical challenges and tasks of enrollment of people into the task of the dissemination of propaganda. It is even irrelevant whether the propagandist believes in their ideology or not, whether it is true or false, or whether it even makes any sense at all. All that matters is that propaganda is disseminated to a narrowcasted population. This results in free speech being dissolved into the project of disseminating propaganda to the extent that propaganda is indistinguishable from free speech in the minds of propagandists and propagandees alike. It simply becomes a matter of its reinforcement of the psychological need for its reinforcement. It is a vicious circle of addiction, as slogans, myths, and sentiments become grafted on to public discourse and debate, regardless of whether the content involves politics, economics, or celebrity gossip, as the focus of the individual becomes on of self-identification with a group, the reinforcement of their own sense of self-righteousness, and the intensification of public outrage and contempt, which flits from issue to issue, all with good conscience in its own truth, without any real understanding of its content, meaning, logic, evidential justification, or truth.

Inconsistency and incoherence generate the kind of mental confusion that is not only the product of propaganda, but intensifies the level of irrationality to the point of creating mass dependency on propaganda. Propaganda becomes a good in itself. This results in public discourse and debate not only degenerating into slogans (of the sort that one can see on Twitter or Facebook), without any real regard for their implications and meaning, and reducing the perception of reality to one of myth, but it results in the atomistic fragmentation of public debate. Ultimately, political discourse and debate has no more meaning or significance that the croaks of bullfrogs in a swamp. Evocative of emotions, "free speech" itself becomes nothing more than a series of affirmations of allegiances, without having any meaning outside of this. The number of likes or shares is the only meaning given to any slogan, and each and every slogan can become interchangeable or replaceable without any consequence at all. This invokes conditional responses in the same way that Pavlov's famous bell caused a dog to salivate, but without any prospect of feeding to follow, simply because the aim has become one of ringing the bell for other people in response to the bell being rung for oneself. The dissemination of propaganda becomes its own reward. The individual no longer consciously acts within the framework of a well-understood ideology, but only from the impulse to share propaganda and receive group reinforcement for doing so. The individual remains completely ignorant of the social and psychological factors at play in the ideologies, doctrines, and beliefs that underwrite the truth of the propaganda they disseminate. Anything not involving propaganda is simply not taken seriously because it has no social or psychological value for satisfying an intensification and reinforcement of belonging to a group mentality. Ideological critiques of public policy or new proposals no longer invoke any response at all, until they are reduced to a clever slogan or sound-bite that can be shared and disseminated. In the face of modern propaganda, public intellectuals are completely ineffective and ignored, even in the face of ongoing genocide, torture, and the gross violation of rights.

180

This can also be seen with the use of religion as a propaganda tool. No longer are the teachings and tenets of the religion meaningful at all, except when used to provide slogans, myths, and justifications for the propagandist. It is irrelevant, for example, what Jesus would do, when politicians invoke Christianity as a justification for public policy; just as it is not relevant what Darwin said in his theory of evolution when politicians denounce it. It is tempting to see the irony of these politicians, who denounce evolution and affirm Christianity, as they simultaneously declare themselves to be Christians and call for public policies based on eugenics, social Darwinism, and the harshest treatment of the poor, sick, disabled, elderly, and vulnerable. Yet, there is no real irony here at all; it is a consequence of the domination of propaganda as the means to disseminate those policies and their justification. Hence it becomes possible for even the most fundamentalist evangelical Christian in America, once they have been politically propagandized, to see no contradiction in militarism and austerity policies and the teachings and words of Jesus of Nazareth. Of course this is hypocrisy, pure and simple, and within the terms of their own faith a consequence of Satan, but it is also a direct consequence of the erosive effect of propaganda on the individual mind; they no longer have any demand for consistency or coherence in their worldview, as their mind has become partitioned and irrational due to the influence of propaganda, and they are consequently incapable to integrating their religious beliefs with their political ones, and feel no need to do so. The same is as true of leftist political ideology as it is for religious doctrine. When propaganda uses leftist ideology it erodes it and makes it devoid of any meaningful content. This can be seen in the Leninist (and later Stalinist) use of Marx and Marxist ideology in its propaganda, ultimately reversing and contradicting itself, at every turn, with only a concern with the political expediency of the message of the day and the justification of the infallibility of the communist leadership. Black is white, up is down, and left is right; the language of dialectics was used both to mystify, conceal, and inoculate party propaganda against all possible criticism and analysis. Western Marxist critics of the Soviet Union, such as Chambre, de Lefèvre, and Lukács, have discussed this at great length. Lukács termed this erosion of doctrine by propaganda as "evisceration." Propaganda ultimately replaces doctrine and ideology with itself, and it can be anything at all, and it becomes quite impossible to establish any solid and logical foundation for political discourse. What is viewed as an absolute or self-evident truth yesterday, especially the axiomatic assumptions of political theory, tomorrow are considered to be nothing other than a lie spread by the enemy or counter-revolutionary reactionaries. George Orwell made this point very well in his novels *Animal Farm* and *1984*. Ideology is an instrument for propaganda, not the other way around, as the content of ideology is completely replaceable and contingent on the needs of the propagandist and the party.

"We already know well that the methods of the totalitarian states have gained footholds in the democracies. Police regimes, internment camps, and uncontrolled, all-powerful administration, systematic elimination of dissenting opinions and minorities are some of the signs that, on the level of public opinion stereotypes such as 'the course of history' (which is only ideological camouflage for the autonomy of political affairs), 'things are as they are,' or 'work means freedom,' or 'laws spring from necessity' have been accepted." (Ellul, p. 89)

As Schumpeter argued, the stability and efficiency of "the democratic method" are the paramount consideration, which shows that for him politics was not only autonomous from moral or ideological considerations, but that *should be* autonomous. Again, this is not to say that politicians and citizens will not invoke morality, but that invocation is itself a justificatory construct rather than a motivation. While the administrative and operational spheres of political action have become autonomous—within which the bureaucrat and politician are functionaries and have no real decision making power—politics itself has become little more than superficial theater, designed and performed to present the illusion of public consent and being responsive to public opinion. Politics is a charade; operational through mass media distraction. In this respect, propaganda is no longer directed with the aim of manipulating and controlling public opinion, but instead is directed and coordinated towards presenting the illusion that public opinion *matters*. The media framing of talking points and sloganeering is simply reproduced to provide content and present the illusion that there is any kind of public debate. Of course the reality is that there is none at all. The individual is conditioned, through narrowcasting and rubber-stamping, to feel satisfaction and catharsis through group-identity while simultaneously becoming inoculated and quite oblivious to any other opinions and worldviews. This understanding of other opinions and worldviews is itself a simulacrum—a straw man—that is fed to him through narrowcasted media in such a way that he feels superior and vindicated as an *a priori* and armed with "off-the-rack" responses to the talking points of *them* as presented to him through narrowcasted media. At no point does she enter into any conversation with anyone, except those who already agree with her and are members of the same social group, political party, religion, class, etc. Here we see that the task of contemporary propaganda is not to manipulate and control public opinion, but rather to prevent it happening at all. Rubber-stamping and sloganeering function as means by which opinion can be repressed—driven into the silence of the private realm—while presenting the illusion of political competition, free speech, and media diversity. It simply does not matter what the individual thinks and says, providing the individual does not know that. The individual is left with the choice of either conforming to the utterances of the group—itself little more than consolatory bleating and indignant barking—or remaining silent and alone with his questions, concerns, and doubts.

In this situation, with the autonomy or political action coexisting with the theater of politics, both "the general will" and "sovereignty" or "the people" are myths—themselves useful only to propagandists—and "democracy" simply does not exist (except within rubber-stamps or slogans). The masses are kept distracted and placated, especially when they are most polarized and agitated, by participating fully in the pantomime of political theater; while not even knowing how to begin to involve themselves in political action, and definitely being unable *to interfere* with the work of bureaucrats and politicians to better integrate public policy with the needs and operations of corporations, big business, and moneyed interests. Both TTIP and TTP are examples of how media silence, concealed by distractions such as "the War on Christmas" or "twerking" pop stars, co-exists with the operations of corporate-government partnerships behind closed doors. Politicians themselves are either complicit in these operations or participate in utterly irrelevant political theater. When Ellul wrote,

"Now that the masses have entered political life and express themselves through what can be called public opinion, there can no longer be any questions of either pushing the masses out of political life or of governing against public opinion. This particular piece of evidence must be our point of departure if we want to understand the profound political transformation wrought by propaganda." (Ellul, p.97)

he remained under the spell of Bernays' model of modern propaganda as a means of manipulating public opinion and manufacturing consent. Propaganda has undergone a profound transformation itself since the mid-twentieth century. It is now the means by which the masses can be distracted from political action by presenting them with a simulacrum (a puppet show) of political life, complete with heroes, villains, conspiracies, plots, twists and turns, and the enduring promise of change and freedom. Governing does not occur against public opinion or by manipulating it. Governing occurs without any regard for public opinion at all.

None of the above is meant to imply that mass media does not provide people with facts. It does. But it is how it provides those facts that is of importance. It provides them in a piecemeal and isolated fashion; avoiding any analysis of either the historical conditions for those facts or how those facts are interconnected. It is for this reason that Saddam Hussein was a friend of the United States in the 1980s—reported as a matter of fact—and in the 1990s he was an enemy—also reported as a matter of fact. Once the latter fact was currency, the former fact was forgotten. There was no discussion or analysis of how this change occurred. Nor was there any discussion or analysis of the connections between the Bush Administration, the oil companies, and arms manufacturers, and their involvement in arming the Hussein regime. There was no discussion or analysis how this "new Hitler" had come to power and was supported by American money, arms, and intelligence. There was no discussion or analysis of America's involvement during the Iraq-Iran war. The Iranian distrust of the U.S. is inexplicable—expect they must "hate our way of life." And, despite presenting the fact that the Hussein regime used chemical weapons against the Kurdish people, itself presented as a justification for U.S. intervention, there was no discussion or analysis of how the Hussein regime obtained those weapons in the first place, even though it was a fact during the 1980s that the Iraqi military used chemical weapons during the Iraq-Iran war. These weapons had undoubtedly been provided by the United States.

How does mass media achieve this forgetfulness regarding the facts? It achieves this in two ways: (1) shifting the focus of public attention; (2) providing a new set of rubber-stamps for use in forming and presenting opinions within social groups. Knowledge becomes divorced from experience—despite the repeated juxtaposition of certain facts and images on the TV news—and transformed into an abstract and general character, which can be presented and disseminated as a meme, a headline, or a slogan, all truncated enough to fit in the space of a news headline or slogan on a t-shirt, or in a pithy and sharp Tweet. In this way, the audience can absorb this fact, make it their own, and use it to display themselves as someone *in the know*—an informed person—and ally themselves with likeminded others. Older facts or facts that don't fit with the contemporary narrative can simply be discarded and forgotten like unfashionable clothing or tunes. It is naïve to accept the facts presented by media at face value. All media sources select, interpret, and spin the facts in accordance with their agenda. The facts, as presented by media, are those facts that the owners of media want to see presented and they are the facts that the consumers of media want to receive. Facts are selected in accordance with their propaganda-value by both propagandist and propagandees. Undesirable facts can both be ignored and dismissed "as propaganda" by those people who are already preconditioned by propaganda and narrowcasted media to accept only those facts that reinforce their prejudices and worldview. Today, they are denounced as "fake news." As Ellul put it, "Testimony by those who have experienced the fact can neither prevail on public opinion, nor form or inform it, for these individuals do not control the means of communication." (pp. 100-1) Facts are only accepted as facts when they support the *a priori* convictions or those already predisposed towards believing them. "The fact then has no existence except through a system of predetermined references that affirm it as facts, or deny existing facts because they do not square with predetermined existence." (p. 102) It is important to realize that even the most informed reader or viewer simply cannot confirm the facts as presented to her by modern media. How can the reader of newspapers and Internet blogs hope to confirm or refute the allegations made about NSA spying us? As made by whistle blowers like Edward Snowden? How can the public evaluate whether these revelations are genuine or whether they are misinformation? Quite simply, we can't. One would need to be an NSA insider to confirm or refute these allegations.

It is for this reason that *even if all the facts were presented to the public via Internet*, only those facts acceptable to their receivers would be accepted as facts, which again would result in a balkanized, factionalized media wherein narrowcasting and rubber-stamping are the norms. Taking the above into account, we can see that even if the Internet remains a publically accessible network for the dissemination of information, this would not be sufficient for the development of an informed and democratic public. What would be required is that the public *already* has a democratic attitude: valuing communication as a means of learning from others (especially those with different experiences and backgrounds) to learn how to understand and solve common problems and shared matters of concern. This is not a technological problem; it is a pedagogical problem. The irrationality of public discourse, itself intensified by narrowcasted mass media propaganda, is one of the primary obstacles to democracy. Of course we must not forget that there are anti-democratic forces at work to undermine and prevent the possibility of democracy, but we need to acknowledge the extent that "the public" has become fragmented and incapable of democratic participation in communicating public problems and coming together to solve them. While education remains the main method to democratize the public, it needs to be acknowledged that mass media propaganda and anti-democratic forces have successfully undermined public education and attempts to awaken an enlightened citizenry capable of critical thinking, autonomy, and corporative community organization. Most citizens either conform to indoctrinated patterns of consumptions, or to the prevailing narrative of their political party, or they are isolated and alienated from the political process completely. This has been deliberately achieved in order to perceive the status quo and the privileges of the ruling elite. We need to address the facts that propaganda (1) has become dominant mode of mediation between people; (2) has become all-pervasive throughout mass media; (3) fulfils psychological needs and is required by the public before any political action is possible. Tempting as it is to see counterpropaganda made with good intentions as being the solution here, nothing could be further from the truth. The use of counterpropaganda intensifies public irrationality, regardless of the intentions of the propagandist, and therefore the use of propaganda cannot counter its effects. It can only intensify them.

The argument presented above is that the individual will tend to grant or deny truth status to any fact if it accords with his political opinions, prejudices, and worldview. Furthermore, in newspapers, television punditry, and blogs the facts are presented in narratives interweaved with interpretations, assumptions, and assertions, often without any substantive political-economic analysis or sources, or placing them within historical context, so how is the reader or viewer to ascertain the facts? She is either forced into the role of sceptic, or compelled to rely on trust or faith. The former throws the reader or viewer into a state of sophisticated self-importance and ignorance; the latter leaves the reader or viewer open to media narrowcasting and propaganda.

"... the informed man's beliefs are fruits of anterior propaganda which creates the prejudice that make people accept or reject information. When a prejudice is established and the stereotypes will set, when a mental pattern exists, facts are put into their places accordingly and cannot, by themselves, change anything." (Ellul, p. 111)

Any facts that contradict these prejudices will be ignored or dismissed as propaganda or lies. Political problems, how they are evaluated (selected and interpreted) and prioritized must be understood psychologically. Distracted from the facts of experience the citizen only receives distortion. Substitution of an imaginary universe for lined world of experience—everything translated into slogans and images. Disconnected from the real world the propagandized citizen inhabits virtual world or hologram. An illusionary universe.

"Man caught in a web of press, cinema, and radio can no longer differentiate between what is of personal concern to him and what exists in society outside of himself or, in the category of facts, what is real and what is not. These astonishing media, particularly radio, render the most distant and disparate events immediate and contemporary. At the moment a speaker speaks, or an event takes place, the listener is witness. The whole faith is no longer anything but one point at which everything is within reach. Prime is no longer anything but an indefinite extension of 'now' for the listener. Radio and the press—just consider the excitement of the public over the 'latest edition'—synchronize the varying lengths of events and lives." (Ellul, pp. 114-15)

Once truth becomes politicized and personalized, as a mark of individual identity and expression in relation to the social group, as a statement of belonging and sharing common prejudices and a worldview, propaganda becomes the creator of almost all political problems. There is hardly a current political problem that was not originally created by propaganda; at least not in the sense that it exists objectively by itself. Most political problems become viable "problems" only when propaganda creates their "solution." Politicians sell "the problems" for which they already have "the solutions" in order to create a demand for "the solutions" that the politicians can satisfy, and use narrowcasted media channels to promote those solutions. Propaganda creates crises and "a crisis" provides opportunities for politicians to provide "solutions" and push the agenda (or the agenda of their party or paymasters). Selected and interpreted facts are disseminated by mass media by "experts." Propaganda is used to form public opinions about those facts by giving ready-made interpretations and implications. Media "debates" and "discussions" are framed so that only permissible "discussions" form the poles of "debate." Talking points and rubber-stamps are established and disseminated as the options people can be "for" or "against." It is thereafter possible for politicians and media pundits to sell "the problems" to their target demographic, who in turn will seize upon them, in the light of the facts and their opinions, to divide themselves into opposing political camps, each of which demands a particular "solution" or set of "solutions" to "the crisis" at hand. This is reinforced by mass media politicians and pundits selling these "solutions" in "response" to "the crisis," thereby presenting *the illusion* that they are responding to public demand and some objectivity real state of affairs. At this stage, a fragmented and narrowcasted public can argue among themselves, thereby reinforcing those talking points and rubber-stamps, and creating a stock of momentary concerns, emotional responses, and demands.

One can establish anything at all within propagandized social groups via political ideologies and theories, and even the once cherished tenets of religion, are expendable, revisable, and replaceable, even with their opposite, and can be used to justify anything. When everything is reduced to rubber-stamps and the message of the day; individuals continually reinforce their group identity through those ever-changing opinions and messages, without any regard to how they have changed or what they once were, what they mean, or whether they are true. Everything is in flux and the individual simply attunes to that flux. Of course, this has a profound impact on how "democracy" operates in society. Political views and positions are not the outcome of rational public debate and deliberation, the product of a balanced examination of the evidence and its interpretation and explanation; instead, they are the outcomes of the organization of groups and the reinforcement of group identity and the politics of contempt, by satisfying the psychological needs of belonging, certainty, and self-justification, all through narrowcasted media. When individual "citizens" are subjected to propaganda in the context of narrowcasting, rational communication and public discourse are not even possible. Not only is there no rational communication whatsoever between political opponents and dissenters, but self-examination and reflection are also completely absent. The possibility of an enlightened *demos* is quite impossible, once it has been replaced by propagandized and partisan groups incapable of any thought except reactionary utterances, repetition, and rubber-stamping. The ideals of the *polis* have been replaced by cable TV, talk radio, Facebook, and Twitter. Thumbs up, press the share button, move on.

This is not even mere self-assertion, as there is no longer any self. Political speech has become nothing other than the utterance of group identity through the dissemination of shared propaganda. Empty of logic or truth, both of which are utterly irrelevant, political speech has less meaning than the croaking of amphibians, which at least has some significance for mating and reproduction of the species. Furthermore, there is no longer any intention behind the relation between propagandist and propagandee, as both are interchangeable disseminators of propaganda, without any awareness of the propaganda they disseminate. It is merely the dissemination and repetition of slogans, sound-bites, and clever associations, without any regard to their truth value or status. Group identity is now the standard by which the value of all and any utterances are to be judged. There is no negotiation and exchange of meanings. Thus mass media (especially the Internet) has become the substance and foundation of how "communication" has become structured and disseminated throughout modern society. The outcomes of modern "communication" are the same in any mass society: identity, catharsis, and conformity. This has been well known for over half a century.[27] Taking all this into account shows that it no longer makes any sense to talk about private or subjective opinions. There is no connection between the private realm of thought and the public realm of speech. There are merely opinions that the individual affirms or rejects based on which social group utters them. "We" are always right, "they" are always wrong. This is not to suggest that individuals do not have private thoughts, beliefs, or opinions; it highlights the extent that all such private thoughts remain unexpressed and unarticulated even in private thought. They are nothing other than vague feelings or impressions that cannot be expressed or clearly reflected on until they are put into the framework of public speech, in its terms, and using its structures. The expression and articulation of private thoughts is not only transformed by this framework, but it anything that does not conform to the certainties and opinions of the group must be repressed and silenced, relegated to the realm of vague dissatisfaction and inexpressible dissent. In this way, propaganda alienates the individual from themselves most of all,

---

[27] See Leonard W. Doob *Public Opinion and Propaganda* (New York: Henry Holt, 1948), chapter 5.

concealing that alienation under the mask of group identity, certainty, and permissible opinions. Through this alienation, convictions become rubber-stamped into statements of group-identity and belonging; ideas are transformed into stereotypes and archetypes, talking points, stock questions and their associated answers, and endless self-justifications to deal with contradictions and inconsistences, if the individual is aware of them at all. Thought becomes impossible. The simplification of problems, the dramatization of crises, and the demonization of others, accompanied by the reinforcement of the factionalization of society into propagandized groups, intensifies the irrationality of society to the point where democracy is impossible and illusionary. Politics itself becomes negated—possibly to the point of civil war and the descent into barbarism—and consumptive of its own self-negation in the form of social media entertainment. Such a society is not only characterized by its shallowness and inauthenticity. It is completely irrational and amoral, fragmented and disorganized, and doomed to collapse.

Whereas the rational society (as an imaginary ideal) is one that tends towards universal solidarity, political equality, and democratic inclusion, the irrational society tends towards factionalization, political inequality, and alienation, with all its pathological consequences, such as alcoholism and drug addiction, fetishism and consumerism, child abuse and domestic violence, criminality, sexual perversion, suicidal tendencies, animal abuse, etc. In the irrational society, which should not be equated with anarchism, the individual is suppressed almost to the point of complete negation (and in many cases actual suicide) and identifies completely with the norms and values of a highly hierarchical and authoritarian society. Thinking is reduced to dogma and its reproduction, and freedom is equated with power and its rewards for conformity. The irrational society—regardless of its pretensions to progress via technology—remains a feudal, superstitious, and brutal collection of struggling and competing social groups, be they clans, families, tribes, religions, political parties, or corporations, that are possessed with "magical thinking" and absolutely intolerant of any group identity apart from their own. In this respect, propaganda should be viewed as the means by which people are themselves dis-organized into the irrationalization of society, and the descent into stupidity and barbarism. At the same time as the illusions of global communication and the information age arise, society divides into baying and hysterical packs demonizing each other and glorifying themselves, each only identifying itself in terms of not being the other, obsessed with identity, without having any coherent or consistent philosophical understanding of their identity and what it means. Without any concern for the future of society, beyond some vague sense that it has all gone wrong (due to "them," whoever that might be), without any vision or notion of that future, driven entirely by kitsch and myth, certain in their own self-justification and self-righteousness, all the while society tended towards nothing at all. Mass nihilism and the intellectual promiscuity of relativism are the inevitable result of this erosion of civilization and descent into barbarism and collapse. This Bedlam—this mass asylum society—is beyond hope, beyond redemption, due to its addiction to the very same forces that cause its madness. The situation has become hopeless and quite desperate for genuine democracy and the future of humanity. Meanwhile, through the operations of propaganda, hatred, racism, misogyny, and fanaticism have intensified in direct proportion to the extent of narrowcasting mass media, especially social media, and mass alienation from politics. Random and otherwise inexplicable acts of violence, cruelty, depravity, and stupidity become commonplace as acts of propaganda by the deed (such as rioting, mass shootings, terrorism). Leaders become mere conduits of propaganda and foci for group identity; unquestioning loyalty to the leader (even in the face of the leader's own exposed immorality and hypocrisy) becomes intensified within a cult of personality and infallibility, even when the leader's own words and actions are diametrically opposed, and yet remain seen as confirming one another, as if by definition the determination of the leader's genius and strategic foresight should always be deferred to some (never reached) future wherein it will always be confirmed.

If there is any merit to what I have said above, we can see that in a propagandized society, all critical faculties are eroded and lost, or even treated with outright hostility as suspect (and possibly criminal), and "the free press" is itself a myth. Once political action becomes mass factionalization, wherein group identity is only secured (rubber-stamped) through propaganda, then all political participation becomes utterly dependent on propaganda. A vicious circle of dependency is established, which further drives society into irrationality, leading to the further degeneration of society into a series of crises, and further eroding the capabilities of society to respond to those crises, except by intensifying them. State terrorism and its justification becomes the response to terrorism, and any resistance to the state is by definition an act of terrorism. Further environmental destruction becomes the normal response to the scarcity generated by environmental destruction. Further borrowing and spending becomes the only possible government response to debt and inflation, whereas even austerity policies and the rollback of social services and provisions, must be accompanied by a massive increase in the industrial military complex and its inextricable relations with government. War becomes the means to peace—requiring greater commitments to new and never-ending wars. The militarization of the police and prison complexes becomes the means to justice—all despite causing and intensifying mass social unrest and dissent. Propaganda becomes the means to democratic truth and participation—all despite making all communication and democracy quite impossible. There is always some "enemy" or "opposition" against which the leader's followers will always rally against; they will even compete with each other to outdo each other's hostility and irrationality, where any indication of impartiality or critical thinking is itself indicative of treason. Divisions, enemies, and opposition all become the eternal "them" against which propaganda can operate as a means of social cohesion and identity within the group. Social degeneration and collapse become inevitable.

Narrowcasted propaganda is most pernicious for democracy when it is disguised as news and investigative journalism—as the free press. Under the guise of the free press, its propagation intensifies irrationality and conformity, suppressing the critical faculties and rational communication of propagandized people, which are the very same faculties that are essential for democracy. Without these faculties, democracy is impossible. Counterfeit news (and clickbait headlines) create a pseudo-free press, whereby a simulacrum of free speech presents the illusion of a politically vigilant and critical free press. It does not matter how seemingly critical any media source is of the government if its content is based on propaganda and falsehoods, as it ultimately will have no effect whatsoever. It is *faux* news. This merely feeds the anti-government sentiments of its target audience, giving them a sense of catharsis, but, by misrepresenting the workings of the government, it conceals them and distracts people away from the means by which they could effectively oppose the government and change it. The target audience simply becomes further alienated from government, from even the possibility of good government and how to achieve it, and disengages them from the political process altogether. Beyond affirming rubber-stamps and slogans, such an audience either retreats into the private realm or participates in absurdity or theater, disillusioning themselves with the belief that they are actually participating in political action, when their actions will have no effect whatsoever, if we understand political action as directed towards changing peoples' minds, negotiating solutions to shared problems, making government accountable and representative, and discovering common values and concerns among people of different political persuasions. Spectator politics, absurdity and theater, and astroturf movements, largely comprised of staged rallies and protests, accompanied by costume wearing, flag waving, and (misspelled) slogans on placards achieves absolutely nothing, except allowing further media distractions. People may appear to be political mobilized and active, but it is more akin to a religious cult, wherein the individual submits to group identity and becomes pacified by it. Pathos replaces politics. Under these circumstances, with propaganda designed to maintain an irrational and divided population, as well as suppress new ideas and genuine alternatives, the population is distracted by artificial issues and is increasingly out of touch with reality. This seriously damages the political process and the mental health of society, if society can be said to have such a thing, and the ability of society to adapt to changes and complexities. Combined with an erosion of public education and the middle class, as the corporate takeover shifts its strategy to outsourcing to China and the Third World (first in production, second in marketing and information technology, and third in consumption), as well as asset stripping and reducing the taxation burden in America, plundering both the natural world and the treasury without regard for consequences. This will inevitably result the collapse of America into barbarism (and possibly civil war) under an increasingly authoritarian and terroristic fascist state, which will resort to violence under the guise of "emergency measures" by suppressing democratic movements, unrest, popular protests, and opposition voices.

The solution only lies in the development and dissemination of enlightened critical thinking through education and philosophical self-examination. Communication requires dialog and social dialectics in which people can change and develop (transform, evolve, shift) their understanding of each other and the shared world in which we all live. It is only on this foundation that democracy is possible. How this can be achieved? Is it too late? Are we doomed? What can be done to overcome narrowcasting? How can we counter propaganda?

Propaganda and Counterpropaganda:

Arguably, one of the greatest propaganda achievements of the C20th was the turning of the working class against unions and organized labor. The ability to create hostility within the working class towards "socialism" and even "the working class" itself, generating a set of prejudices and worldview in opposition to the class-interests of the working class in favor of the class-interests of capitalists. This demonstrates the power of propaganda and mass media ownership. It would be nigh on impossible to reverse 'head-on' this by using counterpropaganda. Instead, the counter-propagandist has two alternatives: (1) avoid the terms and language of "socialism," "unionization," and "class," all of which will invoke suspicion and resistance, and all the rubberstamp responses, and instead use neutral or unfamiliar terms, such as "free association" or "organization;" (2) use the nationalistic rubberstamps to generate a predictable reaction against neoliberalism and corporate outsourcing, to generate a sense of solidarity amongst American workers and support for products "Made in America," for "protectionism" and trade tariffs, and for "putting Americans first." However, counterpropaganda has its limits and undesirable results. The use of counterpropaganda can result in reinforcing divisions and irrationality within society, further intensifying the factionalization and narrowcasting on the population, and can result in psychological civil warfare. This is likely to lead to unpredictable results (including the possibilities of increased violence and even actual civil warfare) and also the projection of hostilities and resentments (scapegoating) along racial and gender lines, or towards minority groups (such as homosexuals) or immigrants, or the rise of populist movements and demagogues. It is also worth reminding the reader that, in America, religion has been successfully used by propaganda to create a partition between thought and action, and a counterpropaganda campaign against religion is doomed to failure, at best, and is more likely to result in an intensification of the sense of persecution (regardless of the reality) among the targeted religious groups, which will result in an intensification of their group identity and resistance towards outside influences. Counterpropaganda is little more than agitation propaganda.

In this kind of propaganda-led media environment (heavily narrowcasted and oppositional) within which a divided and irrational population ignore all facts or interpretations that do not match their rubber-stamps or talking points, and do not reinforce their prejudices and worldview (let alone challenge them!), it is possible to feed the public deliberate lies and fabrications if they reinforce prejudices and already accepted "truths."

"Let us take incidents in conjunction with a strike, reported only by one newspaper. Irrefutable (but invented) testimony is presented in its columns because the labor press cannot possibly prove the opposite, it will seek and excuse the fact—and it certainly is amazing to see a debate arise over the interpretation of a non-existent fact. If, after long examination, it is found that the fact does not exist, the public is in no way affected by the reaction; it has forgotten the fact, but has retained a general impression of the affair and the debate." (Ellul, p. 123)

Information fragmentation and inoculation are both the main consequences of narrowcasting; total disruption of the possibility of democracy once communication between people of different experiences and worldviews becomes impossible. The attempt to counter propaganda with counterpropaganda is doomed to failure. Propaganda and counterpropaganda do not cancel each other out, except by generating a high degree of agnosticism regarding the facts among some intellectuals, or increase the level of public apathy or cynicism; the tendency being that of creating and reinforcing entrenched oppositional positions that divide the general population against each other, each camp irrationally asserting the self-evident correctness of its own position and the self-evident incorrectness (or idiocy) of those in the opposing camp. As Ellul put it,

"We accept some statements not because we have by experience learned that they are true, but because they correspondent to our prejudices, our milieu, and so on (all the irrational factors that determine public opinions), or because one propaganda was superior to the other." (Ellul, p. 121)

Politics becomes the reinforcement, dissemination, and manipulation of illusions; a parasitical feeding upon the irrationality of mass society via propaganda, which acts as a substitute for reality. All political action in the public sphere is distraction and deception, with the aim of dissipating public energies and dividing people against each other, thereby leaving the public incoherent, divided, and impotent. Attempts to use counterpropaganda to directly challenge the prejudices and worldview of a narrowcasted audience will be dismissed as propaganda or respond to with hostility, and will only be received by a narrowcasted audience that is already predisposed to accept it.

However, all is not lost for the counter-propagandist. Due to the partition between thought and action created by pre-propaganda (education) and reinforced by (narrowcasted) propaganda, a person may act in ways that contradict their prejudices and worldview without knowing they are doing so. While counterpropaganda cannot change prejudices and worldviews, it still, if properly designed not to challenge myths, can motivate action or (non-)action in ways that contradict them. By avoiding specific rubber-stamps or any terms (or slogans) that trigger prejudicial responses, perhaps even developing a whole new terminology, or even using the affirmed rubber-stamps of the target group, it is possible to gain their support for a particular course of action. As Ellul put it,

"Propaganda cannot create something out of nothing. It must attach itself to a feeling, and idea; it must build on a foundation already present in the individual. The conditioned reflex can be established only on an innate reflex or a prior conditioned reflex. The myth does not expand helter-skelter; it must respond to a group of spontaneous beliefs. Action cannot be obtained unless it responds to a group of already established tendencies or attitudes stemming from the schools, the environment, the regime, the churches, and so on." (p. 36)

This is true, in the most part. However, as a result of sustained exposure to propaganda, a juxtaposition and cultural connection between previously unrelated values, ideas, representations, norms, or myths is created. The Nazi propaganda machine was able to juxtapose and connect the already existing anti-Semitism and cultural malaise of post-First World War Germany with its myths of the International Jewish Conspiracy and traditional German identity, and it was on those abstractions that it was able to advance the myth of the Aryan Master Race. Similarly, the contemporary Republican propaganda machine in the United States is able to juxtapose and connect traditional conservative values of Christian, nationalistic, and white Americans with its myths of the free market and American exceptionalism, just as the Democratic Party is able to advance its propaganda on the abstractions of equality and social justice to juxtapose and connect different minority groups, women's rights, environmentalists, progressives, liberals, and unions. Just as the traditional values of family, rugged individualism, and self-reliance are translated into corporatism and militarism, and racism, xenophobia, and bigotry can be represented as nationalism, so can they also be translated into respect for equality under the law, religious freedom, and freedom of speech, conservation, and an opposition to crony capitalism. Just as the cultural failures and erosion of traditional conservative values and institutions can be translated, via sustained propaganda, into the consequences of a mythical conspiracy by liberals, feminists, communists, and atheists to destroy America, so they can also be translated into a respect for constitutionality, American workers, and against political corruption. Propaganda creates the translation between already existing worldviews and a mythical explanation for society's problems and how to solve them, so, by avoiding trigger-words and symbols, can counterpropaganda of integration (rather than agitation) change the actions and concerns of its target demographic. Thus, sustained counterpropaganda can create new behavior by creating the means to translate from the old to the new, thereby reinforcing the old in terms of the new, even though the target populations have not changed their worldviews.

The ability to create this translation depends on the knowledge of psychological mechanisms and how to manipulate them. The counter-propagandist will play on fears and pride, for example, to create self-justifications and explanations that both reinforce those fears and sense of pride and also facilitate their projection onto a specific group of others. The counter-propagandist thereby connects the propagandee's own sense of identity with those self-justifications and explanations of the reasons for the way of the world to get the individual to change their course of action Once the propagandee identifies with the counterpropaganda, it can be refined and developed into an intellectualization of both the self and the world, thereby allowing the propagandee to translate their already existing beliefs and values in terms of whatever ideology and worldview the counter-propagandist is promoting. This can lead to a shift to a new worldview. The actual means of translation are themselves arbitrary and the connections between the old and new worldviews are irrational and without any logical foundation, but the transition has been made nonetheless. Hence, like propaganda, counterpropaganda requires constant reinforcement, via all-pervasive cultural repetition and mass media domination, and the rubber-stamps of group identification and membership.

One of the major consequences of narrowcasting is that the partisan selection of information through the lens of whether or not it reinforces one's prejudice and worldview, allowing the individual to affirm the information that does and reject the information that does not, and this results in an intensification of irrationality and the inability to see obvious contradictions in the worldview one is buying into. Instead of recognizing and reaching these contradictions, the narrowcasted audience cherry-picks from a clothes-line of news stories, punditry, opinions, and slogans, without questioning them and thinking-through their implications for the consistency of their worldview. In short, people believe what they want to believe, regardless of whether any particular belief they hold contradicts other beliefs they hold. It is this intellectual partitioning and fragmentation that results in an irrational mentality and cultural schizophrenia. Mass media audiences have succumbed to an ideological "culture war" within which they identify with their narrowcasting sources and the assembly-line of propaganda those sources provide. Not only is any critical relation to these sources suspended, providing that they continue to reinforce the prejudices and worldview of the target audience, but the whole intellectual relation to media and information is mystified. The narrowcasted individual offers no mental resistance to becoming a conduit for mass media propaganda, and, by being so, disseminates it among their peers as an expression of their group identity, and further reinforce it as truth. This leaves the target audience lost within a pseudo-reality of myths and wishful-thinking, opposed to anyone and anything that threatens their truths, and utterly incapable of developing the intellectual and critical skills to comprehend reality and deal with the inconsistencies and contradictions in their worldview. Counterpropaganda will not resolve this portioning (as it too feeds on it) and cannot be used to overcome narrowcasting.

Hence, instead of merely offering counterpropaganda or information that opposes or challenges the propaganda or information offered by others, we need to offer an alternative pedagogical means of analyzing media sources, comprehending the complex relations between sources and information, and creating a new political economy of mass media to oppose the hegemony of corporate domination, narrowcasting, and propaganda-driven consumerism. This requires a new paradigm of mass communication. We need to give people the tools to question and challenge mass media propaganda, alongside the tools to articulate and comprehend their own reality and truths, that works from within any worldview they already hold to reveal and test its limits and inconsistencies (say between nationalism and the uncritical acceptance of economic globalization, or between patriotic militarism and the bad treatment of veterans) to not only reveal the contradictions in this worldview,

198

in its own terms, but help people discover, in their own terms, a way to resolve these contradictions by evolving and questioning their own worldview. We need to reach out to narrowcasted audiences to show them how their concerns cannot be addressed within their worldview by helping them to evolve their worldview in a way that addresses their concerns. The results could be surprising. It is an error to dismiss their concerns. For example, instead of dismissing concerns about illegal immigration as an example of the reactionary racism held by ill-informed bigots and xenophobes, it is better to accept those concerns as legitimate but show how immigration policy or lack of its enforcement has been deliberately engineered by politicians in order to scapegoat immigrants while exploiting them, drive wages down, divide working people against one another, and distract the nationalistic population away from the real problems that the politicians are either unable or unwilling to solve. By taking the concerns as a legitimate starting point and broadening the understanding of the problem, the focus can be shifted away from the immigrants and towered political economy itself. This dialectical approach ultimately leads to an evolution of how concerns are understood by those people who have them. Once this evolution has occurred it becomes possible that the most nationalistic and even racist person could discover, for themselves, in their own terms, some degree of commonality and solidarity with working immigrants against the same source of exploitation, and thereby, come to see for themselves how their own nationalism or racism is questionable and problematical given the social reality of their situation. From this standpoint, it becomes possible for a person to see the double standards and hypocrisy in their own worldview, and how their nationalism and racism have been blinding them to the real causes of their hardship and dissatisfactions. However, this is extremely difficult to achieve using counterpropaganda, as the likelihood is that it will simply be dismissed as propaganda and ignored.

The factionalization of society created by propaganda undermines its stability, adaptability, and creativity by undermining the possibility of diverse, pluralistic, and critical exchanges of viewpoints, experiences, values, ideas, knowledge, and skills. This possibility is essential for democratic participation to have practical value and maximize the overall adaptability of society to unforeseen events and changes in an open-ended, complex, and changing world that does not conform to human intentions.[28] Taking this into account, we can see that propaganda retards society. It cultivates a society based on ignorance and closed-mindedness, wherein people only talk to like-minded people, only to reinforce their own sense of certainty and self-righteousness, and only to secure the totalitarian hologram within which they exist. In such a society, everybody talks and nobody listens, intensifying alienation, and the isolation of the individual as one who is always self-justified and accusatory of others. The increasingly high cost of running propaganda campaigns in mass media has resulted in corporate domination of both propaganda and counterpropaganda. The effect has been an intensification of irrationality and hostility, as the divisions within the public sphere have become increasingly entrenched, while the population is increasingly distracted from the corporate takeover of media and the political realm, as well as societal infrastructure, national security, public services, and, of course, the economic realm. Just as media has become narrowcasted, politics has become privatized. Without a strong public organization of politics, resulting in a government that represents the people and that acts as a check and balance against corporate power, without any public owned mass media, there is nothing that could stop the privatization of the political realm. It has been a gradual erosion since before the Second World War, but it is tantamount to a coup d'état. America was always a plutocracy, even before the American Revolution and the founding of the nation, but, with the erosion of public sector, nothing could prevent the corporate takeover of governmental institutions at every level, thereby transforming the American plutocracy into a full-fledged corporate state.

Among a highly propagandized, narrowcasted, and fragmented population, wherein the individual is bombarded with propaganda and counterpropaganda from all directions, the individual either retreats into the private realm or seeks out only those media sources that reinforce his own prejudices and worldview. This helps the individual maintain her sense of certainty and self-righteousness, though in reality this amounts to a narcissistic eroticism and political alienation. The only alternative is confusion or silence, and this results in the individual being thrown into a state of shock and confusion—at best concluding that both sides are as bad as each other, as if there are only two sides to the political spectrum.

---

[28] Rogers, *Participatory Democracy, Science and Technology*

Propaganda and counterpropaganda do not cancel each other out, even when they contradict each other. They have a cumulative effect in the same way as being hit with a left hook by a boxer after being hit by a right hook does not return a person to a state of normality and clear-headedness. The individual is left groggier and punch-drunk. This shock effect results in a disruption of consciousness and the propagandized individual further retreating into the private realm of political apathy and indifference. Cynicism and nihilism become the common responses. Any alternative, in so far as any can be permitted within a narrowcasted framework, is rapidly eroded by a feeling of impotence and frustration, and propagandized individuals flee into group identity and participate in the dissemination of propaganda and counterpropaganda merely as a way of venting their impotence and frustrations, which takes the form of scapegoating, extremism, and irrationality (even to the far extreme of advocating violence and terrorism) projected towards either individual political candidates or other public personas.

This shows us why propaganda cannot be negated by counterpropaganda. The idea that this negation is even possible is itself based on little more than the antiquated (and false) notion of *mithridatization* (which holds that a person can be made increasingly tolerant and immune to poison by gradually administering and increasing the dose of the poison). The result of this is that the critical faculties of the propagandized individual are eroded and destroyed—completely desensitized—and clings to the status quo and develops political indifference and inertia. This can result in the propagandized individual becoming a zealot for propaganda or counterpropaganda. She might become an activist, but her actions remain irrational. The greatest likelihood, especially in a culture of social media, is that he will participate in the dissemination of propaganda or counterpropaganda to the extreme, becoming a proselytizing propagandist. Under these circumstances, the individual is addicted to propaganda and simply cannot think or communicate without it. Their whole identity is shrouded in propaganda and made meaningful by it. He will spend her whole day on social media "activism." This should be viewed as a form of psychosis.

Propaganda is a form of coercive communication—used as a weapon of psychological warfare—that undermines the conditions and possibility for free speech. A narrowcasted media is the opposite of a free press. The only genuine alternative to propaganda is a process of *sensibilization*. This is a process of increasing the individual's awareness of propaganda, whereby the individual becomes highly agitated by it and begins to see it in all its forms. The individual is driven into a state of hyper-awareness of propaganda, and thereby begins the process of deconstructing it (and detoxifying themselves from it). The individual becomes a critic of media and the uses of propaganda, thereby becoming aware and sensible in their understanding of how the framework and content of public and political discourse are constructed. This is a crucial step towards their liberation. However, there is a danger in this. As the agitated and disrupted individual begins their liberation from propaganda, they will lose their sense of self-importance and self-righteousness, in the same way that a drug addict suffers withdrawal, boredom, and a loss of meaning. This all stems back to the problem of alienation. Any method to overcome propaganda and liberate people from its grip must understand how the individual uses propaganda to overcome their sense of alienation. Only when people act through democratic organizations and coordinated mass action can hope to recover sovereignty over the political process and national infrastructure through direct democratic participation and resistance to corporate domination. This involves building the people's capacity for self-reliance and democratic participation. That will not happen by magic. Corporations will not be passive in the face of popular resistance. At first the tactics of legal and administrative methods, alongside the threat of outsourcing and capital flight are used against organized labor; this is combined with a massive propaganda onslaught, coming from both seemingly left and right wing sources, against all popular resistance, and to divide people against each other. Democratic movements are either demonized or censored in corporate media. If these legal, economic, administrative, and propaganda methods fail to suppress popular resistance, the corporate state readily resorts to police state tactics and the use of paramilitary forces to suppress peaceful protests and democratic movements. If all else fails, the corporate state will simply wage war on the domestic population, often in the guise of a war against an external enemy (real or shadow), using methods of state terrorism, mass arrests and imprisonment, torture and indefinite detention, and the imposition of martial law. In such a state, corporations are above the law and society typically degenerates into a fascist state.

The movement towards a rational understanding of the world is one that leads us to understand universal truths about our shared conditions and existence as human beings. It involves learning and teaching the truth about the world, society, and the human condition. Critical thinking, skepticism, doubt, suspension of judgment, and a philosophical concern with the immediacy of thought and experience, erodes the feeling of certainty and absolutism, and thereby erodes the power of propaganda to act as something that satisfies the human need to know the world and belong to something greater than the individual. When the individual rejects critical and philosophical thinking and questioning, thereby dismissing the value of doubting and deconstructing narrative, and rejecting the rigors of critical reflection and research, the individual has an *irrational relation* with knowledge and truth. He would rather "know" what he does not in fact know than not know at all. This irrational relation is not only the psychological route for a susceptibility to propaganda but it erodes the possibility of critical thinking and reflection, and, as a result, erodes the ability to resist and recognize propaganda. It is for this reason that we should not fall into the trap of countering propaganda with alternative or better propaganda. Admittedly it is always tempting to consider using propaganda as counter-propaganda, as being better than nothing at all (which allows the propagandist to get away with disseminating their propaganda), but counter-propaganda, like all propaganda, is also based on an irrational relation and a substitute for knowledge, communication, and dialogue, and further erodes the ability of the individual to develop a rational relation with knowledge and truth. If there is any truth to this claim, the only real counter to propaganda is for the individual to develop a rational relation with knowledge and truth. This is a matter of education, intellectual rigor and honesty, and the cultivating the practice of critical thinking. It starts with not knowing and consciously examines the foundations upon which knowledge is acquired, organized, and further developed. The individual must confront and challenge what she thinks that she knows to be true. This must be done on the basis of her own experiences. He needs to doubt what he thinks and examine how he knows in order to determine whether he knows something or not. This needs to be done in the individual's own terms, as part of self-examination and self-analysis, rather than in terms of abstracts or rubber-stamps, slogans, and formulae or equations, given to her from third party sources. Can everyone or anyone do this? It does seem to run counter to so much of our "education" and media culture within mass society. Has propaganda already caused too much damage to the human ability to think?

While counterpropaganda prevents propaganda from becoming totalitarian, by giving alienated individuals and alternative worldview and set of prejudices, as well as showing the limits of propaganda, it does not really change people who have already succumbed to propaganda. A narrowcasted audience cannot be liberated through a counterpropaganda campaign, no matter how well-crafted and applied it might be. The consequences of counterpropaganda is that of psychological civil warfare; partisan and factionalized media; intensification of the divisions and irrationality within society. The only way a narrowcasted audience can be liberated from the grip of propaganda is if they are able to recognize the inconsistencies and contradictions within their own worldview, prejudices, and myths. This must be done in their own terms and in relation to their own experiences. Outsiders can only hope to challenge the limits of any worldview through engagement and dialog, by testing its consistency and limits, to get the person to explore these for themselves, and to discover for themselves the limits and gaps in their own worldview. This cannot be achieved through counterpropaganda or confrontation using "the facts." The narrowcasted individual is inoculated against both counterpropaganda and opposing arguments and facts. This will be either dismissed out or reacted to with hostility. Ultimately, the narrowcasted individual can only save themselves, but what is required by others is to give them somewhere else to go. It needs a new paradigm. Of course, this is easier said than done, but the basis of a new democratic society must be founded on people discovering and exploring meaningful human relations and activities for themselves, within a cooperative and practical community, to learn how to share recourses and decision-making with others, and live a satisfying and good life. This cannot be achieved through rubber-stamping, propaganda, and counterpropaganda. It can only be achieved through open dialog and reflection, in a culture of mutual respect, and directed in accordance with the common question of how to solve shared problems and resolve shared concerns. Hence, instead of using counterpropaganda, to show "the opposition" the errors of their prejudices and worldview, it is better to advance a new paradigm based on genuine knowledge of practical and organizational value to give people somewhere else to go. This knowledge can take the following forms:

- Education

- Technical knowledge

- Practical skills

- Communication and dialog

- Reflection

- Community shared problems and concerns

- Methods to achieve mutual respect

It is better to transcend the use of counterpropaganda (even though it remains useful to disrupt the totalitarianism of established propaganda and offer alienated and dissatisfied people an alternative set of myths and prejudices, as well as rubberstamps, opinions, facts, slogans, and arguments to oppose established propaganda) and instead offer and develop a genuine, practical, and meaningful alternative that brings thought and action together through dialog, reflection, and rational communication. Education and technical skills are needed for people to build a genuinely democratic alternative economy and society, as well as organizational and communication skills, and by giving people somewhere else to go—an alternative and practical basis for human life. In this way, the totalitarian worldview can be replaced with something better, within which the individual can discover for themselves human meaning, without requiring the myths and certainties of propaganda, and the need to conform to group thinking.

One of the biggest problems facing us is how to revive critical thinking and judgment among people who have become subject to propaganda. Once these faculties have been repressed and eroded, they are difficult to revive, especially when the propagandized individual will deny they need reviving and will resist all efforts to do so. Propaganda inoculates the individual against fact-based and rational communication that contradicts or challenges his prejudices and worldview. Counterpropaganda will usually be rejected as being propaganda, and such efforts merely reinforce the partitions of a heavy narrowcasted and factionalized population, further entrenching group-identity and the divisions between people, and leaving prejudices and worldviews untouched. Even in the unlikely event of being successful, counterpropaganda continues to erode the capacity for critical thinking and judgment, thereby intensifying the irrationality of the target population, and merely replaces one form of propaganda with another. The propagandized individual is no more authentic and free than they were before, and, if anything, they are further damaged and it is even less likely that their capacity for critical thinking and self-reflection can be revived.

While a humanistic education remains the silver bullet as far as children are concerned, in adults their only real hope is that they can revive themselves through an awareness of the contradictions between their own experiences and their worldview. Propagandized adults must come to see for themselves the flaws in their paradigm. Rather than arguing against it, it is better for critics to work within it and push it to its extremes in order to reveal its inadequacies, contradictions, and limits. Propaganda is undermined and exposed when the propagandized individual can discover for themselves, in terms of their own experiences, how propaganda has effected them and their group identity. War, economic collapse, natural disasters, illness, violence, and horror can all disrupt and undermine the kinds of explanations and rationalizations used by propagandists when their consequences are completely at odds with the expectations, myths, and symbols that propaganda depends on. Soldiers returning from war often see for themselves how the propaganda in favor of war is at odds with the sacrifice and patriotism it appealed to. It is when the propagandized individual becomes aware of the inadequacy of what they have been told—when they begin to sense that they have been fed a "pack of lies" or "bullshit"—that it becomes possible for them to revive their own sense of criticality and liberate themselves from the grip of propaganda. Thinking becomes possible again.

However, this is the greatest point of danger for the individual. They can liberate themselves from the hologram and its worldview and prejudices; they can relearn to exercise their critical faculty that is needed to identify and rediscover their organic self and subjectivity. But where do they go from there? They are left with nothing, at the place of not-knowing, and face the real danger from counterpropaganda filling the void. Freedom and enlightenment are not guaranteed. The individual needs to live in the world and cooperate with other people. Emptiness is difficult to sustain, without withdrawing from human society and living a solitary existence within Nature. When she comes down from the mountain and out of the wilderness, she needs somewhere to go. The risk is that the individual will need propaganda to function in modern society. Through group activities and discourse the individual will become reintegrated into the hologram—a different facet, but the same hologram nevertheless. If the individual is to sustain herself, she must continue to exercise her criticality and deconstruct the hologram, its prejudices and worldview. This is why propaganda cannot be countered with propaganda. It can only be countered with the ruthlessly honest and consistent application of critical self-examination, moral conscience, and rational communication based on truth, humility, and intellectual virtue. Propaganda can only be countered with truth and a philosophical way of life. What this cannot tolerate is any double-standard and we must expose it. Intellectual and moral consistency are essential if we hope to communicate without resorting to propaganda. These are the hallmarks of free speech: speech free from propaganda is based on truthful, consistent, and self-examined discourse. It is free from shortcuts and contradictions. It exposes them.

The only way to counter propaganda is not with counterpropaganda (which will be ignored or opposed) but through a dialog within which a tension is revealed between the worldview, as expressed by people in their own terms, and the course of action associated with it. While it is essential that there exists a diversity of ownership of mass media, we need to remain aware that mass media is not the only means of propaganda. It also pervades personal conversation, conferences, education, and art works. Games, jokes, and entertainments are also means of disseminating propaganda. Censorship and framing are essential to propagandists, which requires all-pervasive media control, and thereby shaping the premises and assumptions underlying policies, regulations, and laws, and these influence everyday speech. We must avoid attacking propaganda in everyday speech frontally, as this will merely reinforce it. It is better to concentrate one's efforts on the creation of psychological conditions for free speech, so that the desired result seems to come from them naturally.[29] A person who is capable of understanding that different interpretations of the same events are not only equally valid but necessary for a full understanding of those events is exactly the kind of person on whom propaganda does not work. Intellectual pluralism and seeking broad understandings opposes propaganda because these not only

---

[29] C. MacDougall, *Understanding Public Opinions* (New York: Macmillan, 1952)

respect the coexistence of different interpretations but requires them, especially when they are inconsistent or opposing perspectives. The existence of diverse viewpoints is a necessary condition for there to be any possibility of intellectual freedom and the development of comprehensive understandings that can transcend subjective interpretations, and this is itself a prerequisite for the possibility of rational reflection and communication on any moral or epistemological question and the framework within which that question can be asked and answered. Such a person seeks out a wide variety of sources of information and opinion, people of different convictions and perspectives, and as many interpretations and worldviews as possible; this is a prerequisite for the possibility of developing a broad understanding of things and events in a complex and changing world, which respects that human beings are both fallible and limited in their perspective. Such an individual seeks to discover flaws and inconsistencies in their own worldview, and discover their own presumptions and preconceptions by learning about counterfactuals, contradictions, exceptions, and limits. Such a person is almost impossible to propagandize.

Propaganda, Democracy, and Media:

One of the enduring myths of modern society is that propaganda only a feature of authoritarian or totalitarian regimes, and does not occur in liberal democracies. Nothing could be further from the truth. Liberal democracy is premised on the Enlightenment myth that man is a rational individual, capable of thinking and living according to reason and knowledge, controlling his passions, and basing his behavior on scientific facts, and choosing his own course of action. This myth seems opposed to the covert and subliminal operations of propaganda, and its appeals to the irrational and emotional factors of human nature, yet it has concealed the all-pervasive operations of propaganda within liberal democracy, especially in the United States of America. It has ignored the close relation between the dissemination of knowledge and the accumulation of power. It has often been claimed that, at least since Machiavelli, politics has been the pursuit of power. This may well be true. If so, it would mean that all other considerations (e.g. ideology, religion, morality, and virtue) are subordinate to the pursuit of power. Politicians may well use these considerations in rhetoric and propaganda, but they are only means to this end. These considerations can be used in two ways: (1) to gather support for the politician from groups for which these considerations are ends; (2) to distract people from the real intentions of the politician. This is not simply a matter of manipulating the masses—even though that clearly is a factor—but it is a compulsory demand placed on the politician who must adopt these seemingly deceitful methods in order to present both the pursuit of power and the use of force as necessary means to realize virtues and ideals within society. If the politician does not do this, she places herself in an aloof position from the vast majority of people, which not only runs the risk of alienating them, but also risks delegitimizing the whole political process. Otherwise he will be seen as nothing more than a puppet or cog in an autonomous technocratic system that transcends human beings and uses them only as resources for the consolidation of power for its own sake. In this respect, standing for something is a necessary illusion, as Chomsky would put it, for the political system to appear representative of the people. If this illusion was exposed successfully to the masses, the inevitable results would be nihilism, anarchism, and revolution.

In mass media, "democracy" is itself a myth, alongside the myth of "the free press." These myths become more than symbols as they conceal the absence of any real referent. They are empty abstractions acting as substitutes, which can mean anything and nothing simultaneously. Their function is to be used by a largely passive and conformist people to affirm themselves as somehow, vaguely sovereign, to align themselves with "the national interest" and "the nation," and to promote a mythical tale of history and its actuality. This creates the hologram—a mass delusion—that not only can be used to cover up the harsh realities of life, but also promote the false belief that all is well. It can be used to conceal the antidemocratic nature of "democracy," systemic racism and sexism, oppression, injustice, inequalities, and poverty throughout society, all the while presenting a delusion that progress is being made. Not only this, but it makes the ideals upon which its myths are based as tools of oppression, while the oppressed pin their hopes and the very forces that oppress them. The myth of "democracy" is the opposite of democracy. The more deeply the mythical nature of this myth is concealed the perception of it as a reality—often appealing to classical ideas that were never put into practice or golden ages that never existed—the more "democracy" promotes a regression to a regressive mentality, regardless of material progress. "Free speech" is tolerated because it is highly circumscribed and largely given to the majority of the population as a set of opinions and facts, from which they can choose from, and is largely irrelevant. It is little more than a form of catharsis and rubber-stamping group identity. It has no relation to political action at all. If we can entertain this very pessimistic view further, it becomes quite evident that politicians are little more than actors, reading (or Tweeting) one-liners and sound-bites, delivering snappy slogans and talking-points. All this is done to present political theatre and the illusion that public opinion matters, when in actuality it matters no more than when children watching pantomime boo at the clearly identified villain and cheer at the unambiguous hero.

The aim of propaganda in a "democracy" is to introduce and reinforce limits to the public perception of democracy and limit its potential. It divides people against each other, and deepens the alienation of people from government. It turns off people from politics, except in a shallow and passive relation between them. It partitions the private doubts and questions of the individual off from public discourse, leaving the individual limited options for permissible expression via talking-points and the rubber-stamps of their group identity. Propaganda alienates the individual from others, government, *and herself*. It makes open discourse and rational communication impossible, and undermines the conditions for free speech and the existence of a free press. It is the opposite of free speech and paralyzes genuine participatory democracy. Even in a representative democracy, the use of propaganda in the run up to elections results in a cult of personality around candidates and leaders, rather than vetting of candidates and the election of accountable leaders. Party politics filtered through mass media leads to politics taking the form of entertainment and a spectator sport in which people do little more than cheer for their team and boo their opponents. Myths, symbolism, slogans, and lies abound, all of which acts as a substitute for evidence-based debate and deliberation; propaganda acts as a substitute for truth and counter-propaganda acts as a substitute for critical thinking. Constituents are entirely distracted and manipulated by mass media, which, of course, acts on behalf of its owners and the elite. The people only relate to a mythical and symbolic image of the political process, an illusion and abstraction of how government works, while behind the scenes the real government—the invisible government (the owners of industry, finance, technology, and media)—pulls the strings and conducts the workings of government unseen. Anti-government conspiracy theorists also participate in this illusion by creating the belief in an all-powerful government over which the people have no control whatsoever. This allows the invisible government to operate with impunity. In this way, the elite transforms government and media into instruments to consolidate and extend their power and privileges, while the attention of the masses gazes at whatever spectacles or scandals media disseminates. The *Wizard of Oz* is an illuminating parable here, except mass media controls the curtain and prevents it from being pulled across to reveal the stage magician pulling levers and turning dials to create the illusion of the wizard.

It is for this reason that sensational stories and scandals dominate the whole political process, rather than any real discussion of the issues. This presents the illusion of a vigilant media watchdog, while misdirecting public focus away how government really works, and how political candidates and representatives are actually selected and funded, and towards the for-or-against pantomime of spectator politics-as-entertainment. Dramatization, fake scandals, and sensationalism are the dominant mode by which public focus is channeled, and in the increasingly shallow point-and-click world of social media, it creates a framework so well constructed as a distraction that it simply does not matter what public opinion is on any issues or policy ideas. It is nothing more than catharsis. In this way, the classical idea of "government by the consent of the governed" is achieved simply because the governed have no idea what they are consenting to, or even of whom the government is comprised or what it does. People consent to an abstraction of government, dressed in personalities, color-coded party politics, and perennial wedge-issues. The public consents to its own distraction and manipulation. It participates in it. It is only in this way that the people believe that public opinion matters. Whether or not votes are even counted after elections is irrelevant when elections are constructed that only candidates who satisfy the interests of the elite run for public office, and only those voices which satisfy those interests are given any coverage at all. Even media scandals about isolated incidents of electoral fraud are essential to maintain the illusion that elections matter, and the outcome is decided by the people, yet such scandals never (or rarely) have any follow-up, investigation, or change in the outcome. This is all directed to leave the people with the belief that they are the electorate; that their vote and opinion selects their "representatives," and there is real competition within the political process, rather than an illegitimate sham. The whole purpose of the media coverage of the election campaign is to foster the public belief that something is at risk, that change is possible, that their voices and concerns will be heard, and that the media are acting as a watchful and critical eye on behalf of the public; all the while, the interests of a tiny minority are satisfied and corporate media is complicit in manufacturing "the election" results.

It is during election campaigns that the power of mass media is most evident. The media-generated cult of personality around presidential candidates is a very effective propaganda tool for concealing the invisible government. By focusing on personality, mass media can distract the population from issues and policies, as well as use fake news and scandals to misrepresent where candidates and parties stand on problems and their solutions. Unworkable solutions, scapegoating, sensationalism, and trivialities (such as the candidates clothing or favorite sport) can act as the focus of public rancor and dissatisfactions, without any follow-up discussion or analysis of the real agenda of the candidates, their record, or their own financial interests and backing. The realities of the mechanisms of government are completely ignored. In this way, media discussion of proposed "solutions" can ignore the fact that they will never be implemented, even if the candidate wins, simply because it would not be a power of the president to implement them. Thus candidates for the presidency can talk about reducing taxes, "tearing up treaties," or introducing tariffs (or building walls across the US-Mexico border) when these are powers of Congress, and this constitutional fact is completely ignored within mass media. The entirety of the "debate" during the election can be reduced to a "for or against" the candidate framework, taking sound-bites and slogans at face value, without any substantive discussion or analysis of whether the candidate would be able to implement them or even really intends to. This not only allows the candidate to campaign on issues over which the executive branch has no authority, but it also distracts the population from congressional campaigns and the actual consequences of the election of that person to the presidency. The myth of the President as an all-powerful leader is maintained, representing him as if he would be the totality of government, the architect of policy, and the person in command of the nation—this idea of the President as "the father of the nation" or "the savior," or someone single-handedly out to destroy it, is one of the enduring myths of presidential campaigns that date back to Jefferson v Adams. Time and time again, the media propagates the myth that the President is the source of all-power, as if the executive branch was a monarchic institution governed in accordance with a single man's personality and whim. The President is turned into a monarch, open to fact-free hyperbole, dramatization, and mass hysteria, all while the real nature of the government is concealed.

The reality that the President is only a single actor, operating in a highly complex arrangement of actors and institutions, with competing supporters and opponents, all with their own agendas and policies, is brushed aside. The notion that, in many respects, the President is little more than a figurehead and doesn't have any real power at all (or even limited executive power within a circumscribed jurisdiction) is a notion that cannot be entertained in mass media coverage of elections and the nature of governance. Such a notion would lead people to question where power actually resides. Who pulls the President's strings? Who pulls Congress's strings? Who decides policy? Who writes the laws? How are they implemented in practice? Who benefits from them? Where does the money come from? Where does it go? These are not tolerable questions within mass media because they threaten to expose the invisible government that owns mass media. To ask these questions would open the proverbial can of worms. If they are asked at all, perhaps on marginal websites or by little known journalists in low circulation publications, they are skipped over in a superficial way—that there is something fishy or sinister going on, but it is all a mystery or attributed to abstractions. It is important for this concealment of the nature of government that the government remains unitary and unanimously embodied in a single person, in whom everyone finds themselves focused on (even in opposition), on whom everyone pins their hopes and dreams (or scapegoats and vilifies), on whom everyone can project themselves (as a savor or tyrant), and for whom everything is permissible and possible (or suspect and evil).

Propaganda pervades all media. Television and radio are still powerful instruments for the dissemination of propaganda, as are also newspapers and magazines, but today the Internet is the new frontier for the propagandists. "Rubber-stamping" is central to social media sites, like Facebook, and Internet-based clicktivism. Personal identity and self-presentation are infused with propaganda as the individual declares their allegiance with groups, leaders, and political parties through rubber-stamps. Memes, slogans, images, headlines, talking-points, and off-the-peg arguments are disseminated ("shared") through social media, forming both opinions and identities through the dissemination of propaganda, allegiances with personalities, and group membership. With the rise of media narrowcasting, whereby niche media feeds and reinforces the prejudices and worldview of a target demographic, increasingly the population has become divided against each other and inoculated against any fact or opinion that they don't already agree with. Even though, undoubtedly, people are becoming aware of the methods which are being used to mold their speech and action, there is the tendency for this awareness to be directed towards "propaganda" used by people they do not agree with, and remain oblivious to the propaganda used on and by them. People remain blissfully ignorant of the extent to which they are both propagandees and propagandists. Hence, even when the public is clearly better informed about the processes of life, technical information, and scientific theory and fact, people remain more receptive to appeals to its own group mind and tribal politics, even when those appeals contradict their own interests. No matter how sophisticated, how cynical people may become about the use of propaganda in mainstream media, the propagandist is still able to reply on basic appeals to self-interest, blaming others for failures to satisfy one's needs, amusement and distraction, the longing for leadership, the need for belonging, etc.

When media has genuinely diverse and independent ownership—when a wide variety of sources reflect a wide variety of views without any centralized control—there is genuine competition and choice between sources and we can say that *a free press* exists. But in a context of intense media consolidation, when the largest proportion of media sources are controlled and coordinated by very few people, we do not have a free press and modern propaganda becomes increasingly all-pervasive and dominant. As Ellul noted,

"To make the organization of propaganda possible, the media must be concentrated, the number of news agencies reduced, the press brought under single control, and radio and film monopolies established. The effect will be still greater if the various media are concentrated in the same hands. When a newspaper trust also externals its control over films and radio, propaganda can be directed at the masses and the individual can be caught in the wide net of media... Only through concentration in a few hands of a large number of media can one attain true orchestration, a continuity, and an application of scientific methods of influencing individuals. A state monopoly, or a private monopoly, is equally effective." (Ellul, *Propaganda*, pp. 102-103)

It is for this reason that media consolidation opposes the free press. Propaganda must be total to be effective and the propagandist must utilize all of the technical means at her disposal: books, newspapers, radio, TV, documentaries, posters, meetings, billboards, telephone calls, door-to-door canvassing, movies, and the Internet. Modern propaganda must utilize *all* of these media. The Internet is the new frontier for propaganda, and media consolidation and the systematic coordination of propaganda run hand in hand. So each medium complements and reinforces the others, all the while seeming to provide more information and greater diversity. Within a context of intense narrowcasting and the inoculation of the target demographic against any alternative or opposing source of information, we can explain the totalitarian attitude adopted by individuals, who are simply reproducing the effect that propaganda has had on them. Given that dialog, contradiction, and discussion are demanding, if not fatal, to the effectiveness of propaganda, it is essential that individuals do not participate in such activities, instead being suspicious and even hostile towards anyone who does not share their worldview and its myths. Any opposing faction must be ridiculed, marginalized, or simply ignored as irrelevant. It must remove any awareness of legitimate disagreements or differences, and any inconsistencies or contradictions between the myths of the worldview and the accepted/expected course of action and patterns of speech (including talking-points, opinions, explanatory metaphors, etc.)

The current situation is one in which mass media is accessible primarily to governments, corporations and other powerful groups, like NGOs and churches, all of which can compete through public relations and advertising, as well as through paid-for research and think-tanks, in a battle of propaganda and counter-propaganda. The individual citizen remains in a passive relation with this, even when using social media. While the Internet does afford some opportunities for individual participation, it too has become dominated by governments, corporations, and other powerful groups. Media consolidation and corporate domination over mass media has removed the relevance of individual freedom of expression, given the passive role of the individual as an information and entertainment consumer. The consolidation of media allows corporations to buy up local media sources, across all kinds of media, to use a national platform and the Internet to suppress opposition to privatization, as well as to disseminate covert propaganda and "exposures" of governmental over-reach and interference, thereby maintaining the illusion of a free and critical press. The Internet, however, does permit the individual to communicate with others, and it is in this respect that free speech is contingent on the means to communicate beyond face-to-face communication. Yet, due to narrowcasting and group-thinking on the Internet, now referred to as "data bubbles," the factionalization of the Internet has resulted in the reduction of communication and media to propaganda channels; little more than the exchange of propaganda and counter-propaganda, media narrowcasting, and the uncritical belief in "fake news" if it reinforces one's prejudices and worldview alongside the declaration of "fake news" about any story that contradicts or problematizes them. This situation is the opposite of free speech. Although Net Neutrality is essential to maintain opportunities for individual participation—and a public-owned ISP is a possible means to do this—this is not enough.[30] What is needed is a transformation of the *quality* of communication between individuals. This is not a technological problem; it is a cultural problem. People need to shift from thinking of free speech as the assertion of opinion; shift towards thinking of it as open and shared communication, involving listening as well as speaking. Speech without listening is noise. Not listening is censorship. The duality of "us v them," listening only to people who echo back our own opinions, needs to be transcended and dissolved through the development of a culture of listening to others; a culture of tolerance, mutual respect, and rational communication between people who do not agree. The possibility of the transformation itself depends on whether we can shift away from partisanship and hostility towards solidarity and good will.

However, none of the modern propaganda techniques would work unless the individual propagandee was *complicit* in its reception. Modern propaganda would not work—could not work—unless individuals bought newspapers, radios, televisions, etc., and absorbed the information and opinions they receive through these media. Understanding the psychological need for propaganda in mass society is essential for us to understand propaganda at all. If the population were simply to stop reading newspapers, turn off their radios and television sets, and disconnect from the Internet, modern propaganda would fail immediately. The population could destroy propaganda through *strike action*, simply by boycotting mass media and mass communications technologies. Yet, a propagandized population could no

---

[30] Karl Rogers, *Media Consolidation and Net Neutrality in the U.S.*

216

more do this than all drug addicts could "just say no." In mass society, propaganda *becomes* culture and education provides the skills (i.e. reading) and preconditioning required for individuals to be receptive to propaganda. Without independent critical thinking and the immediate experiences of practical life, the more cultured and educated the individual is, the more propagandized they are, and the more they need propaganda. The individual in mass society is dependent on irrationality received myths and ideology— received as "self-evident truths" or "absolute values"—in order to situate him or herself within culture and society. It becomes a matter of identity. Propaganda gives the individual meaning, values, and a worldview; resistance to propaganda takes the individual down the path of alienation, existential angst, and skepticism (which readily can become nihilism within the mass society). Propaganda becomes the means by which the isolated individual can become integrated within mass society and operate with a sense of solidarity with the collective as an individual. In this respect, the distinction between information and propaganda cannot be based on the content or truth-status of the message, but is based on how it is received. If the message is received critically and rationally analyzed in terms of immediate experiences, while retaining a conscious awareness of its contingency and the necessity to check its sources and assumptions, we can consider the message to be primarily one of information, but if the message is received uncritically and used to explain away immediate experience or formulate opinions based on the mediated and second-hand experiences of others, without checking sources and assumptions, thereby by treating the message as if it were "self-evidently" or "absolutely" true, we can consider the message to be primarily one of propaganda. In most cases, the distinction between information and propaganda is ambiguous and the rationality or irrationality of mass society is open to question and critical analyses as being likewise ambiguous.

The main mechanism of controlling public opinion is through creating and framing *crises* that can be used to capture the public attention and feed it a range of possible responses and opinions. Typically individuals will respond with the rubber-stamps appropriate to their group-identity, especially their party alignment, and selected facts and interpretations can be fed to them to reinforce these rubber-stamps. In this way, government and politicians can create the problems they already have solutions for. The public can either be manipulated into demanding these solutions, of the range of possible solutions can be framed along party lines, thereby heavily proscribing possible compromise solutions and selling these to the public as responses to the diversity of public opinion. Through the use of propaganda, political parties can channel public attention and structure it in accordance with existing formulas—thereby framing it—polarizing it in terms of the "them v. us" rhetoric that is characteristic of party politics, thereby establishing the range and set of public opinion in accordance with group-identity, rather than logical or practical criteria. Once this has been achieved through mass media and communication, individuals can speak as freely as they like because they will tend towards narrowcasted media sources and partisan groups that will shape and constrain opinion in accordance with the propagated range and set. Anyone who expresses thoughts that outside this range or do not correspond to an appropriate opinion (within the set of opinions propagated through media and groups) will soon find themselves marginalized and isolated.

Thus the government does not need to sensor or punish dissent. It can use propaganda to give the public its opinions, including critical and oppositional opinions, and maintain the illusion of democratic participation, representation, and accountability. When the government is itself increasingly an instrument of corporate interests, alongside corporate control over mass media and telecommunications, wherein corporations act as "gate-keepers" of the political process and public opinion, while also controlling the economic sphere of life, individuals simply have no alternative but to comply and conform (while feeling themselves to be free), or become an isolated voice in the wilderness. This is the nature of a modern totalitarian corporate-state: It empowers those who support it and disempowers all those people for whom it has no use. In the unlikely event that people will organize against it, the corporate-state as a militaristic police-state at its disposal and will resort to oppressive tactics and state terrorism. In this way, the corporate-state degenerates into fascism if it cannot maintain its power through propaganda alone. The armed forces, usually maintains as an instrument for securing corporate interests abroad, can rapidly be turned on its own population.

"For a long time the theory of the people's sovereignty was believe to be tied to the concept of democracy. But it should be remembered that when that doctrine was applied for the first time, it led to the emergence of the most stringent dictatorship—that of the Jacobins. Therefore, we can hardly complain when modern dictators talk about the sovereignty of the people." (Ellul, *Propaganda*, p. 129)

Through modern propaganda and mass media control, elections have become little more than a ceremonial act of mass compliance in the legitimacy of government, as well as a means to distract the focus of the masses and channel it into party-politics and group think. Even the most authoritarian and terroristic regimes, like the Soviet Union or Nazi Germany, could not operate without public compliance and the facade of popular support.

As I have argued above, propaganda has become central to the political and administrative operations of so-called Western democracies, which is reality tend towards being either *adhocracies* or corporate-states, in order to maintain the compliance of the people to the system as a whole and the status quo of the social order, including its inequalities and injustices. With corporate-owned mass media having a vested interest in the status quo, as well as being a gate-keeper over the political process, the existence of "a free press" is simply an illusion. In a nutshell, the problem is as follows: propaganda involves propagating an irrational relation with information, and as such can only work with the complicity of the propagandee. How can we overcome this irrational relation? We must first of all recognize the psychological need for propaganda in mass society. No one consciously feels themselves to want or need propaganda. The pejorative and sinister connotations of the word "propaganda" are enough to lead to a general sense of abhorrence regarding propaganda. Individuals—especially educated individuals—consider themselves to be free and capable to seeing through propaganda. They consider themselves to be immune. Yet, as I have already discussed, in a mass society, individuals crave to feel some sense of belonging and being informed. Individuals need mass media and group-identity; they need to identify with the issues and events of the day, in relation to other people and groups. It is this need that leaves the individual susceptible to propaganda, which satisfies those needs, wards off possible criticisms and attacks, and gives the individual a sense of knowing and catharsis (releasing tensions and uncertainty). The problem of propaganda stems from the problem of alienation. Through intensifying alienation and offering itself as a solution to this problem, propaganda undermines the possibility of democracy and instead enhances conformity and irrationality. Propaganda creates the conditions under which totalitarianism and fascism flourish, even when the content of propaganda is anti-totalitarian and anti-fascist in its message. It does this by undermining the critical faculty of people, their ability to engage in rational communication with people of the same worldview and perspective, let alone people they disagree with, and their ability to resist mass media manipulation and distraction. Propaganda weakens people intellectually by atrophying and stifling their capacity for conscious reflection, questioning and thinking, making informed decisions, and conducting their own research. Thought control through propaganda is particularly effective when the education system also stupefies the population, leaving children incapable of developing rational thinking, critical judgment, and lateral thinking; leaving them lacking in research and communication skills, and the knowledge of how to cooperate and coordinate with others.

Taking this into account, we can see that the role of propaganda and counterpropaganda in mass media is to absorb the public focus. In this sense, it is not correct to say that mass media distorts the truth; *mass media is the distortion.* Mass media does not create and disseminate distractions; mass media is the distraction. It is for this reason that the only solution is to switch it off. People need to turn away from their addiction to mass media and return to interpersonal communication and personal reflection. It was for this reason that Herbert Marcuse considered it necessary for radical movements in opposition to the status quo of corporate capitalist society to create new political discourse capable of countering the double-speak propagated by mass media.[31] This involves rebuilding community-based media and genuine democratic media, dedicated to facilitating rational communication, critical thinking, sharing knowledge through the open and meaningful sharing of experience and truths, sharing real concerns and problems, rigorous and honest reasoning based on facts and evidence, all with the aim of helping people talk to and learn from each other. What is needed is a *re-appropriation* of the technologies of mass media communication to create a genuinely free press within which people exercise free speech and the exchange of information with the purpose of better organizing themselves, coordinating and cooperating with each other, sharing and exploring their visions of a better society, and democratically working towards a shared future. In this way, the people—the *demos*—become the free press. This act of re-appropriation could be termed as a democratic free press movement.

Of course it needs to be understood that propaganda does not exist in a cultural vacuum. The prejudices and bigotry manipulated by the propagandist

---

[31] Cf. *An Essay on Liberation* (Boston: Beacon Press, 1969), pp. 74-7

are often cultural inheritances learned from childhood from one's parents, teachers, and community. The propagandist takes advantage of these cultural beliefs by justifying and reinforcing them. However, the individual can also fabricate their own justifications. The use of propaganda as a means of self-justification of one's own selfishness, ignorance, prejudices, and bigotry is an important aspect in the reception of propaganda. Some people will accept and believe anything—no matter how absurd and irrational—if the outcome of accepting that belief is that the person feels vindicated in their own thoughts and behavior. One of the individual's greatest needs is to feel that he is right in his own eyes, thereby reducing his own feelings of uncertainty and anxiety by asserting his own self-righteousness, and convincing himself that he is doing and saying what he thinks to be true, and therefore he is worthy of self-respect and the respect of others. She needs to feel right in the eyes of those around her, her family, friends, and her community, church, co-workers, and country. He needs to belong to a group, which he considers to be right and just, noble and good, and like him. Her self-righteousness is not absolute righteousness (true and authentic justice) because it does not matter whether the group is actually just or good; it demands no self-sacrifice or struggle whatsoever. All that matters is that the individual and group are seen by themselves to be just and good, that they have reasons by which they can assert their justice and goodness, and that they share these reasons among each other. It is this group-think self-righteousness that has become the driving force in American political discourse, which, of course, leads to a cultural deafness towards people who think or speak differently, alongside the willingness to accept falsehoods and lies providing that they justify the sense of self-righteousness and give it more material for its expression.

It is the refusal to accept error or misjudgment—to admit when one is wrong or unfair—and to change one's attitudes, behavior, and goals, which allows propaganda to provide the rationalizations and self-justifications that *reinforce those attitudes, behavior, and goals*, especially when they run counter to experiences, evidence, and reason. The individual would rather live in a fiction—in the hologram—than confront a reality within which his beliefs are false and his explanations are self-serving lies that he tells himself to make his conduct feel right to himself. Through propaganda, the individual not only defends herself against criticism, but also against her own tensions and anxieties, thereby transforming failure into success, asserting her own sense of right and wrong, especially when she is being hypocritical in her own terms, and allowing justice and injustice to become interchangeable and ambiguous. In this manner, the individual can disguise his own conformity and hypocrisy under the masks of self-righteousness and moral conscience, freedom of expression, and patriotism. When others share the same rationalizations and self-justifications, the individual's self-deception becomes reinforced through conformity with group-identity. Ironically, self-justification only attains its effectiveness in relation to the individual's conformity with group-identity, which is so all-pervasive that even the victims of prejudice and hypocrisy go along with it. For example, the racist justifies his prejudice by saying that the "inferior race" is lazy, anti-social, immoral, or biologically inferior; and in many instances members of the stigmatized group will accept such assertions and experience a feeling of inferiority that justifies their own experiences of discrimination. They too use the same propaganda to explain their conditions and world. In this way, propaganda can help the individual resolve the contradictions between their worldview and experiences of reality by helping them understand that these contradictions in terms of some explanation that further justifies and reinforces their worldview. The failures of neoliberalism, deregulation, and free-trade agreements, for example, can be explained away as a failure of government to implement these policies properly, "crony capitalism," and union "protectionism," and therefore justify the need for further deregulation and the implementation of neoliberal policies and free-trade agreements. The failures of socialism can always be explained away in terms that demand the further implementation of socialist policies and reforms. Propaganda is always available to provide ready-made explanations of the failure of any ideology or policy, regardless of whether it is political or religious in nature.

Under the current conditions, the idea that there exists a "free press" that defends democracy by acting as a watchdog to counter governmental overreach or corporate malfeasance is itself a myth that is the product of propaganda. Democracy itself has become a myth. According to Chomsky, the term *democracy* "refers to a system of government in which elite elements based in the business community control the state by virtue of their dominance of the private society, while the population observes quietly. So understood, democracy is a system of elite decision and public ratification, as in the United States itself. Correspondingly, popular involvement in the formation of public policy is considered a serious threat."[32] The system is able to use propaganda to counter any democratic threat against the status quo. Conservative think-tanks and foundations have been set-up since the seventies to counter the possibility of mass democratic participation and "the excesses of democracy."[33] However, the main mechanism used to counter democratic participation can be seen in the public education system. It is a myth about public education in America, as well as many other Western Countries, that it is progressive and geared towards teaching democratic values, good citizenship, and critical thinking. The reality is that of a bureaucratic mode of education (obedience training) in which both intellectual and personal aspects of education and teacher training are lacking and devalued. The primary objective of a bureaucratic mode of education is to de-intellectualize and de-personalize teachers and students to frame their discourse and activities within an unquestioned system of procedures and techniques. Education is reduced to a series of meaningless exercises and tests, justified by a political interpretation of statistics and a system of propaganda based on psycho-babble, pedagogical doctrine, and ideology. Such a system suppresses democratic values, good citizenship, and critical thinking. Schools are institutions for indoctrination, "for imposing obedience, for blocking the possibility of independent thought, and [that] they play on institutional role in a system of control and coercion."[34]

For John Dewey (*Democracy and Education*), the aim of education is the production of free human beings associated with one another in terms of equality; well-adapted members of the community and citizens, capable of critical thinking and enlightened democratic participation. This humanistic conception of the purpose of education grew out of The Enlightenment and the classical liberal tradition—human beings have intrinsic value and the task of the educator is to aid the child to grow and bring-forth their own potential and nature. This conception grew out of the Renaissance revival of the Socratic approach (*Meno*). This democratic model of education is an anti-authoritarian and cooperative pedagogy, concerned with democratic values

---

[32] Noam Chomsky, *On Power and Ideology* (Boston: South End Press, 1987), p. 6
[33] Noam Chomsky, *Language and Politics* (New York: Black Rose Books, 1988), p. 671
[34] Noam Chomsky, *On Mis-Education* (Lanham, MD: Rowman & Littlefield, 2004). pp.137-8; see also Sylvia Ann Hewlett's UNICEF study *Child Neglect in Rich Societies*, 1993 on how Reaganite and Thatcherite policies have been disastrous for children and families in the US and UK.

and human freedom, which ideally forms the basis for an enlightened and free society. In contrast, the bureaucratic mode of education not only anesthetizes the minds of students by indoctrinating them into the tedium of the working day—as the norm—but it alienates them from the social and dialectical processes of questioning and reflection required to discover, communicate, and resolves their dissatisfactions and limitations. It leaves students isolated, disempowered, and resigned to their state o being. Such students are well molded for their lot in the labor market, or if they fall into criminality or drug-use, they are fodder for the highly profitable private prisons industry. Students are trained to become obedient workers, reactionary consumers, and compliant subjects of a corporate state. Their alienation and isolation leaves them inarticulate and frustrated, repressed and resentful, and incapable of acting as informed, active, and critical citizens of a democratic republic. They are left to descent into the private realm of patterns of consumption, drug abuse, alcoholism, television, domestic violence, sexual perversion, child abuse, competitive team sports and spectator party politics, and animal cruelty; meanwhile the system of power and capital accumulation continues unchallenged and unopposed by the vast majority of people.

Schools remain based on what Paulo Freire termed as the "banking" approach that instructs students to acquire a stock of information and techniques, without involving either teachers or students in questions and reflection on what an education is *for*. At best, such an approach trains students in how to work within the labor market, but it does not develop their ability to question and understand the world, to understand the reasons and causes behind appearances and the facts. At worse, it leaves students alienated and dysfunctional, ill-equipped to even respond to appearances, and ignorant of the facts. As Freire put it, the bureaucratic mode of education reproduces "practices by which one strives to domesticate consciousness, transforming it into an empty receptacle. Education in cultural action for domination is reduced to a situation in which the educator as 'the one who knows' transfers existing knowledge to the learner as 'the one who does not know.'"[35] Philosophical, personal, and social questions and reflections, alongside research skills and critical thinking, are sidelined a favor of

---

[35] Paulo Freire, *The Politics of Education* (South Hadley, Mass: Beryn & Garvey, 1985) p. 114

standardized tests and rote memorization. By doing this, teachers uncritically act as agents of state policy, reinforcing the political economy and the status quo. Teachers reproduce the class-based system in the classroom. When teachers encourage their students to question and analyze the social and political structures that shape their existence, to discover reality and truth for themselves, and to challenge their received wisdom, these teachers do so by stepping outside of the curriculum. And they run the risk of being censored, disciplined, or even fired for doing so.

All of this is justified by the system of propaganda, indoctrinated through party politics and teacher training, that superimposes "the needs of the market" over education, as if it were an unquestionable absolute that *this* was obviously what education is for. Once the debate becomes reduced and framed to how to reform education to better serve "the needs of the market" then the whole system becomes totalitarian. If the social costs of this system cannot be exploited by some for-profit industry, say the private prisons or pharmaceutical industry, they are left neglected, contributions to social decay. The purpose of transforming the student into an empty receptacle is not to instruct or inform the student, but to control the student and erode any possibility that he or she could escape the private realm of their own thoughts or doubts. The purpose of the bureaucratic mode of education is to transform the individual's relation to the public realm into one of passivity and receptivity. Once this has been achieved, the only opportunity for activity and participation afforded the individual is to adapt to the objective structures and methods of the system. When the individual does this, they are considered to be "successful" and rewarded accordingly, as Pavlov rewarded his dogs, and if they do not, they are considered to be "failures" and dumped on skid row. The threat of homelessness or prison conditions behavior and obedience, just as B.F. Skinner learned how to condition the behavior of rats by electrocuting them. In this respect, poverty and unemployment become "the stick" that needs to be shown to the working and middle-classes to get them to chase after "the carrot" of wage-labor.

It is not only imperative for the bureaucratic mode of education to suppress all questions of democracy, citizenship, and the purpose of education, but it must also divorce the content of education from the social realities of the student's existence. It must be seemingly pointless and valueless to the students, as something compulsory to be endured for an allotted period of the day, for an allotted number of years. In this way, it indoctrinates the student into *not having a choice* but to adapt to the discipline of mindless work as the norm. The system of rewards is structured to benefit most those students best able to adapt to tasks *not of their choosing.* Not only is creativity stifled, but self-determination is punished. Within such a system, obedience is synonymous with self-motivation. As Freire put it, "the so-called good student who repeats, who renounces critical thinking, who adjusts to models, should do nothing other than receive contents that are impregnated with the ideological character vital to the interests of the sacred order." (*Politics of Education*, p. 117) The choice presented to students by the bureaucratic mode of education is either adapt to the system or be alienated from it with nowhere else to go. Of course, there are always gangs, religious cults, and extremist groups waiting in the wings to offer alienated and dysfunctional young adults a home. The lessons of Charles Manson have not been learned. In addition, it is essential for the ideological indoctrination of students that they are taught a series of myths about their history, the political system, and the American way of life. Not only are these myths an appealing and simplistic version of complex reality, but their propaganda function is to inoculate the students from the truth of their condition and social reality. The myth presents such a pleasant and comforting version of reality, that those who question or challenge it are viewed as a psychological threat to the identity to the student. They are seen as unpatriotic and un-American, or marginalized as cranks and conspiracy theorists. The myth becomes a solace for the sacrifices the individual has made, and when a person questions or challenges the myths, they question and challenge those sacrifices; they question and challenge the whole identity of those who have bought-into the myths and adapted to the system. And without somewhere else to go, what is a person left with? Cynical nihilism? As Friedrich Nietzsche put it, "We would rather believe anything than believe in nothing." It is for this reason that the real challenge facing educators concerned with the democratic future of America and the rest of the world is to provide a genuine alternative to the bureaucratic mode of education. We must give students, parents, *and teachers* somewhere else to go. There needs to be an alternative paradigm. Without an alternative, individuals will remain susceptible to propaganda and the status quo. Without this, there is no possibility of free speech. Without free speech, there cannot be a free press.

The problem facing democracy is a deeper problem than ownership or control over mass media and communications technology. The real problem is a core a problem of realizing the potential and conditions of free speech within us all. It is a problem of the suppression of our capacity for enlightened reflection, critical thinking, mutual respect, tolerance, intellectual rigor and honesty, and, above all, our need to listen to and share experiences with others, especially those people with a different worldview. The solution to this problem involves developing a sense of solidarity alongside the awareness of the value of learning from each other's experiences and aspirations. It requires intellectual virtue, humility, and empathy. Taking this into account, the view that free speech is the assertion of opinion is a shallow understanding of it—although one is entitled to that opinion—but, much more importantly, revealing of a special kind of relation with others, a free relation, which not only involves a freedom from censorship (including persecution and oppression), but a freedom from ignorance and prejudice (and other forms of repression). Ignorance and prejudice are not forms of free speech at all, but in fact stifle it. An ignorant and prejudiced person is not free at all, but is a slave to ways of thinking (or not-thinking) over which they have no control whatsoever. They are in an unfree relation with their own thought and belief. They have an unfree relation with themselves. It is the freedom from ignorance and prejudice that allows one to escape the limits and boundaries imposed on thought and belief by others, indoctrinated and reinforced since childhood, and this escape can only be achieved by challenging one's preconceptions and assumptions in relation to being open to difference with others. It involves a relation with otherness that transcends the ego, towards which the self-justificatory and self-reinforcing power of propaganda is directed.

The individual may well reject any particular propaganda, but she will remain susceptible to and need propaganda in general. In order for propaganda to be effective, the old organic, traditional groups and communities must be dismantled or destroyed (either by economic means or through authoritarian tactics used by the state) to create isolated individuals within mass society. Hence, one of the ways to counter modern propaganda is for individuals is to disconnect themselves from mass media and mass communications, and organize and communicate at a grassroots, local level to reconstruct organic groups and communities based on interpersonal 'face to face' communications and sharing direct experience. In and of itself, this does not prevent prejudices and irrational commitments to any number of possible worldviews, but it does prevent these from being reinforced by propaganda and makes them more difficult to sustain in all but isolated and homogeneous groups. While religious cults and white supremacist groups, for example, can continue to maintain group identity through rubber-stamping and the use of totalitarian myths and propaganda, these are difficult to sustain within organic and heterogeneous communities, and almost impossible to sustain over generations. Even though leaders and dormant personalities can impose preponderant opinions and ideas onto groups based on interpersonal relations and communications, such groups are more constrained by and responsive to local conditions, experiences, and reality than charismatic individuals. This places tensions and contradictions upon the dominant discourse, which make it more susceptible to being tested, opposed and undermined by the facts of experience, contrary discourse, and alternative worldviews, each of which are also susceptible to local conditions, experience, and reality. Decision-making has to be made in direct relation to the problems and concerns of the group, which cannot be simply dictated or explained away, if that group hopes to survive and flourish within the world.

In order for democracy to work, there must be a public commitment to discovering the truth through rational communication and critical reflection in the public realm. The social discovery of values is fundamental to democracy and this cannot happen when this is relegated to the private realm of subjective choice between political products, nor when value judgments are reduced to a set of rubber-stamps to demonstrate group identity. Despite the appearance of "the free press" and "free speech" in modern mass media, presenting itself as "the marketplace of ideas," corporate media consolidation and narrowcasting have profound implications for democracy in America. They disrupt it by suppressing it and undermining the conditions under which it is even possible. Corporate domination of media, the dissemination of propaganda, and narrowcasting should be considered as anti-democratic forces. The discovery of truth and values, whereupon visions of a good society can be constructed, are fundamental aspects of democratic deliberation and the democratic process in general, wherein a diverse and pluralistic population *comes together* to share and explore each other's visions of the good life, a good society, and good governance. Democracy is the political process through which people can make a shared future for themselves and each other.

228

Knowledge of science, philosophy, and history, as well as technical and practical knowledge of all kinds, are essential for meaningful democratic participation, which is itself an educational process; the hostility, ignorance, and alienation generated by propaganda and narrowcasting, even when they celebrate "democracy" and encourage "voting" and "citizenship," as slogans, undermine the kind of discourse between people, with different perspectives and experiences, which is required for democracy to have any practical meaning or value. The use of propaganda by the State in whatever form, including a corporate state, alienates the population from democratic participation, reduces democratic skills and inclusion, increases the irrationality and conformity of the population, increases hostility and factionalization among the population, reinforces prejudices and ignorance, and thereby tends towards a totalitarian and anti-democratic society. Alternatives are simply suppressed or become unthinkable. An anti-democratic state, even when masquerading as a democratic state, is maintained by propaganda, especially when it uses the constant threat of attack from some "enemy" or "terrorists," and needs to justify being in a permanent state of crisis or war. The methods used by such a state to control or distract the population undermine the possibility of democracy.

Once we realize that free speech and propaganda are antithetical, and the use of propaganda undermines the possibility of democracy, there is a compelling public need to resist and prevent propaganda. Anti-trust legislation and its enforcement to break up media consolidation would help greatly to do this. Better public media and a publicly-owned ISP would also help. Increase media diversity and access are essential for democracy, but, due to the effects of narrowcasting, none of these things would help democracy at all. On their own, they would simply continue the masquerade and illusion of democracy. What is also needed is increased public awareness of propaganda itself. People need to be educated about propaganda and how it works. They need to develop critical thinking and rational communication skills. By promoting and analyzing public debate about propaganda, without using propaganda to do this, there is the possibility of raising consciousness and criticality, both of which undermine the effectiveness of propaganda; this restores the possibility of open-minded and rational communication between people with different worldviews. Not only do people need to turn off the sources of propaganda, but also restore a culture of mutual respect and tolerance between people, wherein free speech and listening become possible, and people can actually learn from each other. An often neglected aspect of free speech is the possibility of being heard; an essential condition for the possibility of free speech is that people listen without prejudice to what other people are saying, with the aim of understanding why someone has the view that they do, even when one does not agree with it.

Democracy does not require that we suspend judgment or agree with everybody. What it requires that instead of dismissing everyone who has a different worldview as being wrong, or treating them with suspicion, thereby reinforcing the group's sense of rightness and superiority, people must attempt to discover the truth and values of other people's worldviews, and the ideals they entail. This not only respects and tolerates differences, but affords the possibility of discovering *common values and ideals* that are given different expression. People with different worldviews can share common values and ideals, such as wanting to live a good life, to live in a just society, to be free, and, to be happy, but have different understandings about how to achieve these aims in practice. Through respect and tolerance, we can learn different approaches to common aims and aspirations, which means that people can learn how much we share in common, bringing a sense of solidarity among the population, but it also means that we can foster opportunities to learn from each other how to improve and evolve our understanding of ourselves, our world, and how to live life well. It is this possibility of learning from each other's differences that provides a practical core to a pluralistic society, which transforms cultural diversity and differences into a resource for the democratic development of communities and society in general.

Clearly intellectual honesty, humility, open-mindedness, curiosity, and rigor are the intellectual virtues that need to be practiced to counter propaganda. The practice of these virtues provides the conditions under which free speech occurs and through which a free press becomes possible. Freedom of speech and the press require not only tolerance and mutual respect within a diverse marketplace of opinions and interpretations, but also a psychological need for diverse and problematizing ideas, experiences, and perspectives, within an intellectual culture of empathy, intuition, and imagination directed towards 'Otherness' as a vital source of broadening one's mind and understanding of the world. It is impossible to propagandize people capable of rational inquiry and communication, and whether the conditions for free speech and the free press are met are perpetually under scrutiny and at stake, challenged and open to critical thinking, question and testing, as well as a wide variety of opinions and viewpoints. This recognizes that the individual needs to attend to the experiences and perspectives of others, through listening and respecting others, in order to learn anything at all. In this regard, only a society based on mutual respect, tolerance, pluralism, open-minded criticality, and valuing differences provides the conditions for rational thinking and communication, and therefore for free speech and the free press.

Free Speech and the Free Press:

What would a democratic free press look like? As a first approximation, we would expect to see a large percentage of the population with the freedom and the means to discover and share knowledge and experience with anyone else, without fear of persecution from government or any other large organization, be it commercial or criminal. A free press also needs for people to have widely available and affordable means to share their ideas and discoveries—as well as raise questions and bring concerns to the attention of others. Otherwise a person is left with their own voice and is limited to anyone within earshot. Without the means to record and communicate information, we are left with the power of our own memory. The Internet is akin to the sum of billions of telephone exchanges, therefore if whoever controls the fiber-optics and microelectronics claims to own the content of the Internet, it would be the same as the telephone company claiming to own all the conversations along its lines and switches. To paraphrase George Orwell, whoever controls information controls history and the public record. This is why the Internet is both a wonderful and dangerous invention, as all great inventions are. It provides an accessible and low cost means of communication for billions of people around the world, but whoever controls the infrastructure and the means to access it, controls it all. It is an unfortunate fact of life, but a free press really needs to be owned by the people who comprise it, otherwise they are as beholden to commercial considerations other than the free interests of people. In our first approximation of the free press, we should expect to see diversity of ownership, as well as diversity of forms of expression and points of view, as well as all the rights of freedom of association and religious free exercise thereof. At first approximation, a free press would appear to be a free market of human exchange and expression, free from fear of persecution, with only the commercial constraints being those involved in maintaining the means of communication. A free press should be free of political and commercial constraints, excepting those involved with communicating with other people in whatever form anyone can muster.

What of freedom of political speech? In the realm of political speech, a free press is a vital counterbalance to both powerful political and economic groups, which are often vying with each other. This is why the press is specifically mentioned in the First Amendment alongside the right of the people to free speech. This does not work when a cartel owns the press. It also does not work when the government acts like a puppet of that cartel. In order for there to be a balance, there needs to be some dynamism to this three way tug of war between the people, telecom corporations, and the government. The people need to start tugging. Remember that if the Internet doesn't work for us, we can always turn it off. A mass Internet boycott would throw a wrench in the works—An Internet strike! Is that even possible anymore? However, we need to look at this first approximation closer and ask ourselves, what does media diversity mean? Even in the early years of the Soviet Union there were hundreds of different newspapers and radio stations, and eventually television with many channels, and many millions of books were published and sold cheaply. The problem was that all of these seemingly independent media were all controlled by the Communist Party, Central Committee, and ultimately a few persons, or even one man, during Stalin's dictatorship. What difference does it make if the few people who control the press call themselves communists or capitalists, if the end result is that a few people can manipulate their power to further enrich and empower themselves at the further expense of everyone else? Is this really media diversity? The people need to be able to respond actively to media, to take it over, adapt and modify each and every mode of media. Without the means for anyone to communicate, there is no free press. And, without a free press there is no watchdog on politicians, corporate control over media—over the content and access to media of any kind, including the Internet. Can we consider mass media to be independent—the free press—if it is beholden to its owners' financial interests? No. Can we consider mass media to be independent if it is beholden to a government, political party, or an ideology? No. A free press must be autonomous and democratic. The idea of the free press is closely connected to that of free speech and participatory democracy. For free speech to occur, citizens not only need to be exposed to a wide diversity of views, often antagonistic views in contradiction with each other, but citizens must also have the freedom to communicate and explore their own views without censorship or persecution.

While the U.S. government and telecoms corporations haggle over who controls the Internet, no one currently controls the Internet. There is a window of opportunity for people to use the Internet freely to communicate and organize in defense of net neutrality, the ability to associate freely and petition their government, to run grassroots campaigns for independent candidates and third parties, and to share knowledge about how to organize and provide genuine alternatives to the status quo. If the Internet is the last bastion of the free press, it might even be beneficial to have powerful telecom corporations controlling communications infrastructure to counterbalance powerful political ambitions in government, but only if the interests of the owners of those corporations remain economic and technical, and the government has the wherewithal to threaten to nationalize the telecom industry under eminent domain if they do not serve the public interest. These corporations should have no vested interest in or control over content. There is a social contract between the people, government, and ISPs that must be respected if government is to be legitimate and an Internet-based free press to be even possible. But is it even possible for the government to nationalize the telecoms industry should it break this contract? Even in the days of Theodore Roosevelt there was little political will to nationalize industries, but we do have to ask whether the government is capable of independent agency on behalf of the people or the nation? Or has it become entirely taken over in serving corporate operations, providing subsidies and contracting, and clearing away any obstacles to increasing profits? Who does government serve? The citizenry needs to ask themselves these questions with an open mind.

People need to look at and educate themselves in how propaganda works, but not to counter propaganda with opposing propaganda. Not only does narrowcasting prevent counterpropaganda from working, given the degree of inoculation that the narrowcasted demographic has to alternative ideas, but it undermines the very conditions under which people can develop the means to recognize propaganda for themselves and overcome it. Free speech provides the means to counter propaganda because it requires a level of critical thinking and intellectual honesty that undermines the irrational and passive mentality that is required for propaganda to work. This is why brainwashing often induces stress, malnutrition, and exhaustion to prepare the subject for propaganda techniques. This is why educational pre-conditioning undermines critical thinking and communication skills. However, once we can freely explore a plurality of diverse alternative views—the wilderness of opinion—and all their contradictions and implications, we can reveal the internal inconsistencies, anomalies, and inadequacies within any worldview generated through the use of propaganda. This provides a method to undo brainwashing by helping its victims see for themselves, in terms of their own experiences, the flaws and contradictions in their own worldview, and help them see its inadequacies as a means of making their values and reflections meaningful and consistent with their experiences. This can lead to what is often termed as *a paradigm shift*, but this is only possible if people have "somewhere to go" once they discover the inadequacies of the old paradigm. To make this shift, it is essential that people can find new ideas, new knowledge, and new ways of understanding their experience, including new practices and experiences, and to develop a better paradigm as a result. This leads to consciousness raising and intellectual liberation—even if it is only a stage in the ongoing development and maturation of a person. It is for this reason that propaganda needs to be countered with knowledge, challenges, ideas, and questions, rather than opposing propaganda, no matter how ideologically well-intended.

Hence, as a second approximation, the possibility of free speech depends on the ability of human beings to exercise it and respond to it. This requires a certain level of critical thinking and rational intellectual development which, if lacking, leaves a person fairly powerless to deal with propaganda and misinformation. The idea of free speech implies that people are capable of using reason free of any constrains or distortions imposed by others. But people do not exist in a vacuum. In order to be able to exercise free speech, people must have open access to the ideas of other people. This is what is often termed as the marketplace of ideas. It presupposes that people are able to deliberate and decide for themselves, during discussions with others, which ideas are the best available ideas, and that through exploring the marketplace of ideas, good ideas will be discovered and prevail. Such a notion requires that good ideas will not be suppressed and that people are capable, given enough time, to work out for themselves which are the good and bad ideas by listening to others, questioning them, and exploring ideas. The more diversity of experience and knowledge brought to the marketplace of ideas, the better chance of discovering the means by which human beings can work out how to come together to improve society, solve common problems, deal with common concerns, and if participation in this marketplace is inclusive, this provides the basis for democratic governance. To silence any opinion is to preempt the outcome of the processes of discovering, and thereby undermine the possibility of discovering truth, knowledge, and new experiences. As John Stuart Mill said in his 1859 book *On Liberty*, "If all mankind minus one, were of one opinion, and one and only one person were of the contrary opinion, mankind would be no more justified in silencing that one person, than he, if he had the power, would be justified in silencing mankind."[36]

Misinformation, propaganda, and censorship undermine the marketplace of ideas because they undermine the human ability to be rational, critical, open-minded, and judge good from bad ideas. Propaganda undermines the human ability to test the soundness of ideas and their implications, and eventually a narrowcasted audience when subjected to relentless propaganda will become retarded in their intellectual ability to the point of idiocy or even insanity. This may well take a few generations, as each generation becomes the bearer of a culture of propaganda disguised as education and personal beliefs passed on to their children, but destruction of the intellectual ability of the population under its sway is inevitable. It is in this sense that we can consider propaganda to be contrary to the idea of an enlightened democracy, which very much depends on the ability of people to rise to the intellectual challenges brought by living in a complex and changing world and to work out how to cooperate to resolve the problems people share. Contrary to propaganda, free speech and the free press are public activities that involve responding adequately to the challenges and questions brought up by others, as the means for discovering truth, meaning, values, and the public interest, as well as enhancing the wellbeing of society by opening up the possibility of discovering and developing good public policies, relations, institutions, and practices based on reasoned deliberation, critical thinking, and open inquiry.

---

[36] John Stuart Mill, *On Liberty* (Simon & Brown, 2012), first published 1859

Everything is at stake. Providing that people wake up, we can recover our freedom to cooperate to realize the potential for democratic participation. It is impossible for any centralized and small group of people to predict the future. No one can know which knowledge or ideas are going to be valuable or important in the future. Human needs, innovation, and invention are impossible paths to predict, and hence it benefits society when people are free to discover these. The practical value to society of the availability of diverse skills and knowledge is indubitable and best satisfied by leaving it to people to decide their educational or training paths for themselves. Hence, rather than indulging in the fantasies of science fiction, government planning, or corporate strategy, human discovery is best achieved through free inquiry and experimentation. When people can choose for themselves how to organize the efforts and resources of society, say during and emergency or crisis, more often than not, people cooperate according to need and plan tasks in relation to their ability to share resources, experiences, skills, and knowledge.

Ordinary people may well be at a disadvantage when talking about science or technology with experts in those fields, which makes it even more difficult to trust scientists when people do not have any education in sciences and feel alienated from the scientific tradition. However, ordinary people are no different from most politicians in this respect. Given the disdain for science shown by a disturbingly high number of politicians in recent years, it seems many politicians do not see the need to acquire any expertise or knowledge at all to make policy decisions regarding technical or scientific matters. The congressional committees dealing with SOPA and PIPA, for example, deliberated these laws to prevent piracy on the Internet, yet spent their time debating whether they needed to hear any expert testimony at all, even though they admitted that they lacked any knowledge of how the Internet worked or the implications of the enforcement of either of these bills. It is almost as if the political process no longer requires any knowledge as a qualification for participation in decision-making, instead relying on ideology or political expediency, or even more self-serving interests, and so it allows for government by ignorance and opportunism. Communications technologies will become increasingly complex, as will the levels of organization required to innovate, install, and further develop them, and ignorant and opportunistic politicians are likely to leave these decisions in the hands of the directors and CEOs of telecom giants and lobbyists from the movie and music industries.

Of course these experts from the industries involved are concerned about profits and costs. It is quite impossible for them to be able to predict with any certainty whatsoever how the needs and technologies of the future will arise and what their consequences will be. It is impossible for anyone to know with certainty all the complexities and implications involved in the research and development of nanotechnology, biochemistry, pharmaceuticals, wireless communications, computer science, and genetic engineering, for example. Yet, it seems that scientists are not even needed by politicians and bureaucrats to judge the complexities and implications of laws on any of these brave new sciences. We still have considerable difficulty predicting the consequences for the climate from burning fossil fuels and deforestation. Some people even deny that there are any consequences at all. Whether "global warming" is even happening has become a partisan matter, rather than a matter of looking at the measurements. While there clearly are important moral and aesthetic questions at stake in decisions about the directions of scientific research and exploration, and hence it cannot be left to the dictates of any "scientific elite" to govern society purely on scientific or technical grounds, it seems to me important to take scientific and technical testimony as important when considering how we understand the natural world and the consequences of technological innovation and development.

Informed participation is a condition for effective participation. If citizens have a poor education then their ability to participate meaningfully is handicapped. Not only are they ill-informed, but they lack the skills required to analyze and question expertise, and to articulate their own concerns and experiences. We are simply not in a position to ignore scientific knowledge, even though we should not rely on the foresight of scientists either. The challenge is that of critically and publicly questioning scientific testimony in relation to how we understand our goals and ideals. Rather than close our ears to scientific testimony, we need to open it public reflection and deliberation, incorporating public concerns and criteria into those reflections and deliberations. Given the absence of universally agreed upon moral and epistemological standards (even among scientists), the processes through which we come to understand our own goals and ideals requires democratic participation and open inquiry. Obviously a low level of scientific education among the public is a serious obstacle to democratic participation in deliberating and understanding scientific research and the consequences of technological innovation. Professional politicians and bureaucrats are often as poorly educated in the sciences as most other citizens. However, this problem also extends to scientists outside their area of specialization, as well as concerning broader levels of education in the humanities (including the history of science and technology) and a philosophical understanding of the public interest.[37] The high degree of narrowly specialized and technical education among scientists is also a serious obstacle to democratic participation when scientists decide the criteria under which scientific knowledge is made meaningful to the public. Providing that citizens have the means to communicate with and from the experiences of others, they are capable of learning highly complex forms of knowledge. Take medical knowledge for example. Here we can find case after case where concerned citizens, as parents or patients, can use the Internet to contact groups of people suffering from the same medical conditions, and rapidly and successfully inform themselves about new breakthroughs and the limitations of medical science, as well as alternative remedies and treatments. Once we recognize that democratic participation needs the time, motivation, and resources required for careful deliberation and decision making, as well as opportunities to address the problems caused by social inequality and poor levels of education, then we can remedy these problems by helping each other learn how to communicate with others and improve levels of education, access to public services, and how to participate in the political process.

Corrupting influences are exerted by corporations via experts provided from within their own industries, as well as the influence of lobbyists on the professional politicians. It is also the case that many of the decisions about the policies for the implementation and development of the sciences are not necessarily made with the interest good as being an important consideration. And, even when these decisions are made for the public interest, experts may well have conflicting conceptions with the public about what the public interest is. Bureaucrats, scientists, and politicians are no more impartial or better placed than any other citizen to decide what the best course of action is, given that this course of action requires value judgments, for which there is no such thing as expertise. As a consequence of this, it is imperative that

---

[37] Karl Rogers, *Participatory Democracy, Science and Technology*

the public has greater involvement in decision-making processes, especially when contracts are allocated. The whole political system needs to be more transparent, accountable, and democratic. However, improving representation only prepares the way for greater public participation in the whole political system at every level. Citizens need to have a greater guiding influence on the direction of the formulation, analysis, implementation, testing, and development of public policy. This is required to provide a reasonable level of confidence in representative government as reflecting the plurality and diversity of the citizenry in general. Of course citizens need to have a better education in sciences, technology, and also in politics and citizenship, but what is also essential is that there is greater local democratic participation in government, the removal of obstacles to democracy, and the maintenance of the legal protections of the rights of citizens. Corruption and propaganda should be considered as serious obstacles to democracy and major threats to the rights of citizens. This can only occur if more citizens step-up to run for public office and involve themselves in local politics and school boards. Hence the free press is essential to provide communication between citizens and better inform people about the world and the implications of public policy on people's lives, as well as promote grassroots efforts to run for public office in local elections. A democratic society cannot reply on one-way communication between the government and the governed—via which the citizen is informed—or delegate political decisions to a professional elite. Citizens also need to have opportunities to inform the government about their concerns and ideas by involving themselves in governance. Two-way communication offers the possibility of genuine democratic participation in government by an informed and informing citizenry, which is the basis for the experiment in self-governance.

Public apathy regarding the political process is not the result of some innate inability of people, but is the result of inequalities in the political institutions and the consequence of the sustained use of propaganda on the population. Corporate media is implicated in perpetuating antidemocratic power relations and eroding the social contexts and opportunities for democratic participation. Yet, we all share the same world, with its economic, cultural, ecological, sociological, historical, and technological dimensions, and we all have a stake in the outcome of public policy and the consequences of the political process. The political institution of corporate hegemony creates an autonomy that can resist, suppress, and ultimately erode the public ability and motivation to participate in the political system. Corporate media turns the political process into a spectator sport, with commercial breaks. To a large extent, this has been done deliberately to exclude the public, but also in part it is the consequence of the privatization of the means to provide public services. Hence, democracy and the reinvigoration of the public sector need to occur simultaneously, especially involving public access media and public-owned ISP. This may well be disturbing to some readers, but to a large degree, democracy and socialism need to develop hand-in-hand because democratic participation is quite impossible without a developed public sector to provide equitable access to the infrastructure of society. Of course this does not need to be driven to any ideological extreme of state-ownership, as cooperatives also constitute a model for public ownership, and there are many possibilities for developing a mixed economy wherein both the private and public sector are developed in parallel to each other, sometimes in competition, other times complementing each other. Rather than respond in terms of knee-jerk ideological reactions (which are symptomatic of being indoctrinated by propaganda), we need to develop public policy on pragmatic and technical criteria of how to provide the best public services for the whole population.

We need to develop adequate practical approaches and social procedures to question what kind of society we wish to live in. This is a moral and aesthetic question too. Unless we examine the way that inequalities are built into society, we may well find that any solutions or policies we come up with will not work. If we accept that our actions and identity are shaped by social structures such as family, religion, politics, and economics, then we must also accept that they are shaped by the infrastructure of society itself, how this is maintained and further developed, and by whom. We need to overcome the feudal faith that there is a special class of persons who know best or who somehow—as if by magic—will solve problems for us all. This feudal faith is central to the myth that maintaining the privileges of a few is necessary to maintain the whole of society. In this sense, what is needed is for people to democratize society through democratizing media and providing the means by which people can organize, cooperate, share experiences and knowledge, and provide each other with genuine practical, economic, and technological alternatives to the status quo. By doing this, people liberate themselves and provide the basis for a genuine democratic revolution. In this way, popular mass movements can transcend being limited to protests, strikes, and boycotts, and instead become the basis by which people can provide each other with the practical means to satisfy vital human needs. Once people can satisfy each other's needs, through cooperative and local economic activity, as well as becoming their own free press to provide each other with knowledge and ideas, then people can liberate themselves from their dependency on the economic relations of corporate America, and open up the possibility of a genuinely democratic future.

On a third approximation, the free press is a rational and democratic activity involving the vast majority of the population. Rationality and freedom are social processes, developed in a society for which mutual respect and openness to otherness are values, in order for critical thinking and political discourse to operate as means through which communication occurs as a way of discovering shared problems and how to solve them through cooperative and democratic action. The above intellectual virtues are a prerequisite for democracy to be possible and meaningful as a practical way of living life in a community, and constantly opens the question of how democracy should put into practice through maximizing inclusion. This gives democratic participation an educational value for the improvement of human life and experience, alongside social institutions and structures, by developing meaningful contexts of mutual involvement and critical deliberation to discover and resolve matters of common value and concern, wherein a person is simultaneous required by others and requires others in order to question, explore, and discover how to live a good life within a society, and, in turn, help others do likewise. When democracy is maximally inclusive, ideally involving everyone as having equal moral worth, it remains perpetually vigilant to the question of the nature of rational communication, free speech, and the free press. These remain open to challenge and deliberation in relation to others, all of whom have experiences and reasons that are worth hearing as part of the ongoing and open process of understanding what these terms mean and how to put them into practice. Democracy becomes the cultural method by which the ideas about freedom of speech and freedom of association are tested and challenged, and adapted to new knowledge, values, experiences, ideas, and perspectives. This not only achieves the broadest possible understanding of democracy, but also of humanity and life itself, simply because it recognizes that human beings are not infallible gods and we live on a shared world of different and limited perspectives, all of which have something to offer to all of us.

Democracy is the practical foundation of how to live life well on a shared planet, and, consequently, is the only foundation for workable and lasting political action and discourse. The democratic aim of politics is for people to come together and learn from each other how best to solve common problems and concerns, and respect future generations, in a world that does not conform to human intentions. Democracy is the only political method for transcending the subjectivity of tyranny, which inevitably fails and leads to societal collapse, and forming the objective basis for determining the best course of action within any given context or circumstances. Democracy is nothing less than the political form of social evolution. This is clearly not easy to achieve in practice, and perhaps may well be the outcome of the struggles of human history, but, as an inspiration and ideal, it becomes the asymptote towards which political action achieves its practicality and objectivity for the human species as a whole. The democratic ideal itself imparts a critical force for change, thereby challenging the preconceived notions of the status quo, testing and questioning them in the light of an ongoing and evolving understanding of the human condition and purpose. This ongoing and evolving understanding is itself a living force that involves the spiritual evolution of the human species, with all its physical, historical, and cultural conditions and limits, to the extent that, through the democratic ideal, the nature and meaning of human existence is itself at stake, open to question and deliberation. Who are we? Where are we going? Why are we here? It should be clear that the term "democracy" should not be limited to the election of representatives to the legislature or executive branches of government. It should not be limited to a specific arrangement of the institutions of the State, or even "majority-rule" through 'winner-takes-all' elections, petitions, referenda, and ballot initiatives. When "democracy" takes the form of competitive elitism, in which a minority (elected by the majority) governs with the consent of the governed, media-control and propaganda are required to determine the election of leaders and for those leaders to inform the majority of policies and decisions; as a result, such a system necessarily undermines the possibility of rational communication, and therefore undermines the possibility of democracy through self-governance, resulting in a passive and irrational electorate, which becomes, quite ironically, incapable of determining who is best to lead them. The likelihood is that the populace will elect demagogues or liars, or those who simply serve the interests of the owners of mass media. Oligarchy (or plutocracy) and

242

technocratic dictatorships (or fascism) are the inevitable outcome of competitive elitism in a modern society. The term "democracy" becomes an empty term, without any meaning at all, in such a society, which uses the word within propaganda to conceal its true nature and present the illusion of legitimacy and consent. It is simply a rubber-stamp and any opposition to the political elite cannot be tolerated, as it is represented as sedition against the system itself. The people have no power whatsoever, beyond choosing between which members of the elite class, concerned with only advancing the interests of that class, should rule over the people. When any alternative to such a system becomes unthinkable, it is an inherently totalitarian system; and for as long as resistance exists, the response of the State will take the form of an oppressive fascist police-state, with all the inherent corruption, oppression, and violence that occurs in such a state to indoctrinate conformity within the population through state-terrorism and other methods of social control.

Passivity and conformity, and other forms of irrational commitment to the system, are the products of propaganda and fear, operating under the guise of "democracy" and "consent," and all forms of 'populism' depend on this. The electorate irrationally decides between competing propagandists to determine which member of the elite is less frightening. This is why elections often involve "choosing" between "the lesser of two evils." Hence, in most part, candidates for election are little more than actors within fictional propaganda campaigns within mass media, and serve only the agenda of the invisible government, which owns mass media, irrespective of whatever claims or promises those actors may or may not say. The political campaign becomes little more than the propagation of *pathos*. The tendency for movie stars and entertainers to become politicians should come of little surprise. The relation of the electorate to the elected is akin to a reality TV show or a sporting team, as it becomes based on personality and group-identity, rather than a rational decision based on self-interest or the public good. Elections are little more than a change in characters and coaches, all the while the elite maintain ownership over media and the institutions of government; at most, allowing the electorate to register opinions or approval ratings that are used when deciding whether or not to renew contracts. But the main role of the personality or team is to keep the electorate distracted from the real business of government, while allowing a faux sense of participation and accountability. The choice of the average citizen is to cheer, boo, or watch in silence. Or buy a baseball cap with a slogan written on it.

Hence the real struggle for democracy is not to reject propaganda in favor of public opinion, as public opinion is a construct of propaganda; nor is it to reject propaganda in favor of the individual's opinion, which when based on news and social media is formed of everything and nothing. The real struggle is one with the individual's engagement with reality itself—that the individual is a participant in changing the conditions of their existence—and it is this freedom in relation to other people that is the hallmark of genuine democracy. This not only grants actual meaning to free speech, but it also recognizes that it requires an openness to the speech of others, as having value (or at least possible value) to the individual in making an informed decision about how to live and improve the conditions of his or her life. This involves a recognition and respect for others, as having solidarity with others, as being a fundamental condition for the possibility of freedom of speech, and its practical value for changing the shared conditions of existence through cooperative action. By recognizing the plurality of experience, knowledge, and value at the core of human existence and its conditions, in the light of solidarity and mutual respect, it becomes possible to change reality through democratic participation. Democracy, in its broadest definition, means that the whole population comprises the free press and the State, as people administrate their own affairs, with governance occurring through people coming together in mutual respect and engaging in rational communication to learn from each other, cooperate and organize the administration of society, and to discover what are their shared problems and concerns, and how to solve and satisfy them. Clearly this does not mean that the entire population of the United States needs to be involved in all and every matter, from the national to local level, as that would be quite impossible—even if people were telepathic!—and unnecessary. Democracy begins at the local level and expands outwards through enrolment and inclusion depending on the scope and scale of the problem or matter of concern in question. Enrolment and inclusion occur through an organic political process involving communities, associations, organizations, cooperatives, unions, and whatever social groups that people form to solve shared problems and satisfy their needs. In this sense, "democracy" can be understood as a system of self-organizing, overlapping, and growing networks, given political form through universally agreed principles of

244

mutual respect, solidarity, and equality, alongside freedom of speech and association, and form the conditions through which rational communication is possible. These principles transcend the nation state and connect all human beings within a shared world.

Democracy so-understood is not an ideology or set of institutional arrangements, but it is a practical way of life and co-existence, through which human beings can learn how to cooperate and thrive on this shared planet through communication. It is a practical approach to the question of how to live successfully with other people, wherein people understand and articulate in their own terms what success means for them, and learn from other people how to do things better in a way that satisfies the needs of as many people as is humanly possible. It assumes that all people have an equal right to life (including future generations) and can learn how to develop and refine their own terms and understanding to better communicate and cooperate with other people. Democracy is a *dialectical social process* wherein participation in the process transforms how the political process is realized and developed through practical activity, how enrolment and inclusion occur from the local level outward, and how problems and matters of concern are identified and communicated to other people. It is a process of feedback. Once we recognize the equal right to life, and share that recognition with others, mutual respect and tolerance derive from that recognition, along with all other rights, including the right to liberty and the pursuit of happiness, and the sense of solidarity it requires. Injustice, inequality, exploitation, and oppression are, by definition, irrational, pathological, and hypocritical acts— as they are anti-democratic acts that benefit an individual or a class of people at the expense of others—premised on deception or violence. Such acts are premised on the assumption that one life (or kind of life) is of greater value and has a greater right to life than others; premised on power and privilege. Such a conception is incompatible with democracy and rationality.

What is at stake is the objective engagement with reality itself. Democracy imparts a serious attitude to each citizen when people are compelled to suffer the consequences of their decisions. It is only when there is a sense of seriousness, when the quality of human existence and experience is at stake, can people make rational and responsible decisions regarding matters such as climate change and global warming, for example. While human beings remained cocooned by the hologram created by mass media propagandists, wherein there are no imagined personal consequences for deciding one way or another, apart from group-identity and self-expression, people only engage with a virtual reality, within which deciding one way is as good as deciding another. When there is little regard for the objective consequences of one's beliefs, by appealing to their subjective feel as their ultimate justification ('it's my belief'), there is no possibility of learning or recognizing error, and therefore there can be no correction of belief in relation to reality and the discovery of truth. The erosive consequences of propaganda on human rationality is devastating and its consequence is humanity's extinction as a species, as it removes the very faculties upon which our survival depend. When the response generated by propaganda is one of "self-justification," concealing ignorance under rubber-stamped opinions and convictions, it removes the awareness of human fallibility, vulnerability, and limitation that we need in order to develop a serious attitude towards reality. This presents modern man with an illusion of security that his nature and circumstances simply does not allow him to possess. This falsely equates freedom with subjectivity—with egoism—and casts the individual citizen into the darkness of ignorance and stupidity, all the while presenting her with the illusion of being well-informed and abreast of world events. Propaganda is a formidable power leading towards the destruction of truth and freedom, largely by alienating human beings from them and concealing that any such alienation has even occurred, regardless of whatever good intentions propagandists may or may not have when they use propaganda to manufacture consent and public opinion. Under such circumstances, "democracy" is simply a mass delusion. The only hope for the citizen is to become aware of the fact that they are subjected to all-pervasive propaganda, and what is at stake is their freedom of thought in relation to reality and truth.

Through the use of propaganda in mass media, the politization of life leads to the illusion that everything is within the remit of politicians; it is the exclusive task of the State to order and organize the nation, its infrastructure, its social services, and even its culture, even when politicians call for "Small Government" or "deregulation," which ultimately creates the conditions for the rise of a corporate state. Through mass media, the illusion that the State has a monopoly over social change is presented as a self-evident fact; the individual is left in the role of a petitioner or voter, and nothing else. This illusion results in the belief that it is the task of the State to modify society— social engineering—to identify and solve our problems on behalf of the people. The citizen is relegated to the private realm, and, at most, the State is placed only in a relation of accountability to the citizenry. This propagates a shallow conception of democracy and an increased dependency on the State, which, of course, has resulted in a massive growth of the State and decreased control over the development of society by the people. Totalitarianism of a technocratic and bureaucratic form is the inevitable result. Due to the increased technologization of politics, through reliance on technical experts, bureaucracy, and mass media propaganda methods, increasingly the State is beyond the control of even our representatives. Politicians are increasingly relegated to the role of public relations and image manipulation on behalf of the State, even when they present themselves as being "against the State" and in favor of "Small Government." Consequently, even though the citizen may elect their representatives, they do not control the State. Politics is reduced to a competition to attain and retain position with a system of the operations of the State apparatus. Through media control and manipulation, the public has largely become neutralized as a political force. The desires, wants, and needs of the citizenry are filtered and manipulated, as "debates" are largely reduced to sales pitches and framed in terms of artificial extremes or trivialities. Either way, non-conforming or critical views are suppressed and prevented from emerging into the public arena. Furthermore, while politicians may well talk in terms of value statements and about the problems facing the nation, especially during election campaigns, these are distractions from the ongoing activities of the State in consolidating and extending its power.

However, rather than calling for depolitization (privatization) of society, what I am calling for here is a renewed effort by the people (using the Internet and other sources of media), as a democratic free press, to demythologize "democracy," and develop a deeper understanding of how undemocratic (or even anti-democratic) "democracy" has become through the actions of the State and mass media. A democratic free press needs to engage with politics by creating genuine tensions between government and the people, the military and the citizenry, church and state, and labor and capital. People need to create a space wherein we can build platforms to express our own foci of interests and concerns, discover and articulate our own values and convictions, and restore our faith in the possibility of participatory democracy. We need to act as a political force capable of placing limits on the State and the political realm. These tensions will break up and dissolve self-evident truths, which have been used by the ruling elite to establish complacency on the part of the citizenry not only to conceal how the State has become the instrument of the ruling elite, but that there is even any ruling elite. The invisible government must be exposed. This will open up the possibility of greater public participation in governance and the development of society, leading to new possibilities of change, and dissolve the illusionary belief in the sovereignty of an otherwise passive and insouciant electorate. The lesson of the American Revolution is that sovereignty must be earned by a citizenry willing to exercise it. Rather than work within established institutions of governance, the citizenry must disrupt and deconstruct them with the aim of creating new ones. In a real sense, the popular movement to amend the U.S. Constitution to clarify that the enumerated rights belong to natural persons and not corporations is itself an important step to creating the kind of tensions within the institutions of American politics through which the citizenry can learn how to assert itself sovereignty. The citizenry needs to create a constitutional crisis and follow it through to its resolution, however it may well be resolved. This cannot be achieved by petitioning and relying on the established political elite. It can only be achieved by the people by coming together, organizing themselves, and disrupting the status quo through direct action, cooperation, and democratic participation. This is no easy task. It is not even guaranteed that it is possible. Due to advances in technology and the centralization of power, the State is capable of formidable exercises of power through mass communications, legal frameworks, executive orders, and the use of military-police forces (including their capacity for mass surveillance and tracking). Even if the situation is not hopeless for those of us concerned with genuine democracy, it certainly is stark!

There is no room for complacency. Democracy is not a manifest destiny. It will not happen all by itself or natural forces. The current tendency is towards an increasingly powerful and authoritarian state placed at the service of corporate interests and economic power. The global consolidation of corporate power has already transcended the limits of nation states to the extent that governments are largely nothing more than instruments of administration and control over the people. The invisible government is a cartel of multinational corporations and banks, and the citizenry has become reduced to workers and consumers, and subjects rather than citizens. Via mass media manipulation and distraction, politics has become a kaleidoscope of clichés, myths, and illusions. The electoral process has become so corrupted that it is even irrelevant whether the ballots are actually counted after the polls have closed; the citizenry has become so divided against each other through narrowcasted media that even the shallow conception of democracy as a competition between candidates has become an illusion. There is no competition. The population has become so alienated from politics, passive and apathetic in the face of two nearly identical political parties, each only offering candidates based on their acceptability to the corporate elite, the major donors to the political parties, all the while the owners of corporate media can silence any real opposition or dissenting voices, that the political process has become nothing other than a sham— itself a form of mass media distraction. Major corporations so dominate the political process, donating huge sums of money to fund elections, that only their "guy" will get elected, regardless of which particular candidate is actually elected. This has not only resulted in corporations acting as gatekeepers to public office, but has also increased the cost of elections to the level in which only their candidates can even run for election. This has successfully eliminated third-parties and independent candidates from participating at all, except as spoilers or media distractions, and even a well-meaning and highly competent democratic candidate has to dance with the one who brought her. Under these circumstances, elections are reduced to a multi-billion dollar ritualistic process of rubber-stamping the whole process by which corporations govern America.

"Democracy," "representative government," "popular sovereignty," "free speech," "the republican form of government," and "the free press," have become little more than myths—slogans and idealizations based on a romantic and largely fictional history that no longer have any substantive meaning in modern politics, except as masks to cover up the corporate takeover of governance in America. This myths combine to present an illusion—a mirage—of political life, but they have no correspondence to political reality. In this way, a highly restrained, controlled, and conformist population can consider itself to be free, no matter the degree that their own experiences contradict this illusion. "Freedom" has become so eroded and detached from any meaningful content or practices that it has become an abstract. It too has become a myth. Its only function is within propaganda itself, as a means by which the absence of any real freedom can be concealed. The situation is one of mass wishful thinking and self-delusion, resulting in

249

the pacification of the population and the polarization of all facets of political life. It should be of little surprise that the result is totalitarianism and the rise of a massive governmental apparatus. The true nature of "Big Government" does not rest only in the expansion of the State to regulate all facets of societal development, but in the fact that the State mediates all human relations. All human relations are reduced to mechanisms amenable to political interventions, regulations, laws, and policies, and anything outside of his framework is itself represented as a problem for which politicians must find a political solution. In this way, the absence of regulation of any human activity or practice is itself represented as a political problem. Large sums of money are spent on propaganda techniques to create a public demand for politicians to step in and resolve the "chaos" of an unregulated phenomenon. Even when politicians talk of "deregulation" or "privatization," they do not actually mean that regulations or political oversight should be removed; what they mean is that a very specific regulatory and oversight framework needs to be constructed in order for those activities or practices to be controlled or dominated by a particular group of people, say corporations or industries, unions or banks, or churches. Even the most laissez-faire "free market" libertarian seeks a specific form of governmental mediation when he considers government itself to be a political problem to be solved politically through "deregulation" and "privatization." The "free market" is perhaps the greatest myth of all within the mass hallucination that has become the representation of political life in America.

The real problem with the politicization of all human relations is that it ultimately places human existence in the hands of the State, makes everything a matter of technocratic regulation, and propagates the myth that the political class are somehow more qualified than anyone else to determine the best way to live a human life. In so far as we are thinking about mass society in which the public realm is controlled by the State and represented through mass media, we see human life reduced to an off-the-peg set of abstracts and for-or-against judgments in which the individual becomes the object of everyone else's deliberations, wherein the State is presented as the means by which individual choices can be sanctioned and controlled for reasons of "the public good," without any conception of what that abstract means. Suddenly, everything not given to us by the State as permissible or prohibited is at stake—up for grabs—as a political problem in need of a political solution. Nothing is outside of the jurisdiction of the State. The individual remains a spectator, a passive consumer, within a system of relations, which is what the State now objectively means, and which mediates everything. No matter how intensely felt or passionately expressed, "democracy" and "freedom" are myths and the individual remains controlled, largely unconsciously, by a system over which the individual has no say whatsoever. In modern society, the political realm has become entirely understood in relation to the State, wherein the State assumes all responsibility for the organization of society and the exercise of force. When this responsibility is deemed a "necessary evil," the State becomes totalitarian as any alternative becomes unthinkable. Freedom? Due to the acceptance of the myth of "freedom," given as a birth right rather than something fought for and won, the American people have fallen afoul of the laziest metaphysical notion imaginable, and, as a result, have given up life, liberty, and the pursuit of happiness to the State. With the vaguest faith in the power of ink and paper, named the Constitution, to somehow—magically—protect the people from the very same institutions that retain the monopoly over its interpretation and application, the American people have walked like the proverbial sheep to slaughter. Even the natural urge of individuals to retain autonomy and freedom from the mediation of the State, or live in a way that is outside of the State, is denounced as a bleated *a priori* as "simplistic," "ridiculous," or "adolescent." True freedom has become the modern heresy. What is the alternative? Anarchism? Participatory democracy?—The direct involvement of the people coming together, cooperating, and deliberating the conditions of their own existence and relations with each other meaning nothing while we are still under the dominating control of the system. The genuine democratization of society requires that we deconstruct the system and replace it with an alternative over which we have mindful and conscious understanding and involvement. We need to revive community, free association, and solidarity among a people capable of creating tensions within the established order, and in relation to each other discover how to transform society through cooperative and communicative action. Communication is key here, and that is fundamentally a philosophical problem of existential meaning. This problem cannot be addressed by a passive, lazy, and reactionary consumption of poll data, vote tallies, and petitions, all of which gives all power to the State and its technocrats, but it can only be addressed by a citizenry capable of thinking for themselves, learning from each other, discovering common values and ideals, and open to experimenting with solutions to shared problems. It can only be addressed by a courageous and enlightened people.

The State has no power, except the power we grant to it when we see the flag, the leader, or the slogan of the day. The system exists only in our minds—its only physical reality is that of our actions, loyalties, and passion. It is only through liberating our minds, through human intelligence, cooperative action, and participation can we hope to counter the totalitarian system of the State and its corporate owners. The very human notions of liberty, equality, suffrage, dignity, and personhood all depend on our direct involvement in securing them. The removal of the individual into the private realm is simply an act of surrender to the very same forces she is trying to escape. Yet voting and political speech have become substitutes for democratic participation that actually conceals the system and political apathy under the guise of partisan politics. The alternative is not one of simply buying into the system, as if the sum total of a person's political action should be one of voting in elections and siding with a team, denouncing anyone who refuses to vote as "apathetic," responsible for the "opposition" winning the election, or a "bad citizen." When voting for a third party or independent candidate is denounced as a "betrayal" or "naivety"—or a "wasted vote," as if it was an apolitical act—the totalitarian dominance of the two-party system is legitimated as an *a priori*. This does not mean that, as an individual citizen, a person cannot legitimately recognize that the Democratic or Republican candidate is the best candidate. What is means is that when the choice becomes 'not the other guy,' something has gone very wrong with the electoral process. The choice between "the lesser of two evils" is not really a choice at all, even though it is clearly better to choose the lesser over the worse. Thus is the nature of a totalitarian regime over the human mind, when even the limited channels through which people may protest or seek an alternative are heavily constrained by the State, and denounced by their fellow citizens. It is due to its historical and sociological development in structuring human psychology that the State gains its objective reality, and, once these structures have become embedded in our thoughts, speech, and practices, the power of the State cannot be denied. The individual simply cannot stand alone and deny the existence of the State, for such a subjective response is completely impotent; it is merely an act of alienation—self-exile—and will be dismissed as an act of madness or paranoia. The liberation of people from the State can only be achieved through individuals coming together, as a *demos*, and cooperating and acting in solidarity to create an alternative to the State.

Human dignity, freedom and happiness are not guaranteed outcomes of the autonomous political machinery of the State. They require not only the vigilance of citizenry, but the collective action of the people as a whole, as the overwhelming majority, to ensure that government represents the people, is accountable to the people, and governs with the consent of the governed. However the lessons of propaganda studies teach us that this consent can be obtained deceitfully through the use of propaganda, generating deep divisions and irrationality within society. The use of propaganda simply maintains the illusion of representation and democracy. It is for the reason that the population *cannot* enjoy politics vicariously and by proxy, choosing their champions as they would a sports team, and passively rely on polls and voting to be their method of participation. Nor are protests and petitioning government sufficient. It is *essential* that ordinary citizens come together, organize themselves into grassroots movements, elect their own representatives from among themselves, and participate in the political process from the community level and upwards *to disrupt* the autonomy of professional politics and force it to obey the interests and values of ordinary people. Those values must come from outside the political system: from family, education, personal experience, tradition, religion, philosophy, history, and from life itself. It only is this way that the political system can be subordinated to human dignity, freedom, and a good life (or to life, liberty, and the pursuit of happiness.)

Is the state an illusion? Democracy requires that the citizenry (or the people—the *demos*) exercise control over the State. This depends on the organization, enlightenment, and participation of citizens; upon which also depends the rights of the people and the possibility of self-determination, dignity, and freedom. Education, critical thinking, communication, and rational action, as the basis for the generation of an active and informed citizenry, in solidarity with one another and capable of corporate and organized mass action, have all been taken to be the foundations by which the people can assert sovereignty and take control over the State. This involves more than the individual being an idealized *limiting factor* in the actions of the State. That is an abstraction, without any reality, unless the people are willing, collectively to protect individual rights against the State.[38] It involves the people coming together and collectively taking control over the state, wherein the notion of individual rights acts as a limit on the people, the basis for self-restraint and mutual respect. It should be of little surprise that this possibility has largely been rejected as an impossible dream or an idealization by contemporary political philosophers and theorists since Schumpeter published *Capitalism, Socialism, and Democracy*, it has been taken as a political fact of life that "the people" is a mythical realization as abstract, and direct democratic control over the State is impossible. Not only do the economic and social demands of modern life lead to pressures that prevent the degree of citizen participation that democracy requires, but the majority of people are simply too irrational and ignorant to be up to the task. The ethos of hopelessness and despair has eclipsed the classical dream of democracy, and it is now taken for granted (except by the naïve and foolish) that public participation is limited to giving support for leaders, reforms, and new laws. The dream of "the rule of the people" has been replaced by the modern conception of the state in terms of the rule of law and administrative methods. But, in this modern (post-Schumpeter and post-Weber) conception of State based in reality? Or is it an illusion too? Do laws and administrative methods really govern the operations of the State? Or is the idea of the state itself an illusion that masks the struggle between competing powerful corporations and other groups to use collective recourses to advance their own agenda and interests? Is the state little more than an amalgam of deals and trades? An instrument by which the victorious parties can divide the spoils between each other? The answers to these questions depend on how we understand the nature of law and administration. What is the nature of bureaucracy? What does it serve? What does it mean to engage in politics? To have a choice between options, not all equal, but none clearly preferable; to have a say in how those choices are weighed (analyzed, evaluated) and made; to have a say about the criteria (i.e. moral or practical) under which our choices are discovered, known, and weighed; to cooperate or organize freely with others to realize those choices in life; to make further and new choices possible; to share in the vision of an ideal society and how we work towards making it real. The limits of freedom are the limits of politics, in so far as freedom is a prerequisite for choice and the ability to deliberate. Although

---

[38] Karl Rogers, *Democracy and the Second Amendment* (Los Angeles, CA: Trébol Press, 2012)

politicians often invoke "necessity" in their rhetoric and propaganda campaigns, politics cannot simply follow what is necessary because that precludes choice. Politics is the means by which we make choices between competing goods and actors, and involves deciding both ends and means. Our choices and their consequences endure over time, both as a prerequisite for new choices and as a limit on our further choices, and politics must be viewed as a continuing process of shaping the boundaries and landscape of freedom. That landscape depends on our capacity for free speech, which, in turn, depends on free thought. Propaganda ceases when free thought begins.

As Hannah Arendt observed, leading to her famous idea of "the banality of evil," the essence of totalitarian government, and perhaps the nature of every bureaucracy, is to make functionaries and mere cogs in the administrative machinery out of human beings, and thus to dehumanize them.[39] It is through this lens of bureaucracy (which she called "the rule of Nobody") as a weapon of totalitarianism that Arendt arrives at her notion of "the banality of evil"—a banality reflected in Eichmann himself, who embodied "the dilemma between the unspeakable horror of the deeds and the undeniable ludicrousness of the man who perpetrated them," who appealed to "obeying orders" or "just doing his job" as the justification for his part in horrendous acts by the State. As Arendt put it,

"What he said was always the same, expressed in the same words. The longer one listened to him, the more obvious it became that his inability to speak was closely connected with an inability to think, namely, to think from the standpoint of somebody else. No communication was possible with him, not because he lied but because he was surrounded by the most reliable of all safeguards against the words and the presence of others, and hence against reality as such."

This "reliable safeguard against the presence of others, and hence against reality of such" was the disconnection from reality generated by propaganda. The Nazis, Arendt argues, furnished this deliberate disconnect from reality with what she calls "holes of oblivion." These "holes of oblivion" are generated by propaganda through the erosion of rationality, thinking, and, ultimately, truth itself. Today, we might call this kind of propaganda

---

[39] Hannah Arendt, *Eichmann in Jerusalem: A Report on the Banality of Evil* (Viking Press, 1963); see also, Hannah Arendt, *On the Origins of Totalitarianism* (Schocken Books, 1951)

"alternative facts," and living in a "post-truth era," but it is nothing other than the hologram—the ersatz reality—in which the individual is absorbed into the group mind and has become incapable of thinking, incapable of authenticity, and incapable of being a self in the world. Beneath the veneer of the hologram is nothing at all. The propaganda machine is a manifestation of the banality of evil, which erodes way human consciousness and freedom, leaving nothing in its wake, apart from the kitsch of myths and symbols. It was for this reason that we can call propaganda evil. But it is not a "radical evil" or demonic (superhuman) force. It is an evil that can be extreme or overwhelming in its power, but it does not possess any depth or reality of its own. It is a corruption and erosion of thought and truth, a distorting and promiscuous chaos, but it is ultimately nothing at all. Any "civilization" that relies on it to continue is destined to collapse into ruins. Any politics that relies on propaganda is destined to dissipate and be replaced with something else, as if it never existed at all. Propaganda can grow and lay waste to a "civilization" precisely because it spreads like a fungus on the surface of reality. It is thought-eroding because it undermines thinking, prevents us from going to our depths and the roots of our being, but it is frustrated because there is nothing to it at all. That is its "banality."

To counter propaganda with counterpropaganda is doomed to failure because it simply continues the process of the erosion of rationality to replace one ersatz "truth" with another. The propagandized individual is further driven into nothingness as a result of counterpropaganda. Poison cannot be countered with poison. The addiction is continued, but one drug has been replaced with another. To replace propaganda with propaganda simply continues the corruption and degeneration of "civilization" into barbarity, war, destruction, and collapse. The only way to counter propaganda is with truth. Genuine truth. This does not simply mean that propaganda needs to be countered with facts, though that is a start, or with logic and reason, thought that is also important, but means that the individual needs to experience the return to contemplation, reflection, and intellectual honesty when thinking, when encountering truth from a place of not-knowing. It is a return to conscious innocence and intellectual virtue in the face of an overwhelming barrage of facts, knowledge, opinion, and words. It is an awakening of the part of us that questions what it truly knows or what it has received as knowledge. It is an awakening of conscious mindfulness of truth and discernment of the difference between thinking and passively receiving words as a substitute for thinking. It is knowing when one has accepted a word as a truth, without knowing why it is truth.

Just as the power of propaganda is destroyed when its contradictions and inconsistencies are revealed in the face of experience—especially the horrific and insane experiences of war and other forms of violence cloaked in glorifying narrative and justifications—so the power of propaganda can be destroyed by genuine and authentic thinking, without knowing, without deciding, without partisan commitments to politics, and becomes the existential burden of the individual. It is the route to filling the holes of oblivion left in the survivors of the machine we call the State. The route to counter propaganda involves going within to that inner being that is veiled in silence, beyond the group, beyond power, beyond politics, and beyond the chatter and banality of "the ego-mind." Propaganda is destroyed by revealing it, exposing it and its tricks. Critical and honest thinking is the counter to propaganda. Humanly speaking, no more is required of us, and no more can reasonably be asked of us, than to think for ourselves and to seek the truth, think and speak the truth, and not parrot or repeat "truths" that we receive, no matter how believable or reasonable they might seem. What do you truly know? How do you know it? What is your source? Why do you trust it? How do you know that you haven't been tricked into believing a lie? What is the foundation of your thought itself? Without engaging with truth through thinking without dogma, assumption, and accepting things as granted, we cannot hope to engage rationally with political speech and the call for action. Irrationality leaves us in a state of coercion, hollow and in a state of oblivion, moving this way and that, like puppets on strings, whereas thinking opens up the possibility of freedom of consciousness to flow from a place of not-knowing. It involves listening to one's inner being as an 'Other,' and listen to others (as one would listen to oneself) with openness of mind and heart, to receive their meaning without a priori commitment, without judgment, without testing them for the Shibboleths of ideology and dogma. Openness and not-knowing in the pursuit of truth, without coercion and compliance, are the conditions for free thought.

The lesson of the Nazi Holocaust and the Gulags of Stalinism is that there are always survivors. There is always resistance. There is always opposition. There is always truth. Totalitarianism is doomed to failure, especially when made possible by the ersatz reality created by propaganda.

257

Reality will always crack the hologram, just as a hurricane cracks the self-congratulatory propaganda of the infallible regime. Propaganda will always stutter and stammer in the face of reality as it tries to paste over the cracks within itself. Of course, under the conditions of propaganda—especially the propaganda of terror—most people will comply, but some people will not. Just as the lesson of the Final Solution is that it could happen anywhere, its lesson is that it did not happen everywhere. It failed to be total. It was resisted and opposed as the monstrosity that it was. Just as Nature abhors a vacuum, the holes of oblivion will be filled with consciousness, and consciousness undermines the nothingness upon which propaganda depends. The false idol will always crack and be revealed as empty. Totalitarianism, like all human constructs, is imperfect, because there are simply too many people in the world to make its absolutism sustainable. It is for this reason that propaganda is always directed against the 'Other'; it depends on division between "us" and "them." It is opposed by human solidarity and universal love. There will always be someone who thinks and sees the hollowness of the totality. There will always be someone who asks the "unaskable" questions. There will always be someone left alive to tell their "impermissible" truth.

Without doubt, politics and commerce are dirty enterprises and quests for personal advancement and power, concerned largely with personal status and money. This should be understood by everybody as a matter of fact and commonplace knowledge. But there are also other systematic factions at work. Hostile and violent forces became unleashed throughout "the slaughter-bench of history," as Hegel termed it. The desire for domination and control over natural resources and people is ancient and varied in its methods, but, today, in what could be the last era of human civilization, we witness the consequences of the application of science, technology, and psychologically psychotic motivations to the vast domination of the Earth in its entirety, even to the point of the destruction of all life on Earth. Diabolical and insane motivations such as these could readily be attributed to some supernatural devil or demon, some unspeakable champion of Evil, but these motives are found in the ruthless ambitions of human origin. They are manifestations of greed and ego. Humanity has made its own history; it is the outcome of everything we did and wished for. This is all been of our doing, our choices, but we do not control the consequences of our actions; we do not control reality and how things slip out of control more intensely with unpredictable events happening as a direct result of the intention to control reality through human action. The belief that the desire for domination and power would ever be satisfied was and is the greatest folly, a form of madness, an unleashed and unrestrained evil, call it what you will. Like cannot be fought with like without magnifying the chaos that follows as a result of the struggle that occurs when a force is divided against itself. Non-linear feedback loops and genocidal frenzies notwithstanding, intensified beyond restraint in the twentieth century, and now screeching to the white noise of brutal species-wide violence, all-pervasive and degenerate in its self-generating, chaotic and self-destructive culmination in global war, mass extinctions, and ecocide.

Our next step must be to reclaim the word "democracy" from its current faux or sham usage. The meaning and form of democracy must be at stake, for people to deliberate afresh, debate and explore, define and test, and discover for ourselves in our own terms. We need to create tensions in the hologram and unravel the current meaning of "democracy." We need to resist and challenge the complacent clichés about the people's sovereignty, equality, liberty, and the will of the people. This requires that we, the people, wake up, stand up, and take charge of ourselves, our society, and our future. Otherwise the word "democracy" is without substance or meaning, apart from some utterance or abstract used in propaganda. Here freedom of speech and freedom of association are essential. It is imperative that we become the free press and create our own movement and media for democratic participation. We need to bring technology and the State under democratic control. This may require the people to rise up and resist the State, but it needs to be remembered that a true revolution is one of consciousness and not simply a coup d'état. There is always the risk of bloody revolt and civil war along the route of mass uprising and insurrection, but the real enemy is within our own minds, and it is in our own minds that the democratic revolution must be waged. How can this democratic revolution be achieved? Through communication and cooperation. We must visualize our society and share those visions with each other. We need to discover, imagine, and co-create democratic society as an ideal. What kind of society do we wish to live in? What do we want our future to be? How can we learn to live together and share this planet? What are the forces or elements that stand in our way? How do we overcome them? How should we build our future society? Democracy will not happen by magic, spontaneously, or by historical forces. It will only happen if we make it happen through communication and cooperation. This is why a free press is essential for democracy. It provides the media through which we come together and explore what "democracy" means. It comes down to our vision of what we wish to become—to be. A democratic free press is the means by which the people come together to educate and enlighten each other about our own possibilities and ideals, our visions and imagination, provide practical and organizational knowledge and skills, and provide genuine opportunities to articulate and question each other about what kind of society we wish to build—what kind of people we wish to become in our shared future. Providing we develop critical thinking and rational communication, we can resist propaganda, and develop the free press in the spirit of communication, mutual respect and understanding, and cooperative problem solving, rather than sloganeering, intensifying irrationality and contempt, and dividing people against each other. The democratic revolution will not be easy. We are faced with choice that must be made from within, as a personal choice, from which, in cooperation and communication with others, political and economic transformations become possible.

We must look closely at how we communicate our truths to each other. Are we trying to dominate the other? Are we trying to get one over on them? To win? To show our power? Are we trying to negate them? To censor them? To shut them up? While we use language as a weapon or means of being victorious—reinforcing our vanities and conceits of our egos about our own power—we learn nothing at all. We simply reinforce our own ignorance and folly. We need to stop doing this. It is the source of all our irrationality and stupidity. Instead, we need to use language to understand each other. Freedom of speech requires listening to the other. By broadening our understanding of each other and the world, we open up the possibility of learning from each other and the world, and thereby become freer and more conscious. Humility, respect, rigor, honesty, and courage are the virtues we need to cultivate to overcome the laziness and inertia of the ego, which seeks that which is familiar, easy, and habitual. New possibilities require new ideas, which require new discoveries and experiences; it is for this reason that a democratic revolution requires our conscious evolution, within ourselves, within dialog, and within solidarity with all life. We are at a crossroads as a species. We could take the path to our own extinction, mindlessly, by conforming to the unsustainable and destructive tendencies of the status quo; or we could learn how to share this world with each other (and all other beings) and consciously evolve into free and enlightened beings, mindful of our relations with others and the consequences of our choices. So take heart! Have courage! Let's choose to face the future with joyful honesty and the intellectual optimism required to come together and make our future happen. Let's take the first step together. It is simple. The first step of the democratic revolution is reaching for the TV remote control and pressing the off button.

www.ingramcontent.com/pod-product-compliance
Lightning Source LLC
Chambersburg PA
CBHW060044100426
42742CB00014B/2690